W
A

POCKET
REFERENCE
2011

OTHER TITLES IN THE RANGE

Whitaker's Almanack

Whitaker's Concise Almanack

Whitaker's Almanack Sport Quiz Book

Whitaker's Almanack Quiz Book

Whitaker's Almanack Little Book of Astronomy

Whitaker's Almanack Little Book of Infinity

Whitaker's World of Facts

Whitaker's World of Weird

WHITAKER'S ALMANACK

POCKET REFERENCE 2011

A & C BLACK
LONDON

Whitaker's Almanack published annually since 1868

Cover images: © Getty Images, Shutterstock

ISBN 978-1-4081-2850-3

Editorial Staff

Project Editor: Clare Bryant
Editors: Ruth Craven, Ross Fulton, Matt Munday
Publisher (Yearbooks): Claire Fogg

This book is produced using paper that is made from wood grown
in managed, sustainable forests. It is natural, renewable and
recyclable. The logging and manufacturing processes conform to
the environmental regulations of the country of origin.

Typeset by RefineCatch Ltd, Bungay, Suffolk
Printed in the UK by T. J. International Ltd

CONTENTS

LANGUAGE   **82**

MATHEMATICS   **94**

MONEY   **101**

MUSIC   **110**

PEOPLE   **120**

PLACES 127

ROYALTY 148

SCIENCE 157

LIFE SCIENCES   **175**

SPORT   **184**

TIME 199

WEIGHTS AND MEASURES 214

FOREWORD

If you have a thirst for facts, figures and general knowledge, then
Whitaker's Almanack Pocket Reference is just the book you need.
Published annually in a concise, easy-to-use format, this edition of
Whitaker's Almanack Pocket Reference is the essential tool for quiz
and general knowledge enthusiasts, ideal for use in the home, office
or classroom.

Whitaker's Almanack Pocket Reference covers a broad range of
subjects answering both practical day-to-day and more esoteric
queries. New in this edition are:

• Vancouver Winter Olympics medal table
• A map of French wine regions
• Endangered languages
• Longest-serving heads of state
• Advertising slogans

Political statistics, geographical and scientific data, historical lists,
protocol, definitions … it's all here at your fingertips! Please write
to us with any suggestions for new sections – our readers' feedback
has always proved invaluable when compiling new content.

Whitaker's Almanack
36 Soho Square
London W1D 3QY

whitakers@acblack.com
www.whitakersalmanack.com

ALPHABETS AND SYMBOLS

GREEK ALPHABET

		NAME OF LETTER	TRANS-LITERATION
Α	α	alpha	a
Β	β	beta	b
Γ	γ	gamma	g
Δ	δ	delta	d
Ε	ε	epsilon	e
Ζ	ζ	zeta	z
Η	η	eta	ē
Θ	θ	theta	th
Ι	ι	iota	i
Κ	κ	kappa	k
Λ	λ	lambda	l
Μ	μ	mu	m
Ν	ν	nu	n
Ξ	ξ	xi	x
Ο	ο	omicron	o
Π	π	pi	p
Ρ	ρ	rho	r
Σ	σ	sigma	s
Τ	τ	tau	t
Υ	υ	upsilon	u or y
Φ	φ	phi	ph
Χ	χ	chi	ch
Ψ	ψ	psi	ps
Ω	ω	omega	ō

CYRILLIC ALPHABET

		TRANSLITERATION
А	а	a
Б	б	b
В	в	v
Г	г	g
Д	д	d
Е	е	e, a, ar or ye
Ё	ё	jo or yo
Ж	ж	ž or zh
З	з	z
И	и	i
Й	й	j or ĭ
К	к	k
Л	л	l
М	м	m
Н	н	n
О	о	o
П	п	p
Р	р	r
С	с	s
Т	т	t
У	у	u
Ф	ф	f
Х	х	x or kh
Ц	ц	c or ts
Ч	ч	č or ch
Ш	ш	š or sh
Щ	щ	šč or shch
Ъ	ъ	"
Ы	ы	y
Ь	ь	'
Э	э	ė or é
Ю	ю	ju or yu
Я	я	ja or ya

ANGLO-SAXON RUNIC ALPHABET

The Anglo-Saxon runic alphabet is known as the Futhorc, from the names of the first six letters.

RUNE	MODERN LETTER	NAME OF RUNE	MEANING
ᚠ	f	feoh	wealth
ᚢ	u	ur	aurochs
ᚦ	th	þorn	thorn
ᚩ	o	os	mouth
ᚱ	r	rad	riding
ᚳ	c	cen	torch
ᚷ	g	gyfu	gift
ᚹ	w	wynn	joy
ᚻ	h	hægl	hail
ᚾ	n	nyd	need
ᛁ	i	is	ice
ᛄ	j	ger	harvest
ᛇ	eo	eoh	yew
ᛈ	p	peorð	hearth
ᛉ	x	eolhxsecg	elksedge
ᛋ	s	sigel	sun
ᛏ	t	Tir	Tiw
ᛒ	b	beorc	birch
ᛖ	e	eh	horse
ᛗ	m	man	man
ᛚ	l	lagu	water
ᛝ	ng	Ing	Ing
ᛟ	oe	eþel	homeland
ᛞ	d	dæg	day
ᚪ	a	ac	oak
ᚫ	æ	æsc	ash
ᚣ	y	yr	weapon
ᛡ	ia	ior	beaver
ᛠ	ea	ear	grave

ARABIC ALPHABET

	NAME OF LETTER	TRANSLITERATION
ا	alif	aa
ب	baa	b
ت	taa	t
ث	thaa	th
ج	jiim	j
ح	haa	h
خ	kha	kh
د	daal	d
ذ	thaal	dh
ر	raa	r
ز	zaay	z
س	siin	s
ش	shiin	sh
ص	saad	s
ض	daad	d
ط	taa	t
ظ	thaa	z
ع	ayn	a i u
غ	ghayn	gh
ف	faa	f
ق	qaaf	q
ك	kaaf	k
ل	laam	l
م	miim	m
ن	nuun	n
ه	ha	h
و	waaw	w
ي	yaa	y
ء	hamza	glottal stop

INTERNATIONAL RADIO ALPHABET

Phonetic alphabets were originally developed to avoid confusion when communicating by radio or telephone. The first draft of the International Radio Alphabet was completed by the International Air Transport Association in 1947 and the final version was adopted by the International Telecommunications Union in around 1956.

A	Alfa
B	Bravo
C	Charlie
D	Delta
E	Echo
F	Foxtrot
G	Golf
H	Hotel
I	India
J	Juliett
K	Kilo
L	Lima
M	Mike
N	November
O	Oscar
P	Papa
Q	Quebec
R	Romeo
S	Sierra
T	Tango
U	Uniform
V	Victor
W	Whiskey
X	X-ray
Y	Yankee
Z	Zulu

MORSE CODE

The International Morse Code was formulated in 1852. The spoken code enables radio operators to send messages with their own voices, using the expressions 'dah' and 'di' or 'dit' instead of keying in dashes and dots on their transmitters.

A	. —	di-dah
B	— . . .	dah-di-di-dit
C	— . — .	dah-di-dah-dit
D	— . .	dah-di-dit
E	.	dit
F	. . — .	di-di-dah-dit
G	— — .	dah-dah-dit
H	. . . .	di-di-di-dit
I	. .	di-dit
J	. — — —	di-dah-dah-dah
K	— . —	dah-di-dah
L	. — . .	di-dah-di-dit
M	— —	dah-dah
N	— .	dah-dit
O	— — —	dah-dah-dah
P	. — — .	di-dah-dah-dit
Q	— — . —	dah-dah-di-dah
R	. — .	di-dah-dit
S	. . .	di-di-dit
T	—	dah
U	. . —	di-di-dah
V	. . . —	di-di-di-dah
W	. — —	di-dah-dah
X	— . . —	dah-di-di-dah
Y	— . — —	dah-di-dah-dah
Z	— — . .	dah-dah-di-dit

Dash = dah
Dot = di or dit

BRAILLE ALPHABET AND NUMBERS

BRAILLE ALPHABET

a	f	k	p	u	z
b	g	l	q	v	
c	h	m	r	w	
d	i	n	s	x	
e	j	o	t	y	

BRAILLE NUMBERS

1	4	7	0
2	5	8	
3	6	9	

HALLMARKS

Hallmarks are the symbols stamped on gold, silver, palladium or platinum articles to indicate that they have been tested at an official Assay Office and that they conform to one of the legal standards. With certain exceptions, all gold, silver, palladium or platinum articles are required by law to be hallmarked before they are offered for sale.

Since 1 January 1999, UK hallmarks have consisted of three compulsory symbols: the sponsor's mark, the assay office mark, and the fineness (standard) mark. The date lettermark became voluntary on 1 January 1999. Additional marks have been authorised from time to time.

COMPULSORY MARKS

SPONSOR'S MARK

Instituted in England in 1363, the sponsor's mark was originally a device such as a bird or fleur-de-lis. Now it consists of the initial letters of the name or names of the manufacturer or firm. Where two or more sponsors have the same initials, there is a variation in the surrounding shield or style of letters.

FINENESS (STANDARD) MARK

The fineness (standard) mark indicates that the content of the precious metal in the alloy from which the article is made is not less than the legal standard. The legal standard is the minimum content of precious metal by weight in parts per thousand, and the standards are:

Gold	999	
	990	
	916.6	(22 carat)
	750	(18 carat)
	585	(14 carat)
	375	(9 carat)
Silver	999	
	958.4	(Britannia)
	925	(sterling)
	800	
Platinum	999	
	950	
	900	
	850	
Palladium	999	
	950	
	500	

ASSAY OFFICE MARK

This mark identifies the particular assay office at which the article was tested and marked. The British assay offices are:

 London

 Birmingham

 Sheffield

 Edinburgh

Assay offices formerly existed in other towns, eg Chester, Exeter, Glasgow, Newcastle, Norwich and York, each having its own distinguishing mark.

OPTIONAL MARKS

Gold – a crown followed by the millesimal figure for the standard, eg 916 for 22 carat

Silver – Britannia silver: a full-length figure of Britannia. Sterling silver: a lion passant (England) or a lion rampant (Scotland)

 Britannia Silver

 Sterling Silver (England)

 Sterling Silver (Scotland)

 Platinum – an orb

 Palladium – the Greek goddess Pallas Athene

DATE LETTER

The date letter shows the year in which an article was assayed and hallmarked. Each alphabetical cycle has a distinctive style of lettering or shape of shield. The date letters were different at the various assay offices and the particular office must be established from the assay office mark before reference is made to tables of date letters.

Since 1 January 1975, each office has used the same style of date letter and shield for all articles.

OTHER MARKS

FOREIGN GOODS

Foreign goods imported into the UK are required to be hallmarked before sale, unless they already bear a convention mark (see below) or a hallmark struck by an independent assay office in the European Economic Area which is deemed to be equivalent to a UK hallmark.

The following are the assay office marks used for gold imported articles until the end of 1998. For silver and platinum the symbols remain the same but the shields differ in shape.

 London

 Birmingham

 Sheffield

 Edinburgh

CONVENTION HALLMARKS

Special marks at authorised assay offices of the signatory countries of the International Convention on Hallmarking (Austria, Czech Republic, Denmark, Finland, Hungary, Ireland, Latvia, Lithuania, the Netherlands, Norway, Poland, Portugal, Sweden, Switzerland, UK and Ukraine) are legally recognised in the United Kingdom as approved hallmarks. These consist of a sponsor's mark, a common control mark, a fineness mark (arabic numerals showing the standard in parts per thousand), and an assay office mark. There is no date letter.

The common control marks are:

Gold   Silver   Platinum   Palladium

COMMEMORATIVE MARKS

There are other marks to commemorate special events: the silver jubilee of King George V and Queen Mary in 1935, the coronation of Queen Elizabeth II in 1953, and her silver jubilee in 1977. During 1999 and 2000 there was a voluntary additional millennium mark. A mark to commemorate the golden jubilee of Queen Elizabeth II was available during 2002.

HERALDRY

TERMS

Achievement: The complete pictorial display of arms comprising a shield, helmet, crest, torse, mantling and motto. Supporters, additional mottoes or rallying cries, decorations and insignia of office may also be depicted if the individual is entitled to them.

Blazon: The formula describing the design of arms of a whole achievement; or, used as a verb, to make such a description.

Escutcheon: The shield displayed in a coat of arms.

Inescutcheon: A small shield placed on top of the larger shield.

POINTS AND PARTS OF A SHIELD

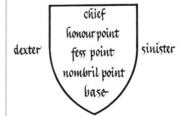

dexter   chief
honour point
fess point   sinister
nombril point
base

ORDINARIES

Ordinaries are simple geometric figures used in armory

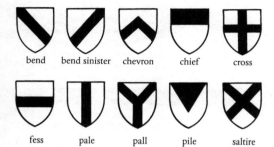

bend   bend sinister   chevron   chief   cross

fess   pale   pall   pile   saltire

DIVISIONS

party per fess
= divided in two
horizontally

party per pale
= divided in
two vertically

Impalement = dividing a shield vertically and placing arms in both halves
Quartering = dividing a shield into four or more equal parts and placing
               arms in each division

TINCTURES

There are six colours, three stains and two metals:

COLOURS

gules	red
azure	blue
vert	green
sable	black
purpure	purple
proper	an animal or object depicted in its natural colours

STAINS

murrey	mulberry or maroon
tenné	tawny orange
sanguine	blood-coloured red

METALS

or	gold; may be depicted as gilt, or painted as yellow or ochre
argent	silver; may be painted as pale grey or be white

FURS

ermine	white field with black spots
ermines	black field with white spots
erminois	gold field with black spots
pean	black field with gold spots
potent	blue and white T-shapes
vair	blue and white bell-shapes

ANIMALS

addorsed	two animals back to back
affronte	whole beast facing forward
at gaze	looking full face (hart, buck, stag or hind only)
combatant	two animals face to face, in the attitude of fighting
couchant	lying, with head erect
coward	with tail between hind legs
dormant	in a sleeping posture
guardant	facing out to viewer
passant	walking, usually with right paw raised
rampant	rearing up with three paws outstretched
reguardant	looking back over shoulder
respectant	two animals face to face
salient	springing up with forepaws raised
sejant	sitting
statant	standing, with all four feet down
trippant	walking, usually with right paw raised (hart, buck, stag or hind only)

Animals are usually facing to the dexter (their right) unless otherwise indicated

BIRDS

close	wings folded in
displayed	fully frontal, wings extended, head turned to the dexter
rising	taking flight, wings raised

Heads of birds are usually shown in profile, except for owls, which are always guardant

THE ARTS

TURNER PRIZE WINNERS

1984 Malcolm Morley	1997 Gillian Wearing
1985 Howard Hodgkin	1998 Chris Ofili
1986 Gilbert and George	1999 Steve McQueen
1987 Richard Deacon	2000 Wolfgang Tillmans
1988 Tony Cragg	2001 Martin Creed
1989 Richard Long	2002 Keith Tyson
1990 no prize	2003 Grayson Perry
1991 Anish Kapoor	2004 Jeremy Deller
1992 Grenville Davey	2005 Simon Starling
1993 Rachel Whiteread	2006 Tomma Abts
1994 Anthony Gormley	2007 Mark Wallinger
1995 Damien Hirst	2008 Mark Leckey
1996 Douglas Gordon	2009 Richard Wright

BOOKER PRIZE WINNERS

1969   P. H. Newby, *Something to Answer For*
1970   Bernice Rubens, *The Elected Member*
1971   V. S. Naipaul, *In a Free State*
1972   John Berger, *G*
1973   J. G. Farrell, *The Siege of Krishnapur*
1974   Nadine Gordimer, *The Conservationist*/Stanley Middleton, *Holiday*
1975   Ruth Prawer Jhabvala, *Heat and Dust*
1976   David Storey, *Saville*
1977   Paul Scott, *Staying On*
1978   Iris Murdoch, *The Sea, The Sea*
1979   Penelope Fitzgerald, *Offshore*
1980   William Golding, *Rites of Passage*
*1981   Salman Rushdie, *Midnight's Children*
1982   Thomas Keneally, *Schindler's Ark*
1983   J. M. Coetzee, *Life and Times of Michael K*
1984   Anita Brookner, *Hotel du Lac*
1985   Keri Hulme, *The Bone People*
1986   Kingsley Amis, *The Old Devils*
1987   Penelope Lively, *Moon Tiger*
1988   Peter Carey, *Oscar and Lucinda*
1989   Kazuo Ishiguro, *The Remains of the Day*
1990   A. S. Byatt, *Possession*

1991 Ben Okri, *The Famished Road*
1992 Michael Ondaatje, *The English Patient*/Barry Unsworth, *Sacred Hunger*
1993 Roddy Doyle, *Paddy Clarke Ha, Ha, Ha*
1994 James Kelman, *How Late It Was, How Late*
1995 Pat Barker, *The Ghost Road*
1996 Graham Swift, *Last Orders*
1997 Arundhati Roy, *The God of Small Things*
1998 Ian McEwan, *Amsterdam*
1999 J. M. Coetzee, *Disgrace*
2000 Margaret Atwood, *The Blind Assassin*
2001 Peter Carey, *True History of the Kelly Gang*
2002 Yann Martell, *The Life of Pi*
2003 D. B. C. Pierre, *Vernon God Little*
2004 Alan Hollinghurst, *The Line of Beauty*
2005 John Banville, *The Sea*
2006 Kiran Desai, *The Inheritance of Loss*
2007 Anne Enright, *The Gathering*
2008 Aravind Adiga, *The White Tiger*
2009 Hilary Mantel, *Wolf Hall*

* Also the winner of the Booker of Bookers prize in 1993 and the Best of Booker prize in 2008

NOMS DE PLUME

Richard Bachman	*Stephen King*	Dietrich	
Acton Bell	*Anne Brontë*	Knickerbocker	*Washington Irving*
Currer Bell	*Charlotte Brontë*	Molière	*Jean Baptiste Poquelin*
Ellis Bell	*Emily Brontë*	Toni Morrison	*Chloe Anthony*
John le Carré	*David John Moore*		*Wofford*
	Cornwell	Flann O'Brien	*Brian O'Nolan*
Lewis Carroll	*Charles Dodgson*	George Orwell	*Eric Arthur Blair*
George Egerton	*Mary Chavelita Dunne*	Saki	*Hector Hugh Munro*
	Bright	Lemony Snicket	*Daniel Handler*
George Eliot	*Mary Ann Evans*	Barbara Vine	*Ruth Rendell*
Nicci French	*Nicci Gerard and Sean*	Mark Twain	*Samuel Clemens*
	French	Mary Westmacott	*Agatha Christie*

SHAKESPEARE'S PLAYS

All's Well That Ends Well (1604)
Antony and Cleopatra (1606)
As You Like It (1599)
The Comedy of Errors (1593)
Coriolanus (1608)
Cymbeline (1610)
Edward III (1595)*
Hamlet (1601)
Henry IV Part 1 (1597)
Henry IV Part 2 (1598)
Henry V (1599)
Henry VI Part 1 (1592)
Henry VI Part 2 (1591)
Henry VI Part 3 (1592)
Henry VIII (1613)
Julius Caesar (1599)
King John (1596)
King Lear (1605)
Love's Labour's Lost (1594)
Macbeth (1606)

Measure for Measure (1604)
The Merchant of Venice (1596)
The Merry Wives of Windsor (1600)
A Midsummer Night's Dream (1596)
Much Ado About Nothing (1598)
Othello (1604)
Pericles (1608)
Richard II (1595)
Richard III (1592)
Romeo and Juliet (1595)
The Taming of the Shrew (1594)
The Tempest (1611)
Timon of Athens (1607)
Titus Andronicus (1594)
Troilus and Cressida (1602)
Twelfth Night (1600)
The Two Gentlemen of Verona (1594)
The Two Noble Kinsmen (1613)*
The Winter's Tale (1611)

* Shakespeare's authorship of these plays is contested

Dates in brackets indicate approximate year of first performance

PILGRIMS FROM CHAUCER'S *CANTERBURY TALES*

Knight	Physician
Miller	Pardoner
Reeve	Shipman
Cook	Prioress
Man of Law	Sir Thopas
Wife of Bath	Melibeus
Friar	Monk
Summoner	Nun's Priest
Clerk	Second Nun
Merchant	Canon's Yeoman
Squire	Manciple
Franklin	Parson

'BAD SEX AWARD' WINNERS

The Literary Review Bad Sex in Fiction Award is given annually to the author who produces the worst description of a sex scene in a novel. The award itself depicts a woman draped provocatively over an open book. It has been presented every year since 1993 and was established by literary critic Rhoda Koenig and the then editor of the *Literary Review* Auberon Waugh.

1993	Melvyn Bragg, *A Time to Dance*	2001	Christopher Hart, *Rescue Me*
1994	Philip Hook, *The Stone Breakers*	2002	Wendy Perriam, *Tread Softly*
1995	Philip Kerr, *Gridiron*	2003	Aniruddha Bahal, *Bunker 13*
1996	David Huggins, *The Big Kiss: An Arcade Mystery*	2004	Tom Wolfe, *I am Charlotte Simmons*
1997	Nicholas Royle, *The Matter of the Heart*	2005	Giles Coren, *Winkler*
1998	Sebastian Faulks, *Charlotte Gray*	2006	Iain Hollingshead, *Twenty Something*
1999	A. A. Gill, *Starcrossed*	2007	Norman Mailer, *The Castle in the Forest*
2000	Sean Thomas, *Kissing England*	2008	Rachel Johnson, *Shire Hell*
		2009	Jonathan Littell, *The Kindly Ones*

POETS LAUREATE

The post of Poet Laureate was officially established when John Dryden was appointed by royal warrant as Poet Laureate and Historiographer Royal in 1668, although Ben Jonson was considered to have been the first recognised laureate after having a pension of 100 marks a year conferred upon him. The post is attached to the royal household and was originally conferred on the holder for life; in 1999 the length of appointment was changed to a ten-year term. It is customary for the Poet Laureate to write verse to mark events of national importance. The postholder currently receives an honorarium of £5,750 a year.

Ben Jonson (1572–1637), appointed 1616
Sir William D'Avenant (1606–68), appointed 1638
John Dryden (1631–1700)*, appointed 1668
Thomas Shadwell (1642–92), appointed 1689
Nahum Tate (1652–1715), appointed 1692
Nicholas Rowe (1674–1718), appointed 1715
Laurence Eusden (1688–1730), appointed 1718
Colley Cibber (1671–1757), appointed 1730
William Whitehead (1715–85), appointed 1757
Thomas Warton (1728–90), appointed 1785
Henry Pye (1745–1813), appointed 1790
Robert Southey (1774–1843), appointed 1813
William Wordsworth (1770–1850), appointed 1843
Alfred, Lord Tennyson (1809–92), appointed 1850
Alfred Austin (1835–1913), appointed 1896
Robert Bridges (1844–1930), appointed 1913
John Masefield (1878–1967), appointed 1930
Cecil Day Lewis (1904–72), appointed 1968
Sir John Betjeman (1906–84), appointed 1972
Ted Hughes (1930–98), appointed 1984
Andrew Motion (1952–), appointed 1999
Carol Ann Duffy (1955–), appointed 2009

* John Dryden, a Catholic, was stripped of his laureateship in 1689 for refusing to swear the oath of allegiance to the new Protestant monarchy.

BRITISH POLITICS

GENERAL ELECTIONS SINCE 1900

YEAR	DATE	PARTY FORMING THE GOVERNMENT
1900	1–24 Oct	Conservative
1906	12 Jan–8 Feb	Liberal
1910	15 Jan–10 Feb	Liberal
1910	3–19 Dec	Liberal
1918	14 Dec	Coalition*
1922	15 Nov	Conservative
1923	6 Dec	Labour
1924	29 Oct	Conservative
1929	30 May	Labour
1931	27 Oct	National Government†
1935	14 Nov	National Government‡
1945	5 July	Labour
1950	23 Feb	Labour
1951	25 Oct	Conservative
1955	26 May	Conservative
1959	8 Oct	Conservative
1964	15 Oct	Labour
1966	31 March	Labour
1970	18 June	Conservative
1974	28 Feb	Labour
1974	10 Oct	Labour
1979	3 May	Conservative
1983	9 June	Conservative
1987	11 June	Conservative
1992	9 April	Conservative
1997	1 May	Labour
2001	7 June	Labour
2005	5 May	Labour
2010	6 May	Coalition§

* Coalition of Coalition Unionist (335 seats), Coalition Liberal (133) and Coalition Labour (10);
opposition parties 229 seats, including Liberal 28 and Labour 63

† National Government of Conservative (473 seats), Liberal National (35), Liberal (33) and National
Labour (13); opposition parties 61 seats, including Labour 52 and Independent Liberal 4

‡ National Government of Conservative (387 seats), Liberal National (33), National Labour (8) and
National (1); opposition parties 186 seats, including Labour 154 and Liberal 21

§ Coalition of Conservative (305 seats) and Liberal Democrat (57); opposition parties 279 seats,
including Labour 256

PRIME MINISTERS

The accession of George I, who was unfamiliar with the English language, led to a disinclination on the part of the Sovereign to preside at meetings of his Ministers and caused the appearance of a Prime Minister, a position first acquired by Robert Walpole in 1721 and retained by him without interruption for 20 years and 326 days. The office of Prime Minister was officially recognised in 1905.

The Prime Minister, by tradition also First Lord of the Treasury and Minister for the Civil Service, is appointed by the Sovereign and is usually the leader of the party which enjoys, or can secure, a majority in the House of Commons. Other ministers are appointed by the Sovereign on the recommendation of the Prime Minister, who also allocates functions among ministers and has the power to obtain their resignation or dismissal individually.

Over the centuries there has been some variation in the determination of the dates of appointment of Prime Ministers. Where possible, the date given is that on which a new Prime Minister kissed the Sovereign's hands and accepted the commission to form a ministry. However, until the middle of the 19th century the dating of a commission or transfer of seals could be the date of taking office. Where the composition of the government changed, eg became a coalition, but the Prime Minister remained the same, the date of the change of government is given.

YEAR APPOINTED

1721	Sir Robert Walpole	*Whig*
1742	The Earl of Wilmington	*Whig*
1743	Henry Pelham	*Whig*
1754	The Duke of Newcastle	*Whig*
1756	The Duke of Devonshire	*Whig*
1757	The Duke of Newcastle	*Whig*
1762	The Earl of Bute	*Tory*
1763	George Grenville	*Whig*
1765	The Marquess of Rockingham	*Whig*
1766	The Earl of Chatham	*Whig*
1768	The Duke of Grafton	*Whig*
1770	Lord North	*Tory*
1782 *March*	The Marquess of Rockingham	*Whig*
1782 *July*	The Earl of Shelburne	*Whig*
1783 *April*	The Duke of Portland	*Coalition*
1783 *Dec.*	William Pitt	*Tory*
1801	Henry Addington	*Tory*
1804	William Pitt	*Tory*
1806	The Lord Grenville	*Whig*

YEAR APPOINTED

1807	The Duke of Portland	*Tory*
1809	Spencer Perceval	*Tory*
1812	The Earl of Liverpool	*Tory*
1827 *April*	George Canning	*Tory*
1827 *Aug.*	Viscount Goderich	*Tory*
1828	The Duke of Wellington	*Tory*
1830	The Earl Grey	*Whig*
1834 *July*	The Viscount Melbourne	*Whig*
1834 *Dec.*	Sir Robert Peel	*Tory*
1835	The Viscount Melbourne	*Whig*
1841	Sir Robert Peel	*Tory*
1846	Lord John Russell (later The Earl Russell)	*Whig*
1852 *Feb.*	The Earl of Derby	*Tory*
1852 *Dec.*	The Earl of Aberdeen	*Peelite*
1855	The Viscount Palmerston	*Liberal*
1858	The Earl of Derby	*Conservative*
1859	The Viscount Palmerston	*Liberal*
1865	The Earl Russell	*Liberal*
1866	The Earl of Derby	*Conservative*
1868 *Feb.*	Benjamin Disraeli	*Conservative*
1868 *Dec.*	William Gladstone	*Liberal*
1874	Benjamin Disraeli	*Conservative*
1880	William Gladstone	*Liberal*
1885	The Marquess of Salisbury	*Conservative*
1886 *Feb.*	William Gladstone	*Liberal*
1886 *July*	The Marquess of Salisbury	*Conservative*
1892	William Gladstone	*Liberal*
1894	The Earl of Rosebery	*Liberal*
1895	The Marquess of Salisbury	*Conservative*
1902	Arthur Balfour	*Conservative*
1905	Sir Henry Campbell-Bannerman	*Liberal*
1908	Herbert Asquith	*Liberal*
1915	Herbert Asquith	*Coalition*
1916	David Lloyd-George	*Coalition*
1922	Andrew Bonar Law	*Conservative*
1923	Stanley Baldwin	*Conservative*
1924 *Jan.*	Ramsay MacDonald	*Labour*
1924 *Nov.*	Stanley Baldwin	*Conservative*
1929	Ramsay MacDonald	*Labour*
1931	Ramsay MacDonald	*Coalition*

YEAR APPOINTED

1935	Stanley Baldwin	*Coalition*
1937	Neville Chamberlain	*Coalition*
1940	Winston Churchill	*Coalition*
1945 *May*	Winston Churchill	*Conservative*
1945 *July*	Clement Attlee	*Labour*
1951	Sir Winston Churchill	*Conservative*
1955	Sir Anthony Eden	*Conservative*
1957	Harold Macmillan	*Conservative*
1963	Sir Alec Douglas-Home	*Conservative*
1964	Harold Wilson	*Labour*
1970	Edward Heath	*Conservative*
1974 *Feb*	Harold Wilson	*Labour (minority government)*
1974 *Oct*	Harold Wilson	*Labour*
1976	James Callaghan	*Labour*
1979	Margaret Thatcher	*Conservative*
1990	John Major	*Conservative*
1997	Tony Blair	*Labour*
2007	Gordon Brown	*Labour*
2010	David Cameron	*Coalition*

LEADERS OF THE OPPOSITION

The office of Leader of the Opposition was officially recognised in 1937 and a salary was assigned to the post.

YEAR APPOINTED

1916	Herbert Asquith	*Liberal*
1918	William Adamson/Sir Donald Maclean	*Labour/Liberal*
1921	John Clynes	*Labour*
1922	Ramsay MacDonald	*Labour*
1924	Stanley Baldwin	*Conservative*
1924	Ramsay MacDonald	*Labour*
1929	Stanley Baldwin	*Conservative*
1931	Arthur Henderson	*Labour*
1931	George Lansbury	*Labour*
1935	Clement Attlee	*Labour*
1945	Clement Attlee	*Labour*
1945	Winston Churchill	*Conservative*
1951	Clement Attlee	*Labour*
1955	Hugh Gaitskell	*Labour*
1963	Harold Wilson	*Labour*
1965	Edward Heath	*Conservative*
1970	Harold Wilson	*Labour*
1974	Edward Heath	*Conservative*
1975	Margaret Thatcher	*Conservative*
1979	James Callaghan	*Labour*
1980	Michael Foot	*Labour*
1983	Neil Kinnock	*Labour*
1992	John Smith	*Labour*
1994	Tony Blair	*Labour*
1997	William Hague	*Conservative*
2001	Iain Duncan Smith	*Conservative*
2003	Michael Howard	*Conservative*
2005	David Cameron	*Conservative*
2010	Harriet Harman (*acting*)	*Labour*

SPEAKERS OF THE COMMONS SINCE 1660

The Speaker of the House of Commons is the spokesman and president of the Chamber. He or she is elected by the House at the beginning of each Parliament or when the previous Speaker retires or dies. The Speaker neither speaks in debates nor votes in divisions except when the voting is equal.

The appointment requires royal approbation before it is confirmed. The present Speaker is the 157th.

PARLIAMENT OF ENGLAND

YEAR APPOINTED

1660 *Jan.*	William Say
1660 *Apr.*	Sir Harbottle Grimston
1661	Sir Edward Turnour
1673 *Feb.*	Sir Job Charlton
1673	Sir Edward Seymour
1678 *April*	Sir Robert Sawyer
1678 *May*	Sir Edward Seymour
1679	Sir William Gregory
1680	Sir William Williams
1685	Sir John Trevor
1689	Henry Powle
1690	Sir John Trevor
1695	Paul Foley
1698	Sir Thomas Lyttleton
1701	Robert Harley (Earl of Oxford and Mortimer)
1705	John Smith

PARLIAMENT OF GREAT BRITAIN

1708	Sir Richard Onslow (Lord Onslow)
1710	William Bromley
1714	Sir Thomas Hanmer
1715	Spencer Compton (Earl of Wilmington)
1728	Arthur Onslow
1761	Sir John Cust
1770	Sir Fletcher Norton (Lord Grantley)
1780	Charles Cornwall
1789 *Jan.*	Hon. William Grenville (Lord Grenville)
1789 *June*	Henry Addington (Viscount Sidmouth)

PARLIAMENT OF UNITED KINGDOM

1801	Sir John Mitford (Lord Redesdale)
1802	Charles Abbot (Lord Colchester)
1817	Charles Manners-Sutton (Viscount Canterbury)
1835	James Abercromby (Lord Dunfermline)
1839	Charles Shaw-Lefevre (Viscount Eversley)
1857	John Evelyn Denison (Viscount Ossington)
1872	Sir Henry Brand (Viscount Hampden)
1886	Arthur Wellesley Peel (Viscount Peel)
1895	William Gully (Viscount Selby)
1905	James Lowther (Viscount Ullswater)
1921	John Whitley
1928	Hon. Edward Fitzroy
1943	Douglas Clifton-Brown (Viscount Ruffside)
1951	William Morrison (Viscount Dunrossil)
1959	Sir Harry Hylton-Foster
1965	Horace King (Lord Maybray-King)
1971	Selwyn Lloyd (Lord Selwyn-Lloyd)
1976	George Thomas (Viscount Tonypandy)
1983	Bernard Weatherill (Lord Weatherill)
1992	Betty Boothroyd (Baroness Boothroyd of Sandwell)
2000	Michael Martin
2009	John Bercow

CHANCELLORS OF THE EXCHEQUER SINCE 1900

YEAR APPOINTED		YEAR APPOINTED	
1895	Sir Michael Hicks-Beach	1931	Neville Chamberlain
1902	Charles Ritchie	1937	Sir John Simon
1903	Austen Chamberlain	1940	Sir Kingsley Wood
1905	Herbert Asquith	1943	Sir John Anderson
1908	David Lloyd George	1945	Hugh Dalton
1915	Reginald McKenna	1947	Sir Stafford Cripps
1916	Andrew Bonar Law	1950	Hugh Gaitskell
1919	Austen Chamberlain	1951	R. A. Butler
1921	Sir Robert Horne	1955	Harold Macmillan
1922	Stanley Baldwin	1957	Peter Thorneycroft
1923	Neville Chamberlain	1958	Derick Heathcoat Amory
1924 *Jan.*	Philip Snowden	1960	Selwyn Lloyd
1924 *Nov.*	Winston Churchill	1962	Reginald Maudling
1929	Philip Snowden	1964	James Callaghan

YEAR APPOINTED		YEAR APPOINTED	
1967	Roy Jenkins	1989	John Major
1970 *June*	Iain Macleod	1990	Norman Lamont
1970 *July*	Anthony Barber	1993	Kenneth Clarke
1974	Denis Healey	1997	Gordon Brown
1979	Sir Geoffrey Howe	2007	Alistair Darling
1983	Nigel Lawson	2010	George Osborne

FOREIGN SECRETARIES SINCE 1900

In 1782 the Northern Department was converted into the Foreign Office, and Charles James Fox was appointed first Secretary of State for Foreign Affairs. With the merger of the Foreign Office and the Commonwealth Office on 1 October 1968 the post was redesignated as Secretary of State for Foreign and Commonwealth Affairs.

YEAR APPOINTED		YEAR APPOINTED	
1900	Marquess of Lansdowne	1963	R. A. Butler
1905	Sir Edward Grey	1964	Patrick Gordon Walker
1916	Arthur Balfour	1965	Michael Stewart
1919	Earl Curzon	1966	George Brown
1924 *Jan.*	Ramsay MacDonald	1968	Michael Stewart
1924 *Nov.*	Sir Austen Chamberlain	1970	Sir Alec Douglas-Home
1929	Arthur Henderson	1974	James Callaghan
1931 *Aug.*	Marquess of Reading	1976	Anthony Crosland
1931 *Nov.*	Sir John Simon	1977	Dr David Owen
1935 *June*	Sir Samuel Hoare	1979	Lord Carrington
1935 *Dec.*	Anthony Eden	1982	Francis Pym
1938	Viscount Halifax	1983	Sir Geoffrey Howe
1940	Anthony Eden	1989 *July*	John Major
1945	Ernest Bevin	1989 *Oct.*	Douglas Hurd
1951 *March*	Herbert Morrison	1995	Malcolm Rifkind
1951 *Oct.*	Anthony Eden	1997	Robin Cook
1955 *April*	Harold Macmillan	2001	Jack Straw
1955 *Dec.*	Selwyn Lloyd	2006	Margaret Beckett
1960	Earl of Home (later Sir Alec Douglas–Home)	2007	David Miliband
		2010	William Hague

HOME SECRETARIES SINCE 1900

In 1782 the Southern Department was converted into the Home Office. The conduct of war was removed from the Home Secretary's hands in 1794 to a separate Secretary of State for War. Colonies were similarly transferred in 1801 to the Secretary for War and Colonies.

YEAR APPOINTED		YEAR APPOINTED	
1900	Charles Ritchie	1957	R. A. Butler
1902	Aretas Akers-Douglas	1962	Henry Brooke
1905	Herbert Gladstone	1964	Sir Frank Soskice
1910	Winston Churchill	1965	Roy Jenkins
1911	Reginald McKenna	1967	James Callaghan
1915	Sir John Simon	1970	Reginald Maudling
1916 *Jan.*	Herbert Samuel	1972	Robert Carr
1916 *Dec.*	Sir George Cave	1974	Roy Jenkins
1919	Edward Shortt	1976	Merlyn Rees
1922	William Bridgeman	1979	William Whitelaw
1924 *Jan.*	Arthur Henderson	1983	Leon Brittan
1924 *Nov.*	Sir William Joynson-Hicks	1985	Douglas Hurd
1929	John Clynes	1989	David Waddington
1931	Sir Herbert Samuel	1990	Kenneth Baker
1932	Sir John Gilmour	1992	Kenneth Clarke
1935	Sir John Simon	1993	Michael Howard
1937	Sir Samuel Hoare	1997	Jack Straw
1939	Sir John Anderson	2001	David Blunkett
1940	Herbert Morrison	2004	Charles Clarke
1945 *May*	Sir Donald Somervell	2006	John Reid
1945 *Aug.*	Chuter Ede	2007	Jacqui Smith
1951	Sir David Maxwell-Fyfe	2009	Alan Johnson
1954	Gwilym Lloyd-George	2010	Theresa May

LORD CHANCELLORS SINCE 1900

YEAR APPOINTED		YEAR APPOINTED	
1895	Lord Halsbury	1945	Lord Jowitt
1905	Lord Loreburn	1951	Lord Simonds
1912	Lord Haldane	1954	Viscount Kilmuir
1915	Lord Buckmaster	1962	Lord Dilhorne
1916	Lord Finlay	1964	Lord Gardiner
1919	Lord Birkenhead	1970	Lord Hailsham of St
1922	Viscount Cave		Marylebone
1924 *Jan.*	Viscount Haldane	1974	Lord Elwyn-Jones
1924 *Nov.*	Viscount Cave	1979	Lord Hailsham of St
1928	Lord Hailsham (later		Marylebone
	Viscount Hailsham)	1987 *June*	Lord Havers
1929	Lord Sankey	1987 *Oct.*	Lord Mackay of Clashfern
1935	Viscount Hailsham	1997	Lord Irvine of Lairg
1938	Lord Maugham	2003	Lord Falconer of Thoroton
1939	Viscount Caldecote	2007	Jack Straw
1940	Viscount Simon	2010	Kenneth Clarke

The Lord Chancellor's role was significantly altered by the Constitutional Reform Act 2005. The office holder is no longer Speaker of the House of Lords or head of the judiciary in England and Wales, and is a cabinet minister from the House of Commons or the House of Lords (the Secretary of State for Justice).

POLITICAL PARTIES AND LEADERS SINCE 1900

CONSERVATIVE PARTY

In the early 19th century the Tory Party became known as 'Conservative', to indicate that the preservation of national institutions was the leading principle of the party.

Until 1922, when the Conservatives were in opposition there were separate leaders of the Conservative Party in the House of Commons and the House of Lords. In the following list, the leaders in the Commons for the relevant years are given (*).

LEADERS OF THE CONSERVATIVE PARTY

1900	Marquess of Salisbury
1902	Arthur Balfour
1911	Andrew Bonar Law*
1921	Austen Chamberlain*
1922	Andrew Bonar Law
1923	Stanley Baldwin
1937	Neville Chamberlain
1940	Winston Churchill
1955	Sir Anthony Eden
1957	Harold Macmillan
1963	Sir Alec Douglas-Home
1965	Edward Heath
1975	Margaret Thatcher
1990	John Major
1997	William Hague
2001	Iain Duncan Smith
2003	Michael Howard
2005	David Cameron

LABOUR PARTY

Labour candidates first stood for Parliament at the general election of 1892, when there were 27 standing as Labour or Liberal-Labour. In 1900 the Labour Representation Committee (LRC) was set up in order to establish a distinct Labour group in parliament. In 1906 the LRC became known as the Labour Party. From 1922 to 1981, when in opposition, the Parliamentary Labour Party elected its leader at the beginning of each session; most elections were uncontested.

CHAIRMEN OF THE PARLIAMENTARY LABOUR PARTY

1906	Keir Hardie
1908	Arthur Henderson
1910	George Barnes
1911	Ramsay MacDonald
1914	Arthur Henderson
1917	William Adamson
1921	John Clynes

CHAIRMEN AND LEADERS OF THE PARLIAMENTARY LABOUR PARTY

1922	Ramsay MacDonald
1931	Arthur Henderson*
1932	George Lansbury
1935	Clement Attlee
1955	Hugh Gaitskell
1963	Harold Wilson

LEADERS OF THE PARLIAMENTARY LABOUR PARTY

1970	Harold Wilson
1976	James Callaghan

LEADERS OF THE LABOUR PARTY

1978	James Callaghan
1980	Michael Foot
1983	Neil Kinnock
1992	John Smith
1994	Tony Blair
2007	Gordon Brown
2010	Harriet Harman (*acting*)

*Arthur Henderson lost his seat in the 1931 election. The acting leader of the Parliamentary Labour Party in 1931 was George Lansbury

LIBERAL DEMOCRAT PARTY

The Liberal Party was officially formed in 1859 by a group of Whigs, Peelites and Radicals, although the term 'Liberals' had been used informally for many years.

The Liberal Party split in 1916 into two factions, which merged again following the 1922 election. In 1931 the party split into three factions: the Liberals, led by Sir Herbert Samuel; the Independent Liberals, led by David Lloyd George; and the National Liberals, led by Sir John Simon. The Independent Liberals rejoined the Liberals in the mid-1930s; the National Liberals gradually merged with the Conservative Party. After 1981 the Liberal Party formed an alliance with the Social Democratic Party (SDP), and in 1988 a majority of the

Liberals agreed on a merger with the SDP under the title Social and Liberal Democrats; since 1989 they have been known as the Liberal Democrats. A minority continue separately as the Liberal Party.

LEADERS OF THE LIBERAL PARTY

1899	Sir Henry Campbell-Bannerman
1908	Herbert Asquith
1926	David Lloyd George
1931	Sir Herbert Samuel
1935	Sir Archibald Sinclair
1945	Clement Davies
1956	Jo Grimond
1967	Jeremy Thorpe
1976	David Steel

LEADERS OF THE LIBERAL DEMOCRATS

1988	David Steel*/Robert Maclennan*
1988	Paddy Ashdown
1999	Charles Kennedy
2006	Menzies Campbell
2007	Nick Clegg

* David Steel and Robert Maclennan merged their respective parties into the Liberal Democrats and were joint leaders until a new leader was elected

ETIQUETTE

FORMS OF ADDRESS

This list covers the forms of address for peers, baronets and knights, their wives and children, and Privy Counsellors.

Both formal and social forms of address are given where usage differs; nowadays, the social form is generally preferred to the formal, which increasingly is used only for official documents and on very formal occasions.

F— represents forename
S— represents surname

BARON
Envelope (formal), The Right Hon. Lord—; (social), The Lord—.
Letter (formal), My Lord; (social), Dear Lord—.
Spoken, Lord—.

BARON'S WIFE
Envelope (formal), The Right Hon. Lady—; (social), The Lady—.
Letter (formal), My Lady; (social), Dear Lady—.
Spoken, Lady—.

BARON'S CHILDREN
Envelope, The Hon. F— S—.
Letter, Dear Mr/Miss/Mrs S—.
Spoken, Mr/Miss/Mrs S—.

BARONESS IN OWN RIGHT
Envelope, may be addressed in same way as a Baron's wife or, if she prefers (formal), The Right Hon. the Baroness—; (social), The Baroness—.
Otherwise as for a Baron's wife.

BARONET
Envelope, Sir F— S—, Bt.
Letter (formal), Dear Sir; (social), Dear Sir F—.
Spoken, Sir F—.

BARONET'S WIFE
Envelope, Lady S—.
Letter (formal), Dear Madam; (social), Dear Lady S—.
Spoken, Lady S—.

COUNTESS IN OWN RIGHT
As for an Earl's wife.

COURTESY TITLES
The heir apparent to a Duke, Marquess or Earl uses the highest of his father's other titles as a courtesy title. The holder of a courtesy title is not styled The Most Hon. or The Right Hon., and in correspondence 'The' is omitted before the title. The heir apparent to a Scottish title may use the title 'Master' (see below).

DAME
Envelope, Dame F— S—, followed by appropriate postnominal letters.
Letter (formal), Dear Madam; (social), Dear Dame F—.
Spoken, Dame F—.

DUKE
Envelope (formal), His Grace the Duke of—; (social), The Duke of—.
Letter (formal), My Lord Duke; (social), Dear Duke.
Spoken (formal), Your Grace; (social), Duke.

DUKE'S WIFE
Envelope (formal), Her Grace the Duchess of—; (social), The Duchess of—.
Letter (formal), Dear Madam; (social), Dear Duchess.
Spoken, Duchess.

DUKE'S ELDEST SON
See Courtesy titles.

DUKE'S YOUNGER SONS
Envelope, Lord F— S—.
Letter (formal), My Lord; (social), Dear Lord F—.
Spoken (formal), My Lord; (social), Lord F—.

DUKE'S DAUGHTER
Envelope, Lady F— S—.
Letter (formal), Dear Madam; (social), Dear Lady F—.
Spoken, Lady F—.

EARL

Envelope (formal), The Right Hon. the Earl (of)——; (social), The Earl (of)——.
Letter (formal), My Lord; (social), Dear Lord——.
Spoken (formal), My Lord; (social), Lord——.

EARL'S WIFE

Envelope (formal), The Right Hon. the Countess (of)——; (social), The Countess (of) ——.
Letter (formal), Madam; (social), Lady——.
Spoken (formal), Madam; (social), Lady——.

EARL'S CHILDREN

Eldest son, see Courtesy titles.
Younger sons, The Hon. F—— S—— (for forms of address, see Baron's children).
Daughters, Lady F—— S—— (for forms of address, see Duke's daughter).

KNIGHT (BACHELOR)

Envelope, Sir F—— S——.
Letter (formal), Dear Sir; (social), Dear Sir F——.
Spoken, Sir F——.

KNIGHT (ORDERS OF CHIVALRY)

Envelope, Sir F—— S——, followed by appropriate postnominal letters.
Otherwise as for Knight Bachelor.

KNIGHT'S WIFE

As for Baronet's wife.

LIFE PEER

As for Baron or for Baroness in own right.

LIFE PEER'S WIFE

As for Baron's wife.

LIFE PEER'S CHILDREN

As for Baron's children.

MARQUESS

Envelope (formal), The Most Hon. the Marquess of——; (social), The Marquess of——.
Letter (formal), My Lord; (social), Dear Lord——.
Spoken (formal), My Lord; (social), Lord——.

MARQUESS'S WIFE
Envelope (formal), The Most Hon. the Marchioness of—; (social),
The Marchioness of—.
Letter (formal), Madam; (social), Dear Lady—.
Spoken, Lady—.

MARQUESS'S CHILDREN
Eldest son, see Courtesy titles.
Younger sons, Lord F— S— (for forms of address, see Duke's younger sons).
Daughters, Lady F— S— (for forms of address, see Duke's daughter).

MASTER
The title is used by the heir apparent to a Scottish peerage, though usually the heir apparent to a Duke, Marquess or Earl uses his courtesy title rather than 'Master'.

Envelope, The Master of—.
Letter (formal), Dear Sir; (social), Dear Master of—.
Spoken (formal), Master, or Sir; (social), Master, or Mr S—.

MASTER'S WIFE
Addressed as for the wife of the appropriate peerage style, otherwise as Mrs S—.

PRIVY COUNSELLOR
Envelope, The Right (or Rt.) Hon. F— S—.
Letter, Dear Mr/Miss/Mrs S—.
Spoken, Mr/Miss/Mrs S—.

It is incorrect to use the letters PC after the name in conjunction with the prefix The Right Hon., unless the Privy Counsellor is a peer below the rank of Marquess and so is styled The Right Hon. because of his rank. In this case only, the post-nominal letters may be used in conjunction with the prefix The Right Hon.

VISCOUNT
Envelope (formal), The Right Hon. the Viscount—; (social), The Viscount—.
Letter (formal), My Lord; (social), Dear Lord—.
Spoken, Lord—.

VISCOUNT'S WIFE
Envelope (formal), The Right Hon. the Viscountess——; (social), The Viscountess——.
Letter (formal), Madam; (social), Dear Lady——.
Spoken, Lady——.

VISCOUNT'S CHILDREN
As for Baron's children.

ORDER OF POSTNOMINAL INITIALS

Postnominal initials appear in the following order:
1   Orders and decorations conferred by the Crown (see below)
2   Appointments to the Queen, eg PC, ADC
3   University degrees
4   Religious orders, eg OSB, SJ
5   Medical qualifications
6   Fellowships of the learned societies
7   Royal academies of art
8   Fellowships of professional institutions, associations etc
9   Writers to the Signet (WS)
10   Appointments
11   Memberships of the armed forces

ORDERS
Bt.   (Baronet) precedes all other letters after the surname
Kt.   (Knight Bachelor) (postnominal initials not usually used)

DECORATIONS

THE VICTORIA CROSS (1856)
For Conspicuous Bravery

VC

Ribbon, crimson, for all services (until
1918 it was blue for the Royal Navy)

THE GEORGE CROSS (1940)
For Gallantry

GC

Ribbon, dark blue, threaded through a bar
adorned with laurel leaves

ORDERS OF CHIVALRY, ETC.*
Initials in parentheses are of honours no longer awarded, though holders of these
honours may still be alive.

KG	Knight/Lady Companion of the Order of the Garter
KT	Knight/Lady of the Order of the Thistle
(KP)	Knight of the Order of St Patrick
GCB	Knight/Dame Grand Cross of the Order of the Bath
OM	Order of Merit
(GCSI)	Knight Grand Commander of the Order of the Star of India
GCMG	Knight/Dame Grand Cross of the Order of St Michael and St George
(GCIE)	Knight Grand Commander of the Order of the Indian Empire
(CI)	Order of the Crown of India
GCVO	Knight/Dame Grand Cross of the Royal Victorian Order
GBE	Knight/Dame Grand Cross of the Order of the British Empire
CH	Companion of Honour
KCB/DCB	Knight/Dame Commander of the Order of the Bath
(KCSI)	Knight Commander of the Order of the Star of India
KCMG/ DCMG	Knight/Dame Commander of the Order of St Michael and St George
(KCIE)	Knight Commander of the Order of the Indian Empire
KCVO/ DCVO	Knight/Dame Commander of the Royal Victorian Order
KBE/DBE	Knight/Dame Commander of the Order of the British Empire
CB	Companion of the Order of the Bath
(CSI)	Companion of the Order of the Star of India
CMG	Companion of the Order of St Michael and St George
(CIE)	Companion of the Order of the Indian Empire
CVO	Commander of the Royal Victorian Order
CBE	Commander of the Order of the British Empire
DSO	Distinguished Service Order
LVO	Lieutenant of the Royal Victorian Order
OBE	Officer of the Order of the British Empire
(ISO)	Imperial Service Order
MVO	Member of the Royal Victorian Order
MBE	Member of the Order of the British Empire

DECORATIONS*

CGC	Conspicuous Gallantry Cross
DSC	Distinguished Service Cross
MC	Military Cross
DFC	Distinguished Flying Cross
AFC	Air Force Cross

OTHER MEDALS*

DCM	Distinguished Conduct Medal
CGM	Conspicuous Gallantry Medal
GM	George Medal
QPM	Queen's Police Medal for gallantry
DSM	Distinguished Service Medal
MM	Military Medal
DFM	Distinguished Flying Medal
AFM	Air Force Medal
CPM	Colonial Police Medal for gallantry
RVM	Royal Victorian Medal
BEM	British Empire Medal
QPM	Queen's Police Medal for distinguished service
QFSM	Queen's Fire Service Medal for distinguished service

EFFICIENCY AND LONG SERVICE DECORATIONS, ETC.*

ERD	Army Emergency Reserve Decoration
(VD)	Volunteer Officers' Decoration
TD	Territorial Decoration
ED	Efficiency Decoration
RD	Decoration for Officers of the Royal Naval Reserve
(VRD)	Decoration for Officers of the Royal Naval Volunteer Reserve
AE	Air Efficiency Award

APPOINTMENTS

In the following order:

QC	Queen's Counsel (until appointed to the High Court)
MP	Member of Parliament
JP	Justice of the Peace
DL	Deputy Lord Lieutenant

*These lists are not all-inclusive but contain the most commonly awarded medals and decorations

RANKS IN THE ARMED FORCES

(The numbers indicate equivalent ranks in each service)

ROYAL NAVY

1 Admiral of the Fleet
2 Admiral (Adm.)
3 Vice-Admiral (Vice-Adm.)
4 Rear-Admiral (Rear-Adm.)
5 Commodore (Cdre)
6 Captain (Capt.)
7 Commander (Cdr)
8 Lieutenant-Commander (Lt.-Cdr)
9 Lieutenant (Lt.)
10 Sub-Lieutenant (Sub-Lt.)
11 Acting Sub-Lieutenant (Acting Sub-Lt.)

ARMY

1 Field Marshal
2 General (Gen.)
3 Lieutenant-General (Lt.-Gen.)
4 Major-General (Maj.-Gen.)
5 Brigadier (Brig.)
6 Colonel (Col.)
7 Lieutenant-Colonel (Lt.-Col.)
8 Major (Maj.)
9 Captain (Capt.)
10 Lieutenant (Lt.)
11 Second Lieutenant (2nd Lt.)

ROYAL AIR FORCE

1 Marshal of the RAF
2 Air Chief Marshal
3 Air Marshal
4 Air Vice-Marshal
5 Air Commodore (Air Cdre)
6 Group Captain (Gp Capt.)
7 Wing Commander (Wg Cdr)
8 Squadron Leader (Sqn Ldr)
9 Flight Lieutenant (Flt Lt.)
10 Flying Officer (FO)
11 Pilot Officer (PO)

FLAG-FLYING DAYS

The correct orientation of the Union Flag when flying is with the broader diagonal band of white uppermost in the hoist (ie near the pole) and the narrower diagonal band of white uppermost in the fly (ie furthest from the pole).

The flying of the Union Flag is decided by the Department for Culture, Media and Sport (DCMS) at the Queen's command.

On 25 March 2008 the DCMS announced that UK government department buildings in England, Scotland and Wales have the freedom to fly the Union Flag at all times and not just on the established days listed below. In addition, on the patron saints' days of Scotland and Wales, the appropriate national flag may also be flown alongside the Union Flag on Whitehall government buildings.

Flags are hoisted in the UK from 8am to sunset.

20 Jan	Countess of Wessex's birthday	9 May	Europe Day*
6 Feb	Accession of the Queen	2 Jun	Coronation Day
19 Feb	Duke of York's birthday	10 Jun	Duke of Edinburgh's birthday
1 Mar	St David's Day (in Wales only)*	11 Jun	The Queen's Official Birthday (2011)
10 Mar	Earl of Wessex's birthday	17 Jul	Duchess of Cornwall's birthday
14 Mar	Commonwealth Day (2011)	15 Aug	Princess Royal's birthday
17 Mar	St Patrick's Day (in Northern Ireland only)†	13 Nov	Remembrance Day (2011)
21 Apr	Birthday of the Queen	14 Nov	Prince of Wales' birthday
23 Apr	St George's Day (in England only)*	20 Nov	Wedding Day of the Queen
		30 Nov	St Andrew's Day (in Scotland only)*

Opening of Parliament by the Queen‡
Prorogation of Parliament by the Queen‡

---

* The appropriate national flag, or the European flag, may be flown in addition to the Union Flag, but not in a superior position

† Only the Union Flag should be flown

‡ Only in the Greater London area, whether or not the Queen performs the ceremony in person

FLAGS AT HALF-MAST

Flags are flown at half-mast on the following occasions:

- from the announcement of the death up to the funeral of the sovereign, except on Proclamation Day, when flags are hoisted right up from 11am to sunset
- the death or funeral of a member of the royal family*
- the funerals of foreign rulers*
- the funerals of prime ministers and ex-prime ministers of the UK*
- other occasions by special command of the Queen

On occasions when days for flying flags coincide with days for flying flags at half-mast, the following rules are observed. Flags are flown at full mast:

- although a member of the royal family, or a near relative of the royal family, may be lying dead, unless special commands are received from the Queen to the contrary
- although it may be the day of the funeral of a foreign ruler

If the body of a very distinguished subject is lying at a government office, the flag may fly at half-mast on that office until the body has left (provided it is a day on which the flag would fly) and then the flag is to be hoisted right up. On all other government buildings the flag will fly as usual.

* Subject to special commands from the Queen in each case

THE ROYAL STANDARD

The Royal Standard comprises four quarterings – two for England (three lions passant), one for Scotland* (a lion rampant) and one for Ireland (a harp).

The Royal Standard is flown when the Queen is in residence at a royal palace, on transport being used by the Queen for official journeys and from Victoria Tower when the Queen attends parliament. It may also be flown on any building (excluding ecclesiastical buildings) during a visit by the Queen.

The Royal Standard is never flown at half-mast, even after the death of the sovereign, as the new monarch immediately succeeds to the throne.

* In Scotland a version with two Scottish quarterings is used

FILM, TV AND MEDIA

'BEST PICTURE' OSCAR WINNERS

1928 Wings
1929 The Broadway Melody
1930 All Quiet On the Western Front
1931 Cimarron
1932 Grand Hotel
1933 Cavalcade
1934 It Happened One Night
1935 Mutiny on the Bounty
1936 The Great Ziegfeld
1937 The Life of Emile Zola
1938 You Can't Take It With You
1939 Gone With the Wind
1940 Rebecca
1941 How Green Was My Valley
1942 Mrs Miniver
1943 Casablanca
1944 Going My Way
1945 The Lost Weekend
1946 The Best Years of Our Lives
1947 Gentleman's Agreement
1948 Hamlet
1949 All the King's Men
1950 All About Eve
1951 An American in Paris
1952 The Greatest Show on Earth
1953 From Here to Eternity
1954 On the Waterfront
1955 Marty
1956 Around the World in 80 Days
1957 The Bridge on the River Kwai
1958 Gigi
1959 Ben-Hur
1960 The Apartment
1961 West Side Story
1962 Lawrence of Arabia
1963 Tom Jones
1964 My Fair Lady

1965 The Sound of Music
1966 A Man for All Seasons
1967 In the Heat of the Night
1968 Oliver!
1969 Midnight Cowboy
1970 Patton
1971 The French Connection
1972 The Godfather
1973 The Sting
1974 The Godfather Part II
1975 One Flew Over the Cuckoo's Nest
1976 Rocky
1977 Annie Hall
1978 The Deer Hunter
1979 Kramer vs Kramer
1980 Ordinary People
1981 Chariots of Fire
1982 Gandhi
1983 Terms of Endearment
1984 Amadeus
1985 Out of Africa
1986 Platoon
1987 The Last Emperor
1988 Rain Man
1989 Driving Miss Daisy
1990 Dances With Wolves
1991 The Silence of the Lambs
1992 Unforgiven
1993 Schindler's List
1994 Forrest Gump
1995 Braveheart
1996 The English Patient
1997 Titanic
1998 Shakespeare in Love
1999 American Beauty
2000 Gladiator
2001 A Beautiful Mind

2002 Chicago
2003 The Lord of the Rings:
     The Return of the King
2004 Million Dollar Baby
2005 Crash

2006 The Departed
2007 No Country for Old Men
2008 Slumdog Millionaire
2009 The Hurt Locker

'BEST ACTOR' OSCAR WINNERS

1928 Emil Jannings, *The Last Command*
1929 Warner Baxter, *In Old Arizona*
1930 George Arliss, *Disraeli*
1931 Lionel Barrymore, *A Free Soul*
1932 Wallace Beery, *The Champ*; Fredric
     March, *Dr. Jekyll and Mr. Hyde*
1933 Charles Laughton, *The Private Life
     of Henry VIII*
1934 Clark Gable, *It Happened One Night*†
1935 Victor McLaglen, *The Informer*
1936 Paul Muni, *The Story of Louis Pasteur*
1937 Spencer Tracy, *Captains Courageous*
1938 Spencer Tracy, *Boys Town*
1939 Robert Donat, *Goodbye, Mr. Chips*
1940 James Stewart, *The Philadelphia
     Story*
1941 Gary Cooper, *Sergeant York*
1942 James Cagney, *Yankee Doodle Dandy*
1943 Paul Lukas, *Watch on the Rhine*
1944 Bing Crosby, *Going My Way*†
1945 Ray Milland, *The Lost Weekend*†
1946 Fredric March, *The Best Years of
     Our Lives*†
1947 Ronald Colman, *A Double Life*
1948 Laurence Olivier, *Hamlet*†
1949 Broderick Crawford, *All the King's
     Men*†
1950 José Ferrer, *Cyrano de Bergerac*
1951 Humphrey Bogart, *The African
     Queen*
1952 Gary Cooper, *High Noon*
1953 William Holden, *Stalag 17*
1954 Marlon Brando, *On The
     Waterfront*†

1955 Ernest Borgnine, *Marty*†
1956 Yul Brynner, *The King and I*
1957 Alec Guinness, *The Bridge on the
     River Kwai*†
1958 David Niven, *Separate Tables*
1959 Charlton Heston, *Ben-Hur*†
1960 Burt Lancaster, *Elmer Gantry*
1961 Maximilian Schell, *Judgment at
     Nuremberg*
1962 Gregory Peck, *To Kill a
     Mockingbird*
1963 Sidney Poitier, *Lilies of the Field*
1964 Rex Harrison, *My Fair Lady*†
1965 Lee Marvin, *Cat Ballou*
1966 Paul Scofield, *A Man for All
     Seasons*†
1967 Rod Steiger, *In the Heat of the
     Night*†
1968 Cliff Robertson, *Charly*
1969 John Wayne, *True Grit*
1970 George C. Scott, *Patton**†
1971 Gene Hackman, *The French
     Connection*†
1972 Marlon Brando, *The Godfather**†
1973 Jack Lemmon, *Save the Tiger*
1974 Art Carney, *Harry and Tonto*
1975 Jack Nicholson, *One Flew Over the
     Cuckoo's Nest*†
1976 Peter Finch, *Network*
1977 Richard Dreyfuss, *The Goodbye
     Girl*
1978 Jon Voight, *Coming Home*
1979 Dustin Hoffman, *Kramer vs Kramer*†
1980 Robert De Niro, *Raging Bull*

1981	Henry Fonda, *On Golden Pond*	1996	Geoffrey Rush, *Shine*
1982	Ben Kingsley, *Gandhi*†	1997	Jack Nicholson, *As Good As It Gets*
1983	Robert Duvall, *Tender Mercies*	1998	Roberto Benigni, *Life Is Beautiful*
1984	F. Murray Abraham, *Amadeus*†	1999	Kevin Spacey, *American Beauty*†
1985	William Hurt, *Kiss of the Spider Woman*	2000	Russell Crowe, *Gladiator*†
1986	Paul Newman, *The Color of Money*	2001	Denzel Washington, *Training Day*
1987	Michael Douglas, *Wall Street*	2002	Adrien Brody, *The Pianist*
1988	Dustin Hoffman, *Rain Man*†	2003	Sean Penn, *Mystic River*
1989	Daniel Day-Lewis, *My Left Foot*	2004	Jamie Foxx, *Ray*
1990	Jeremy Irons, *Reversal of Fortune*	2005	Philip Seymour Hoffman, *Capote*
1991	Anthony Hopkins, *The Silence of the Lambs*†	2006	Forest Whitaker, *The Last King of Scotland*
1992	Al Pacino, *Scent of a Woman*	2007	Daniel Day-Lewis, *There Will Be Blood*
1993	Tom Hanks, *Philadelphia*		
1994	Tom Hanks, *Forrest Gump*†	2008	Sean Penn, *Milk*
1995	Nicholas Cage, *Leaving Las Vegas*	2009	Jeff Bridges, *Crazy Heart*

* indicates the actor or actress refused the award

† indicates actor or actress won their award appearing in that year's best picture

'BEST ACTRESS' OSCAR WINNERS

1928	Janet Gaynor, *7th Heaven*	1944	Ingrid Bergman, *Gaslight*
1929	Mary Pickford, *Coquette*	1945	Joan Crawford, *Mildred Pierce*
1930	Norma Shearer, *The Divorcee*	1946	Olivia de Havilland, *To Each His Own*
1931	Marie Dressler, *Min and Bill*	1947	Loretta Young, *The Farmer's Daughter*
1932	Helen Hayes, *The Sin of Madelon Claudet*	1948	Jane Wyman, *Johnny Belinda*
1933	Katharine Hepburn, *Morning Glory*	1949	Olivia de Havilland, *The Heiress*
1934	Claudette Colbert, *It Happened One Night*†	1950	Judy Holliday, *Born Yesterday*
1935	Bette Davis, *Dangerous*	1951	Vivien Leigh, *A Streetcar Named Desire*
1936	Luise Rainer, *The Great Ziegfeld*†	1952	Shirley Booth, *Come Back, Little Sheba*
1937	Luise Rainer, *The Good Earth*	1953	Audrey Hepburn, *Roman Holiday*
1938	Bette Davis, *Jezebel*	1954	Grace Kelly, *The Country Girl*
1939	Vivien Leigh, *Gone with the Wind*†	1955	Anna Magnani, *The Rose Tattoo*
1940	Ginger Rogers, *Kitty Foyle*	1956	Ingrid Bergman, *Anastasia*
1941	Joan Fontaine, *Suspicion*	1957	Joanne Woodward, *The Three Faces of Eve*
1942	Greer Garson, *Mrs Miniver*†		
1943	Jennifer Jones, *The Song of Bernadette*		

1958	Susan Hayward, *I Want To Live!*
1959	Simone Signoret, *Room at the Top*
1960	Elizabeth Taylor, *Butterfield 8*
1961	Sophia Loren, *Two Women*
1962	Anne Bancroft, *The Miracle Worker*
1963	Patricia Neal, *Hud*
1964	Julie Andrews, *Mary Poppins*
1965	Julie Christie, *Darling*
1966	Elizabeth Taylor, *Who's Afraid of Virginia Woolf?*
1967	Katharine Hepburn, *Guess Who's Coming to Dinner*
1968	Katharine Hepburn, *The Lion in Winter*; Barbra Streisand, *Funny Girl*
1969	Maggie Smith, *The Prime of Miss Jean Brodie*
1970	Glenda Jackson, *Women in Love*
1971	Jane Fonda, *Klute*
1972	Liza Minnelli, *Cabaret*
1973	Glenda Jackson, *A Touch of Class*
1974	Ellen Burstyn, *Alice Doesn't Live Here Anymore*
1975	Louise Fletcher, *One Flew over the Cuckoo's Nest†*
1976	Faye Dunaway, *Network*
1977	Diane Keaton, *Annie Hall†*
1978	Jane Fonda, *Coming Home*
1979	Sally Field, *Norma Rae*
1980	Sissy Spacek, *Coal Miner's Daughter*
1981	Katharine Hepburn, *On Golden Pond*
1982	Meryl Streep, *Sophie's Choice*

1983	Shirley MacLaine, *Terms of Endearment†*
1984	Sally Field, *Places in the Heart*
1985	Geraldine Page, *The Trip to Bountiful*
1986	Marlee Matlin, *Children of a Lesser God*
1987	Cher, *Moonstruck*
1988	Jodie Foster, *The Accused*
1989	Jessica Tandy, *Driving Miss Daisy*
1990	Kathy Bates, *Misery*
1991	Jodie Foster, *The Silence of the Lambs†*
1992	Emma Thompson, *Howards End*
1993	Holly Hunter, *The Piano*
1994	Jessica Lange, *Blue Sky*
1995	Susan Sarandon, *Dead Man Walking*
1996	Frances McDormand, *Fargo*
1997	Helen Hunt, *As Good As It Gets*
1998	Gwyneth Paltrow, *Shakespeare in Love†*
1999	Hilary Swank, *Boys Don't Cry*
2000	Julia Roberts, *Erin Brockovich*
2001	Halle Berry, *Monster's Ball*
2002	Nicole Kidman, *The Hours*
2003	Charlize Theron, *Monster*
2004	Hilary Swank, *Million Dollar Baby†*
2005	Reese Witherspoon, *Walk the Line*
2006	Helen Mirren, *The Queen*
2007	Marion Cotillard, *La Vie en Rose*
2008	Kate Winslet, *The Reader*
2009	Sandra Bullock, *The Blind Side*

† indicates actor or actress won their award appearing in that year's best picture

BOX OFFICE HITS OF 2009

The following are the highest-grossing films of 2009 in the UK and Republic of Ireland, USA and India.

UK & REPUBLIC OF IRELAND BOX OFFICE 2009	GROSS (MILLIONS GBP)
Harry Potter and the Half-Blood Prince	£50.7
Avatar*	£41.0
Ice Age III	£35.0
Up*	£34.4
Slumdog Millionaire	£31.7
The Twilight Saga: New Moon*	£27.1
Transformers: Revenge of the Fallen	£27.1
The Hangover	£22.1
Star Trek	£21.4
Monsters vs Aliens	£21.4

* Film remained in cinemas beyond 10 January 2010 (not reflected in £ gross)
Source: UK Film Council; Rentrak EDI

US BOX OFFICE 2009	GROSS (MILLIONS USD)
Transformers: Revenge of the Fallen	$402.1
Harry Potter and the Half-Blood Prince	$302.0
Up	$293.0
The Twilight Saga: New Moon*	$284.5
Avatar*	$283.6
The Hangover	$277.3
Star Trek	$257.7
Monsters vs Aliens	$198.4
Ice Age: Dawn of the Dinosaurs	$196.6
The Blind Side*	$196.6

* Film remained in cinemas beyond 31 December 2009 (not reflected in $ gross)
Source: MPPA; Rentrack Corporation, CARA

INDIAN BOX OFFICE 2009	GROSS (MILLIONS GBP)
3 Idiots	£31.0
Ajab Prem Ki Ghazab Kahani	£10.5
Love Aaj Kal	£9.2
Wanted (2009)	£8.6
Kembakkht Ishq	£7.8
Paa (2009)	£7.4
De Dana Dan	£7.4
All the Best	£7.2
Kaminey	£6.9
New York	£6.3

(Refers to films released in 2009: includes takings beyond 31 December 2009)

ADVERTISING SLOGANS

YEAR	PRODUCT	SLOGAN
1928	Guinness	Guinness is good for you
1932	Kellogg's Rice Krispies	Snap! Crackle! Pop!
1957	Kit Kat	Have a break. Have a Kit Kat
1967	Heinz	Beanz meanz Heinz
1969	Coca-Cola	It's the real thing
1972	Andrex toilet tissue	Soft, strong and very long
1973	Carlsberg	Probably the best lager in the world
1973	L'Oréal	Because I'm worth it
1985	Creme Egg	How do you eat yours?
1988	Nike	Just do it
1991	Tango	You know when you've been Tango'd
1994	Orange mobile	The future's bright, the future's Orange
1999	Budweiser	Whassup?
2003	McDonald's	I'm lovin' it
2005	Marks and Spencer	This is not just food...

FILM TAG LINES

Alien (1979)	'In space no one can hear you scream.'
Bonnie and Clyde (1967)	'They're young...they're in love...and they kill people.'
Braveheart (1995)	'The courage to face fear.'
E. T.: The Extra Terrestrial (1982)	'He is afraid. He is alone. He is three million light years from home.'
The Fly (1958)	'If she looked upon the horror that her husband had become... She would scream for the rest of her life!'
Frankenstein (1931)	'A Monster Science Created – But Could Not Destroy!'
GoodFellas (1990)	'Murderers come with smiles.'
Jaws (1975)	'Don't go in the water.'
King Kong (1933)	'The strangest story ever conceived by man.'
The Maltese Falcon (1941)	'A story as explosive as his blazing automatics!'
Psycho (1960)	'A new and altogether different screen excitement!!!'
Some Like It Hot (1959)	'The movie too HOT for words!'
The 39 Steps (1935)	'Handcuffed to the girl who double-crossed him.'
The Usual Suspects (1995)	'Five criminals. One line-up. No coincidence.'
The Wizard of Oz (1939)	'Gaiety! Glory! Glamour!'

BBC TIMELINE

1922 The British Broadcasting Company is formed by six wireless manufacturers with the remit of establishing a nationwide network of radio transmitters to broadcast services nationally. Its first broadcast, from London, is a news bulletin read by Arthur Burrows, director of programmes.

1926 The British Broadcasting Company is dissolved.

1927 The company is reformed as a non-commercial, publicly owned service with a royal charter, and begins broadcasting as the British Broadcasting Corporation (BBC).

1932 BBC headquarters opens at Broadcasting House, London W1. The BBC Empire Service (forerunner of the World Service) is launched.

1936 The BBC Television Service is launched. It is later suspended for the duration of World War Two.

1938 The Empire Service begins foreign-language transmissions; by 1942 programmes are broadcast in all major European languages.

1946 Jan Bussell presents *For the Children*, the first children's programme on British TV.

1951 *The Archers*, 'an everyday story of country folk', is broadcast on national radio for the first time.

1953 Queen Elizabeth II's coronation is watched by an estimated 20 million Britons.

1958 The Radiophonics Workshop is founded, creating pioneering sound effects and theme music.

1964 BBC2 is launched on 20 April. A power failure prevents the channel from broadcasting its intended schedule.

1967 Radio 1 is launched, responding to a government ban on pirate pop music stations. The Light, Third and Home networks are reorganised into Radios 2, 3 and 4.

1974 CEEFAX, the world's first teletext service, is launched; in 1979 it begins broadcasting subtitles for the deaf.

1979 BBC Enterprises becomes a limited company, consolidating the BBC's commercial activities into a single subsidiary (renamed BBC Worldwide in 1994).

1985 'Cor, it stinks in here' is the first line spoken in *EastEnders*, by 'Dirty' Den Watts.

1991 BBC World Service Television is launched. The new service is rebranded as BBC World in 1995.

1997 BBC News 24 (renamed BBC News in 2008), a rolling news service, is launched in the UK.

1998 BBC Choice ('BBC3' from 2003) becomes the BBC's first digital channel.

2002 Five Live Sports Extra becomes the BBC's first digital radio station. 6Music, 1Xtra and Asian Network digital radio stations are launched.

2007 BBC iPlayer is launched, allowing viewers to download or stream programmes online.

MOST WATCHED TV

TITLE	AUDIENCE (MILLIONS)

1950s

Title	Audience
Wagon Train	13.63
Take Your Pick	13.16
Sunday Palladium	13.08
Armchair Theatre: Suspicious Mind	12.74
The Army Game	12.60

1960s

Title	Audience
The World Cup Final 1966	32.20
The Royal Family	30.69
Royal Variety Performance 1965	24.20
News (John F. Kennedy Assassination)	24.15
Miss World	23.76

1970s

Title	Audience
Apollo 13 Splashdown	28.60
FA Cup Final Replay: Chelsea vs Leeds	28.49
Princess Anne's Wedding	27.60
To the Manor Born	23.95
Miss World	23.76

1980s

Title	Audience
EastEnders	30.15
Royal Wedding Ceremony	28.40
Coronation Street	26.93
Dallas	21.60
To the Manor Born	21.55

1990s

Title	Audience
The Funeral of Princess Diana	32.10
Only Fools and Horses	24.35
EastEnders	24.30
Winter Olympics 1994: Torvill and Dean	23.95
World Cup 1998: England vs Argentina	23.78

2000 – present

Only Fools and Horses	21.34
Euro 2004: England vs Portugal	20.66
EastEnders	20.05
Coronation Street	19.40
World Cup 2006: England vs Sweden	18.46

Source: BFI/BARB

NATIONAL GRID POWER SURGES

The following table shows the top ten 'TV pick-ups' – where an advert break or end of a football match results in a surge of electricity as millions of people switch on the kettle at the same time. An increase in demand of 2,800 MW is the equivalent of enough hot water to make three million cups of tea.

DATE	PROGRAMME	MW
4 Jul 1990	World Cup Semi-Final – England vs West Germany	2,800
22 Jan 1984	The Thorn Birds	2,600

21 Jun 2002	World Cup – England vs Brazil	2,570
12 Jun 2002	World Cup – England vs Nigeria	2,340
5 Apr 2001	EastEnders – 'Who Shot Phil Mitchell?'	2,290
20 Apr 1991	The Darling Buds of May	2,200
8 May 1985	Dallas	2,200
22 Nov 2003	Rugby World Cup Final – England vs Australia	2,110
18 Apr 1994	Coronation Street	2,100
3 Jun 1998	World Cup – England vs Argentina	2,100

Source: National Grid

THE ALTERNATIVE CHRISTMAS MESSAGE

The Royal Christmas Message to the Commonwealth has been delivered by the British monarch every Christmas Day at 3pm since 1932, and on television since 1957. Channel 4's Alternative Christmas Message was first broadcast in the UK on Christmas Day 1993, also at 3pm, with a message of seasonal goodwill delivered by a popular or topical figure.

1993 – Quentin Crisp (1908–1999), gay icon and writer
1994 – Rev. Jesse Jackson, US civil rights activist and Baptist minister
1995 – Brigitte Bardot, animal rights campaigner and former actor
1996 – Rory Bremner (as Diana, Princess of Wales), satirist
1997 – Margaret Gibney, Belfast schoolgirl and peace campaigner
1998 – Doreen and Neville Lawrence, parents of murdered black teenager Stephen Lawrence (1974–1993)
1999 – Sacha Baron Cohen (as 'Ali G'), comedian
2000 – Helen Jeffries, mother of CJD victim Zoe Jeffries (1985–2000)
2001 – Genelle Guzman, survivor of 11 September attacks on the World Trade Center
2002 – Sharon Osbourne, star of reality television show *The Osbournes*
2003 – Barry and Michelle Seabourn, stars of reality television show *Wife Swap*
2004 – Marge Simpson, animated matriarch of television show *The Simpsons*
2005 – Jamie Oliver, celebrity chef
2006 – 'Khadija', niqab (face-veil) wearing convert to Islam
2007 – Sergeant Major Andrew Stockton, injured Afghanistan war veteran
2008 – President Mahmoud Ahmadinejad of the Islamic Republic of Iran*
2009 – Katie Piper, former model, TV presenter and acid-attack victim

* Shown at 7.15pm due to the controversial choice of speaker

FREEDOM OF THE PRESS

Countries with the most and least press freedom according to the Reporters Without Borders *Worldwide Press Freedom Index*. The index uses 40 criteria to assess the degree of professional freedom enjoyed by journalists and news agencies.

MOST FREEDOM

2009 RANK	COUNTRY	SCORE	2008 RANK (SCORE)	
1*	Denmark	0.0	14	(3.50)
–	Finland	0.0	4	(2.00)
–	Ireland	0.0	4	(2.00)
–	Norway	0.0	1	(1.50)
–	Sweden	0.0	7	(3.00)

LEAST FREEDOM

2009 RANK	COUNTRY	SCORE	2008 RANK (SCORE)	
171	Burma	102.67	170	(94.38)
172	Iran	104.14	166	(80.33)
173	Turkmenistan	107.00	171	(95.50)
174	North Korea	112.50	172	(96.50)
175	Eritrea	115.50	173	(97.50)

* Ranked equal first

Source: Reporters Without Borders *Worldwide Press Freedom Index 2009*

GOOGLE ZEITGEIST

Most popular searches conducted on Google in 2009.

BY CATEGORY (UK)

NEWS	TICKETS	PRODUCTS	I FEEL...
1 swine flu	1 Lady Gaga	1 iPod	1 love
2 Susan Boyle	2 Michael Jackson	2 TV	2 alone
3 Jade Goody	3 Taylor Swift	3 Xbox	3 fine
4 Robert Pattinson	4 Whitney Houston	4 Wii	4 good
5 Rihanna	5 Pixies	5 Nokia	5 sick

WORLDWIDE

HOW TO...	WHAT IS...?	POPULAR PEOPLE	MOST POPULAR
(USA)	(New Zealand)	(Austria)	(China)
1 kiss	1 love	1 Megan Fox	1 QQ*
2 draw	2 Twitter	2 Angelina Jolie	2 Baidu†
3 knit	3 global warming	3 Britney Spears	3 Baidu (in Chinese)
4 crochet	4 Matariki	4 Zac Efron	4 movies
5 flirt	5 swine flu	5 Emma Watson	5 games

* Or Tencent QQ, a popular messaging service in mainland China
† A Chinese search engine
Source: Google 2009 Year-End Zeitgeist (www.google.com/zeitgeist)

FOOD AND DRINK

ALCOHOL

WINE LABELS BY QUALITY

COUNTRY	TABLE WINE	REGIONAL WINE	QUALITY WINE	TOP QUALITY WINE
France	Vin de Table	Vin de Pays	VDQS (Vin Délimité de Qualité Supérieure)	AOC (Appellation d'Origine Contrôlée)
Italy	Vino da Tavola	IGT (Indicazione Geografica Tipica)	DOC (Denominazione di Origine Controlata)	DOCG (Denominazione di Origine Controllata e Garantita)
Germany	Tafelwein	Landwein	QbA (Qualitätswein bestimmter Anbaugebiete)	Prädikatswein or QmP (Qualitätswein mit Prädikat)
Spain	Vino de Mesa	Vino de la Tierra	DO (Denominación de Origen)	DOC (Denominación de Origen Calcificada)
Portugal	Vinho de Mesa	Vinho Regional	IPR (Indicacao de Proveniencia Regulamentada)	DOC (Denominacao de Origem Controlada)

COCKTAILS

The International Bartenders Association divides cocktails into four categories: pre-dinner cocktails, long drinks, popular drinks and after-dinner cocktails.

COCKTAIL	CATEGORY	INGREDIENTS
Bellini	long drink	Dry white sparkling wine, peach purée
Bloody Mary	long drink	Vodka, tomato juice, lemon juice, Worcester sauce, tabasco sauce, salt and pepper
Buck's Fizz	long drink	Champagne, orange juice
Cuba Libre	popular	White rum, cola, lime juice
Daiquiri	pre-dinner	White rum, lemon juice, syrup

Grasshopper	after-dinner	Crème de menthe, white crème de cacao, whipping cream
Harvey Wallbanger	long drink	Vodka, Galliano, orange juice
Long Island Ice Tea	popular	Vodka, gin, tequila, white rum, Cointreau, lemon juice, syrup, cola
Manhattan	pre-dinner	Rye whisky, sweet vermouth, Angostura bitters
Margarita	pre-dinner	Tequila, Cointreau, lemon juice
Martini (dry)	pre-dinner	Gin, dry vermouth
Pina Colada	long drink	Rum, pineapple juice, coconut milk
Sex on the Beach	popular	Vodka, peach schnapps, orange juice, cranberry juice
Tequila Sunrise	long drink	Tequila, orange juice, grenadine
White Russian	after-dinner	Vodka, coffee liqueur, cream

CALORIES IN ALCOHOL

Bitter, ale, lager and cider values are for half a pint (284ml), wine and champagne are a small glass (125ml), spirits are a small measure (25ml), alcopops are per bottle (275ml) and fortified wine is a standard measure (50ml). All figures shown below are average amounts and can vary.

DRINK	ALCOHOL BY VOLUME (%)	UNITS	CALORIES
Alcopop	5	1.4	193
Ale	4	1.1	97
Brandy	40	1	56
Champagne	12	1.5	95
Cider	5	1.4	125
Gin	37.5	0.9	52
Guinness	4.1	1.2	105
Lager	5	1.4	122
Port	20	1	78
Rum	40	1	56
Sherry	17.5	0.9	77
Vodka	40	0.9	52
Whisky	40	1	56
Wine (red)	12	1.5	85
Wine (white)	12	1.5	93

FRENCH WINE REGIONS

HEALTHY EATING

WATER-SOLUBLE VITAMINS

Vitamins are organic compounds, so called because they are vital to life and are essential in small amounts. Care must be taken in cooking to preserve the water-soluble vitamins.

VITAMIN	FUNCTION	SOURCES IN FOOD
C	Maintains connective tissue such as skin and gums; antioxidant	Potatoes; green vegetables; fruit, especially citrus
B1 (Thiamine)	Releases energy from carbohydrate	Milk; wholemeal bread and cereals; meat, especially offal
B2 (Riboflavin)	Utilises energy from food	Dairy produce; yeast; meat, especially liver
B3 (Niacin)	Utilises energy from food	Wholegrain and cereals; fish; meat, especially liver
B6 (Pyridoxine)	Metabolises amino acids and formation of haemoglobin	Occurs widely; especially in wholegrain cereals, meats, fish and eggs
B12	Maintains growth and metabolism; aids the synthesis of red blood cells	Offal; fish; eggs; dairy products
B9 (Folic acid)	Maintains heart health; helps develop healthy foetuses in pregnant women	Offal; green leafy vegetables; fortified bread and cereals

FAT-SOLUBLE VITAMINS

VITAMIN	FUNCTION	SOURCES IN FOOD
A (Retinol)	Maintains healthy skin and tissues; aids resistance to disease and light perception	Fish liver oil; offal; eggs; carrots; green and yellow vegetables; margarine*
D	Controls and maintains calcium absorption, healthy bones and teeth	Fatty fish; eggs; butter; margarine*
E	Protects cell membranes; antioxidant	Plant sources, especially wheatgerm and green vegetables
K	Aids blood clotting	Green vegetables; egg yolk; liver

* Margarine is fortified by law

FRUIT AND VEGETABLES IN SEASON

MONTH	VEGETABLES	FRUIT
January	Artichokes (Jerusalem), Brussels sprouts, cabbages, leeks, onions, parsnips, potatoes	Pears, rhubarb
February	Artichokes (Jerusalem), Brussels sprouts, cabbages, chicory, endive, greens, leeks, onions, potatoes, swede	Rhubarb
March	Broccoli, cabbages, chicory, greens, leeks	Rhubarb
April	Broccoli, cabbages, cauliflower, greens, lettuce, radishes, sea kale, sorrel	Rhubarb
May	Asparagus, carrots, cauliflower, lettuce, radishes, rocket, sea kale, sorrel, watercress	Rhubarb
June	Asparagus, broad beans, carrots, cauliflower, lettuce, peas, radishes, sorrel, watercress	Cherries, gooseberries, rhubarb, strawberries
July	Artichokes (globe), beetroot, French beans, garlic, kohlrabi, pak choi, peas, potatoes, radishes, spinach, tomatoes	Blackcurrants, cherries, gooseberries, raspberries, redcurrants, strawberries
August	Artichokes (globe), aubergines, beans, beetroot, cabbages, cauliflower, chard, courgettes, cucumber, fennel, garlic, kohlrabi, onions, peas, potatoes, radishes, spinach, sweetcorn, tomatoes, watercress	Apricots, blackberries, blackcurrants, blueberries, nectarines, peaches, plums, raspberries, redcurrants
September	Artichokes (globe), aubergines, beans, beetroot, broccoli, cabbages, carrots, cauliflower, chard, chillies, courgettes, fennel, garlic, kale, kohlrabi, lamb's lettuce, onions, pak choi, peppers, pumpkins, rocket, spinach, sweetcorn, tomatoes, watercress	Apples, blackberries, blueberries, greengages, peaches, pears, plums, raspberries
October	Beetroot, broccoli, cabbages, carrots, cauliflower, celeriac, celery, courgettes, kale, kohlrabi, leeks, onions, peppers, potatoes, pumpkins, spinach, tomatoes, turnips	Apples, grapes, pears, quinces, raspberries
November	Artichoke (Jerusalem), beetroot, cabbages, carrots, celeriac, celery, chicory, endive, greens, kohlrabi, leeks, lettuce, onions, parsnips, potatoes, pumpkins, swede, turnips	Apples, pears, quinces, raspberries
December	Artichoke (Jerusalem), Brussels sprouts, carrots, greens, kale, leeks, onions, parsnips, potatoes, swede, turnips	Apples

GUIDELINE DAILY AMOUNTS

	MEN	WOMEN	CHILDREN (over 5)
Calories	2,500	2,000	1,800
Fat	95g	70g	70g
Saturated fat	30g	20g	20g
Sugar	120g	90g	85g
Salt	6g	6g	4g

BODY MASS INDEX

Body Mass Index is a way to measure weight in relation to height. Calculate your Body Mass Index using:

$$BMI = \frac{Weight\ (kg)}{Height\ (m^2)}$$

The World Health Organisation recommends that a healthy BMI is between 18.5 and 24.9, less than 18.5 is underweight, and over 30 is obese.

TYPES OF CHEESE

CHEESE	COUNTRY	CHARACTERISTICS
Brie	France	Soft, cow's milk, downy rind
Camembert	France	Soft, cow's milk, downy rind
Cheddar	England	Hard, cow's milk, white to yellow
Dolcelatte	Italy	Semi-soft, cow's milk, mould-ripened, blue/green veined
Edam	The Netherlands	Semi-hard, skimmed cow's milk, mild, red wax rind
Emmenthal	Switzerland	Hard, cow's milk, creamy
Gorgonzola	Italy	Semi-hard, cow's milk, mould-ripened, blue/green veined
Gouda	The Netherlands	Semi-hard, cow's milk, mild, yellow wax rind
Gruyère	Switzerland	Hard, cow's milk, small holes
Feta	Greece	Soft, ewe's or goat's milk, salty
Lancashire	England	Hard, cow's milk, white, crumbly
Manchego	Spain	Semi-hard, ewe's milk, mild or sharp
Munster	France	Semi-soft, cow's milk, bacteria-ripened
Parmesan	Italy	Very hard, cow's milk, bacteria-ripened, long cure
Roquefort	France	Semi-hard, ewe's milk, blue veined
Stilton	England	Semi-hard, cow's milk, mould-ripened, blue veined

BEEF CUTS

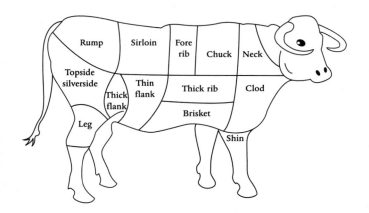

CULINARY TERMS

TERM	DEFINITION
Al dente	Of pasta that is firm when bitten (*trans.* to the tooth)
Aperitif	Alcoholic drink taken before a meal
Au gratin	Covered with breadcrumbs and/or cheese and cooked until golden brown
Balti	Cooked and served in a pan resembling a wok
Béchamel	White sauce infused with carrot, onion, celery, black peppercorns and bay leaf
Blanch	To boil food in water briefly
Bourguignonne	Cooked in a red wine sauce with mushrooms and onions
Braise	To cook slowly with a small amount of liquid
Bruschetta	Sliced ciabatta bread topped with garlic, olive oil, fresh tomatoes and basil
Alla cacciatora	Cooked with tomatoes, mushrooms, onions and herbs
Canapé	Appetiser, small piece of bread or toast with savoury topping
Chasseur	Sauce made with mushrooms, white wine, shallots and herbs
Dhal	Thick, spicy stew prepared with split pulses
En croûte	Wrapped in pastry and baked
Entrecôte	Boneless steak of beef cut from the sirloin
Entrée	Dish served before the main course
Flambé	To cover food with alcohol and ignite before serving
Florentine	Cooked in the style of Florence, usually with spinach
Frikkadel	Fried ball of minced meat
Frittata/Tortilla	Thick omelette often containing potatoes, vegetables, cheese and ham
Gnocchi	Small potato and flour dumplings
Haute cuisine	Fine cuisine, elaborately prepared
Hors d'oeuvre	Appetiser served before a meal
à la Lyonnaise	Sautéed meat or vegetables with chopped onions cooked in butter, vinegar and chopped parsley
Millefeuille	Small rectangular pastries made from thin layers of puff pastry with whipped cream and jam or fruit
En papillote	Food cooked and served in parchment paper
Passata	Italian sauce made from sieved tomatoes
Roux	Cooked mixture of flour and fat used to thicken sauces
Sauté	To quickly fry in a shallow pan
Tagine	Meat or vegetable stew cooked in an earthenware dish with a conical lid
Tapas	Spanish appetisers, can make up a whole meal
Tikka	Meat marinated in yoghurt and spices, cooked in a clay oven
Timbale	A layered rice dish cooked in a tall mould

SHOOTING SEASONS

DEER

The statutory close seasons for deer are listed below; it is illegal to shoot deer during this time.

SPECIES	SEX	ENGLAND AND WALES	SCOTLAND
Red	Stags	1 May–31 Jul	21 Oct–30 Jun
	Hinds	1 Apr–31 Oct	16 Feb–20 Oct
Fallow	Bucks	1 May–31 Jul	1 May–31 Jul
	Does	1 Apr–31 Oct	16 Feb–20 Oct
Sika	Stags	1 May–31 Jul	21 Oct–30 Jun
	Hinds	1 Apr–31 Oct	16 Feb–20 Oct
Roe	Bucks	1 Nov–31 Mar	21 Oct–31 Mar
	Does	1 Apr–31 Oct	1 Apr–20 Oct
Red/Sika	Stags	1 May–31 Jul	21 Oct–30 Jun
Hybrids	Hinds	1 Apr–31 Oct	16 Feb–20 Oct
Chinese Water	Buck	1 Apr–31 Oct	–
Deer	Doe	1 Apr–31 Oct	–

GAME

It is an offence to kill or take game birds between the following dates and on Sundays and Christmas Day (in England and Wales)

GAME BIRD (COMMON NAME)	CLOSE SEASONS
Black game (black grouse)	10 Dec–20 Aug
Capercaillie*	1 Feb–30 Sept
Grouse (red grouse and ptarmigan)	10 Dec–12 Aug
Partridges (grey partridge and red-legged partridge)	1 Feb–1 Sep
Pheasants	1 Feb–1 Oct
Snipe, Common	1 Feb–11 Aug
Woodcock†	1 Feb–30 Sept

* Capercaillie are now fully protected in Scotland
† The close season for woodcock is different in Scotland (1 Feb to 31 Aug)

GEOGRAPHY

THE EARTH

DIMENSIONS

Surface area = 510,069,120 km² (196,938,800 miles²), of which water makes up 70.92 per cent and land 29.08 per cent
Equatorial diameter = 12,756.27 km (7,926.38 miles)
Polar diameter = 12,713.50 km (7,899.80 miles)
Equatorial circumference = 40,075.01 km (24,901.46 miles)
Polar circumference = 40,007.86 km (24,859.73 miles)

Equator = 0°
North Pole = 90° N.
South Pole = 90° S.
Tropic of Cancer = 23°27′ N.
Tropic of Capricorn = 23°27′ S.
Arctic Circle = 66°33′ N.
Antarctic Circle = 66°33′ S.

The Tropics and the Arctic and Antarctic circles are affected by the slow decrease in obliquity of the ecliptic, of about 0.5 arcseconds per year. The effect of this is that the Arctic and Antarctic circles are currently moving towards their respective poles by about 14 metres a year, while the Tropics move towards the Equator by the same amount.

The Earth is divided by geologists into three layers:

Crust   thin outer layer, with an average depth of 24 km/15 miles, although the depth varies widely depending on whether it is under land or sea
Mantle lies between the crust and the core and is about 2,865 km/1,780 miles thick
Core   extends from the mantle to the Earth's centre and is about 6,964 km/4,327 miles in diameter

THE ATMOSPHERE

The atmosphere is the air or mixture of gases enveloping the Earth. Various layers are identified by scientists, based on rate of temperature change, composition, etc. Most weather conditions form in the troposphere, and this is also the layer where most pollutants released into the atmosphere by human activity accumulate. The stratosphere is the layer in which most atmospheric ozone is found.

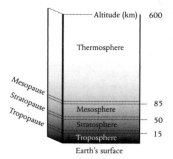

The component gases of the atmosphere are:

GAS	% BY VOL.	GAS	% BY VOL.
Nitrogen	78.10	Methane	0.00017
Oxygen	20.95	Krypton	0.00011
Argon	0.934	Hydrogen	0.00005
Carbon dioxide	0.038	Nitrous oxide	0.00005
Neon	0.00182	Ozone	0.00004
Helium	0.00052	Xenon	0.000009

ATMOSPHERIC POLLUTION

The Framework Convention on Climate Change was adopted by 153 states at the UN conference on environment and development at Rio de Janeiro, Brazil, in 1992. Its aim is to reduce the risks of global warming by limiting greenhouse gas emissions. Progress towards the convention's targets is assessed at regular conferences. Under the Kyoto protocol, which came into force in 2005, 37 industrialised countries agreed to legally binding targets for cutting emissions of greenhouses gases by 5.2 per cent below 1990 levels by 2008–12. EU members agreed to an 8 per cent reduction, and the UK to 12.5 per cent. The political weight of the agreement has been reduced by the failure of the USA, India and China to sign up to its framework. The UN Climate Change Conference held in Copenhagen, Denmark, in December 2009 failed to reach a consensus on a legally binding successor to Kyoto.

The six main 'greenhouse' gases identified by the convention are:

carbon dioxide	hydrofluorocarbons (HFCs)
methane	perfluorocarbons (PFCs)
nitrous oxide	sulphur hexafluoride (SF_6)

GEOLOGICAL TIME

PRECAMBRIAN ERA *c.*4,600 – *c.*542 million years ago

Hadean	Earth uninhabited
Archean	Earth uninhabited
Proterozoic	First primitive life forms, eg algae, bacteria

PALAEOZOIC ERA ('ancient life') *c.*542 – *c.*251 million years ago

Cambrian	Mainly sandstones, slate and shales; limestones in Scotland. First shelled fossils and invertebrates
Ordovician	Mainly shales and mudstones, eg in north Wales. First fish
Silurian	Shales, mudstones and some limestones, found mostly in Wales and southern Scotland
Devonian	Old red sandstone, shale, limestone and slate, eg in south Wales and the West Country
Carboniferous	Coal-bearing rocks, millstone grit, limestone and shale. First traces of land-living creatures
Permian	Marls, sandstones and clays. Glaciations in southern continents. First reptiles

MESOZOIC ERA ('middle forms of life') *c.*251 – *c.*65.5 million years ago

Triassic	Mostly sandstone, eg in the West Midlands. First mammals
Jurassic	Mainly limestones and clays, typically displayed in the Jura mountains, and in England in a NE–SW belt from Lincolnshire and the Wash to the Severn and the Dorset coast. First birds
Cretaceous	Mainly chalk, clay and sands, eg in Kent and Sussex

CENOZOIC ERA ('recent life') from *c.*65.5 million years ago

PALAEOGENE

Palaeocene	Emergence of new forms of life, including existing species
Eocene	Emergence of first modern mammals
Oligocene	Fossils of a few still existing species

NEOGENE

Miocene	Fossil remains show a balance of existing and extinct species
Pliocene	Fossil remains show a majority of still existing species

QUATERNARY

Pleistocene	Glaciations and interglacials Majority of remains are those of still existing species
Holocene	Present, post-glacial period Existing species only, except for a few exterminated by humans

EARTHQUAKES

Movements on or in the Earth generate seismic waves. These can be measured in a variety of ways, and there are a number of different scales for comparing the relative size of earthquakes based on seismic waves, usually called seismic magnitudes. The nature of seismic waves means that any one earthquake can have many different seismic magnitudes. The main magnitude scales are:

NAME	PERIOD OF MEASUREMENT (IN SECONDS)
Richter magnitude	0.1–1
body wave magnitude	1–5
surface wave magnitude	20
moment magnitude	>200

The point of initiation of an earthquake is known as the hypocentre (usually given in terms of latitude, longitude, and depth below the surface). The epicentre is the surface projection of the hypocentre.

RICHTER SCALE

Named after Charles Richter, who invented seismic magnitude scales in the 1930s.

MAGNITUDE	INTENSITY
1	Detectable only by instruments
2	Barely detectable, even near epicentre
3	Similar to vibrations from a heavy goods vehicle
4–5	Detectable within 32km (20 miles) of the epicentre; possible slight damage within a small area
6	Moderately destructive, chimneys fall, houses move on foundations
7	Major earthquake, bridges twist, walls fracture, buildings collapse
8	Great earthquake, surface waves seen, objects thrown in the air
9	Widespread destruction

THE WORLD'S MOST DESTRUCTIVE EARTHQUAKES

(by number of fatalities, Richter scale)

DATE	LOCATION	FATALITIES	MAGNITUDE
23 January 1556	China, Shaanxi	830,000	~8
27 July 1976	China, Tangshan	255,000*	7.5
9 August 1138	Syria, Aleppo	230,000	Unknown
26 December 2004	Sumatra	227,898	9.1
12 January 2010	Haiti	222,570	7.0

* Official number; real figure possibly as high as 650,000

WEATHER

WIND FORCE MEASURES

The Beaufort Scale of wind force is used internationally in communicating weather conditions. Devised originally by Admiral Sir Francis Beaufort in 1805 as a scale of 0–12, it was extended to Force 17 by the US Weather Bureau in the 1950s. Each scale number represents a certain strength or velocity of wind at 10 m (33 ft) above ground in the open.

SCALE NO.	WIND FORCE	KPH	MPH	KNOTS
0	Calm	0–1	0–1	0–1
1	Light air	1–5	1–3	1–3
2	Light breeze	6–11	4–7	4–6
3	Gentle breeze	12–19	8–12	7–10
4	Moderate breeze	20–28	13–18	11–16
5	Fresh breeze	29–38	19–24	17–21
6	Strong breeze	39–49	25–31	22–27
7	Near gale	50–61	32–38	28–33
8	Gale	62–74	39–46	34–40
9	Strong gale	75–88	47–54	41–47
10	Whole gale	89–103	55–63	48–55
11	Storm	104–117	64–72	56–63
12	Hurricane	118–133	73–82	64–71
13	—	134–148	83–92	72–80
14	—	149–166	93–103	81–89
15	—	167–183	104–114	90–99
16	—	184–201	115–125	100–108
17	—	202–219	126–136	109–118

WEATHER RECORDS (UK)

Highest daily temperature	38.5°C	Faversham, Kent (2003)
Lowest daily temperature	−27.2°C	Braemar, Aberdeenshire (1895, 1982) Altnaharra, Highland (1995)
Highest monthly sunshine	383.9hrs	Eastbourne, Sussex (1911)
Highest gust speed (low-level)	123 knots	Fraserburgh, Aberdeenshire (1989)
Highest 24-hour rainfall	316.4mm	Seathwaite, Cumbria (2009)

CLOUD TYPES

Clouds comprise suspended particles of water or ice, or both. The water is condensed from air which rises into levels of lower atmospheric pressure, expands and cools to form water drops. These can remain liquid to temperatures of -30°C but below this temperature start to freeze to ice crystals. Below -40°C, clouds consist of ice crystals alone.

Clouds are classified according to the height of their base from the ground and to their shape. The basic cloud types are:

cirrus (a filament of hair)	high wispy ice clouds
stratus (a layer)	laminar, eg flat
cumulus (a heap or pile)	rounded, with strong vertical structure
nimbus (a rain cloud)	precipitating

The original classification scheme, devised by an English pharmacist, Luke Howard, in 1803, has been expanded to include ten cloud types:

TYPE (BASE HEIGHT ABOVE GROUND LEVEL)	WATER PHASE	DISTINCTIVE FEATURES
HIGH CLOUDS (over 5,000m/16,500ft)		
Cirrus (Ci)	ice	mares tails
Cirrostratus (Cs)	ice	halo cloud
Cirrocumulus (Cc)	ice or mixed	mackerel sky
MIDDLE CLOUDS (2,000m/6,500ft to 7,000m/23,000ft)		
Altostratus (As)	mixed or ice	overcast
Altocumulus (Ac)	liquid or mixed	widespread, cotton balls
LOW CLOUDS (below 2,000m/6,500ft)		
Nimbostratus (Ns)	mixed or ice	low, dark grey
Stratus (St)	liquid	hazy layer, like high fog
Stratocumulus (Sc)	liquid or mixed	widespread, heavy rolls
VERTICAL CLOUDS (1,000m/3,000ft to 5,000m/16,500ft)		
Cumulus (Cu)	liquid	fluffy, billowy
Cumulonimbus (Cb)	mixed	flat bottom, anvil-shaped top

WORLD GEOGRAPHICAL STATISTICS

OCEANS

AREA	KM^2	MILES^2
Pacific	155,557,000	59,270,000
Atlantic	76,762,000	29,638,000
Indian	68,556,000	26,467,000
Southern*	20,327,000	7,848,300
Arctic	14,056,000	5,427,000

* In 2000 the International Hydrographic Organisation approved the description of the 20,327,000km^2 (7,848,300 miles^2) of circum-Antarctic waters up to 60°S. as the Southern Ocean. The division by the Equator of the Pacific into the North and South Pacific and the Atlantic into the North and South Atlantic makes a total of seven oceans.

SEAS

AREA	KM^2	MILES^2
South China	2,974,600	1,148,500
Caribbean	2,515,900	971,400
Mediterranean	2,509,900	969,100
Bering	2,261,000	873,000
Gulf of Mexico	1,507,600	582,100
Okhotsk	1,392,000	537,500
Japan	1,012,900	391,100
Hudson Bay	730,100	281,900
East China	664,600	256,600
Andaman	564,880	218,100
Black Sea	507,900	196,100
Red Sea	453,000	174,900
North Sea	427,100	164,900
Baltic Sea	382,000	147,500
Yellow Sea	294,000	113,500
Persian Gulf	230,000	88,800

THE CONTINENTS

There are six geographic continents, although America is often divided politically into North, Central and South America.

AREA	KM^2	MILES^2
Asia	43,998,000	16,988,000
America*	41,918,000	16,185,000
Africa	29,800,000	11,506,000
Antarctica	13,209,000	5,100,000
Europe†	9,699,000	3,745,000
Australia	7,618,493	2,941,526

* North and Central America have a combined area of 24,255,000km^2 (9,365,000 miles^2)

† Includes 5,571,000km^2 (2,151,000 miles^2) of former USSR territory, including the Baltic states, Belarus, Moldova, the Ukraine and part of Russia west of the Ural mountains and Kazakhstan west of the Ural river. European Turkey (24,378km^2/9,412 miles^2) comprises territory to the west and north of the Bosporus and the Dardanelles

LARGEST ISLANDS

AREA	KM^2	MILES^2
Greenland	2,175,500	840,000
New Guinea	792,500	306,000
Borneo	725,450	280,100
Madagascar	587,041	226,674
Baffin Island	507,451	195,928
Sumatra	427,350	165,000
Honshu	227,413	87,805
Great Britain*	218,077	84,200
Victoria Island	217,292	83,897
Ellesmere Island	196,236	75,767

* Mainland only

LARGEST DESERTS

AREA	KM^2	MILES^2
Sahara	9,000,000	3,500,000
Gobi	1,300,000	500,000
Australian*	1,120,000	460,000
Arabian	1,000,000	385,000
Kalahari	570,000	220,000
Taklimakan Shamo	320,000	125,000

* includes Great Sandy, Gibson, Simpson and Great Victoria

HIGHEST MOUNTAINS

The world's 8,000-metre mountains (with six subsidiary peaks) are all in Asia's
Himalaya-Karakoram-Hindu Kush ranges.

	HEIGHT	
	METRES	FEET
Mt Everest (Qomolangma)	8,850	29,035
K2 (Qogir)†	8,611	28,251
Kangchenjunga	8,597	28,208
Lhotse I	8,510	27,923
Makalu I	8,480	27,824
Lhotse Shar (II)	8,400	27,560

† Formerly Godwin-Austin

The culminating summits in the other major mountain ranges are:

	HEIGHT	
	METRES	FEET
Pik Pobedy, Tien Shan	7,439	24,406
Cerro Aconcagua, Andes	6,960	22,834
Mt McKinley (S. Peak), Alaska	6,194	20,320
Kilimanjaro, Tanzania	5,894	19,340
Hkakabo Razi, Myanmar	5,881	19,296
Citlaltépetl, Mexico	5,655	18,555
El'brus (W. Peak), Caucasus	5,642	18,510
Vinson Massif, Antarctica	4,897	16,066
Puncak Jaya, New Guinea	4,884	16,023
Mt Blanc, Alps	4,807	15,771

BRITISH ISLES (by country)		
Ben Nevis, Scotland	1,344	4,406
Snowdon, Wales	1,085	3,559
Carrantuohill, Rep. of Ireland	1,050	3,414
Scafell Pike, England	977	3,210

LARGEST LAKES

The areas of some of these lakes are subject to seasonal variation.

	AREA	
	KM²	MILES²
Caspian Sea, Iran/Azerbaijan/ Russia/Turkmenistan/Kazakhstan	371,000	143,000
Michigan-Huron, USA/Canada*	117,610	45,300

	AREA	
	KM²	MILES²
Superior, Canada/USA	82,100	31,700
Victoria, Uganda/Tanzania/Kenya	69,500	26,828
Tanganyika, Dem. Rep. of Congo/ Tanzania/Zambia/Burundi	32,900	12,665
Great Bear, Canada	31,328	12,096
Baykal (Baikal), Russia	30,500	11,776
Malawi (Nyasa), Tanzania/Malawi/ Mozambique	28,900	11,150

* Lakes Michigan and Huron are regarded as lobes of the same lake. The Michigan lobe has an area of 57,750km² (22,300 miles²) and the Huron lobe an area of 59,570km² (23,000 miles²)

UNITED KINGDOM (by country)		
Lough Neagh, Northern Ireland	381.73	147.39
Loch Lomond, Scotland	71.12	27.46
Lake Windermere, England	14.74	5.69
Lake Vyrnwy (artificial), Wales	4.53	1.75
Llyn Tegid (Bala) (natural), Wales	4.38	1.69

DEEPEST LAKES

	GREATEST DEPTH	
	METRES	FEET
Baikal, Russia	1,637	5,371
Tanganyika, Burundi/Tanzania/Dem. Rep. of Congo/Zambia	1,470	4,825
Caspian Sea, Azerbaijan/Iran/Kazakhstan/Russia/Turkmenistan	1,025	3,363
Malawi, Malawi/Mozambique/Tanzania	706	2,316
Issyk Kul, Kyrgyzstan	702	2,303
Great Slave, Canada	614	2,015
Danau Toba, Indonesia	590	1,936
Hornindalsvatnet, Norway	514	1,686
Sarezskoye Ozero, Tajikistan	505	1,657
Tahoe, California/Nevada, USA	501	1,645
Lago Argentina, Argentina	500	1,640
Lac Kivu, Rwanda/Dem. Rep. of Congo	480	1,574

All these lakes would be sufficiently deep to submerge the Empire State Building – in the case of Lake Baikal, more than four times over.

LONGEST RIVERS

	LENGTH	
	KM	MILES
Nile, Africa	6,725	4,180
Amazon, S. America	6,448	4,007
Yangtze-Kiang (Chang Jiang), China	6,380	3,964
Mississippi-Missouri-Red Rock, N. America	5,970	3,710
Yenisey-Angara, Mongolia/Russia	5,536	3,440
Huang He (Yellow River), China	5,463	3,395
BRITISH ISLES (by country)		
Shannon, Rep. of Ireland	386	240
Severn, Britain	354	220
Thames, England	346	215
Tay, Scotland	188	117
Clyde, Scotland	158	98.5

HIGHEST WATERFALLS

	TOTAL DROP		GREATEST SINGLE LEAP	
WATERFALL, RIVER AND LOCATION	METRES	FEET	METRES	FEET
Saltó Angel, Carrao Auyán Tepuí, Venezuela	979	3,212	807	2,648
Tugela, Tugela, Natal, S. Africa	948	3,110	410	1,350
Ramnefjellsfossen, Jostedal Glacier, Norway	800	2,625	600	1,970
Mongefossen, Monge, Norway	773	2,535	—	—
Gocta, Cocahuayco, Peru	771	2,531	—	—
Mutarazi, Zambezi, Zimbabwe	762	2,499	479	1,572
Yosemite, Yosemite Creek, USA	739	2,425	435	1,430
Ostre Mardola Foss, Mardals, Norway*	655	2,149	296	974
Tyssestrengene, Tysso, Norway*	646	2,120	289	948
Cuquenán, Arabopó, Venezuela	610	2,000	—	—

* cascades

LANGUAGE

MOST WIDELY SPOKEN LANGUAGES

The number of first-language speakers of the standard form of each language.

LANGUAGE	SPEAKERS (MILLIONS)
1. Mandarin Chinese	845
2. Spanish	329
3. English	328
4. Arabic	221
5. Hindi	182
6. Bengali	181
7. Portuguese	178
8. Russian	144
9. Japanese	122
10. German	90

© SIL, Ethnologue 16th Edition
(www.ethnologue.com)

COMMON PUNCTUATION MARKS AND DIACRITICS

,	comma
;	semicolon
:	colon
.	full stop
?	question mark
!	exclamation mark
'	apostrophe
' '	single quotation marks
" "	double quotation marks
( )	parentheses
[ ]	square brackets
< >	angle brackets
{ }	curly brackets or braces
-	hyphen
—	dash
/	slash/stroke
\	backslash
&	ampersand
*	asterisk
...	mark of omission/ellipsis
á	acute accent
à	grave accent
â	circumflex
ç	cedilla
ë	umlaut or diaeresis
ñ	tilde
š	caron

COLLECTIVE NOUNS FOR ANIMALS

Ants	army, bike, colony, swarm
Apes	shrewdness
Bears	sloth
Camels	caravan, flock
Caterpillars	army
Cats	clowder, cluster
Chickens	brood, clutch, peep
Crows	hover, murder, parcel
Dogs	cowardice, kennel, pack
Doves	dole, flight
Flamingos	flurry, regiment, stand
Flies	business, cloud, swarm
Foxes	earth, lead, skulk, troop
Frogs	army, colony
Goldfinches	charm, chattering
Goldfish	troubling
Grasshoppers	cloud
Hares	down, drove, husk, trip
Hawks	kettle, mews
Hedgehogs	array
Jellyfish	brood, smuck
Larks	exaltation
Leopards	leap
Lions	flock, pride, troop
Magpies	tiding, tittering

REG 01 09 2018 12:55
0001 000063

2X   @1/ 0.60
BOOKS/MEDIA   ·1.20
TL   1.20
CASH   ·2.00
CHANGE   ·0.80

Moles	labour, movement	Seals	harem, herd, pod, rookery
Monkeys	troop	Snakes	nest, pit
Mules	barren, pack, span	Snipe	walk, whisper, wish, wisp
Otters	bevy, family	Sparrows	host, quarrel
Owls	parliament, stare	Spiders	cluster, clutter
Peacocks	muster	Squirrels	drey
Penguins	colony, rookery	Starlings	chattering, murmuration
Pigs	herd, drove	Swans	bank, wedge, whiteness
Rabbits	bury, colony, nest, warren	Tigers	ambush
Raccoons	nursery	Toads	knab, knot
Rats	colony	Turkeys	posse, raffle, rafter
Ravens	unkindness	Turtles	bale, dule, turn
Rhinoceros	crash	Wasps	bike, herd, nest, pledge
Rooks	clamour, parliament	Whales	herd, pod, school

NAMES OF MALE, FEMALE AND YOUNG ANIMALS

ANIMAL	MALE	FEMALE	YOUNG
Ant	drone	queen, worker	larvae
Bear	boar	sow	cub
Cat	tom	queen	kitten
Deer	buck, stag	doe	fawn
Donkey	jack, jackass	jennet, jenny	colt, foal
Elephant	bull	cow	calf
Fox	reynard	vixen	kit, cub, pup
Giraffe	bull	doe	calf
Goat	buck, billy	doe, nanny	kid, billy
Goose	gander	goose	gosling
Gorilla	male	female	infant
Hedgehog	boar	sow	pup, piglet
Hippopotamus	bull	cow	calf
Mouse	buck	doe	kitten, pinkie, pup
Rabbit	buck	doe	kit
Sheep	buck, ram	ewe, dam	lamb, lambkin, cosset
Swan	cob	pen	cygnet
Whale	bull	cow	calf

LATIN FLOWER AND PLANT NAMES

Ash	*Fraxinus*
Aspen	*Populus tremula*
Basil	*Ocimum*
Beech tree	*Fagus*
Bellflower	*Campanula*
Bramble	*Rubus*
Busy Lizzie	*Impatiens walleriana*
Carnation	*Dianthus caryophyllus*
Cypress	*Cupressus*
Daffodil	*Narcissus sylvestris*
Daisy	*Bellis*
Dandelion	*Leontodon*
Fennel	*Foeniculum vulgare*
Foxglove	*Digitalis*
Geranium	*Pelargonium hortorum*
Holly	*Ilex aquifolium*
Honeysuckle	*Lonicera*
Ivy	*Hedera*
Lavender	*Lavandula*
Lilac	*Syringa*
Lily of the Valley	*Convallaria majalis*
Marigold	*Calendula*
Mistletoe	*Viscum*
Pansy	*Viola tricolor*
Peppermint	*Mentha piperita*
Poppy	*Papaver rhoeas*
Prickly pear cactus	*Opuntia*
Snapdragon	*Antirrhinum*
Snowdrop	*Galanthus*
Sweet Pea	*Lathyrus odoratus*
Sweet William	*Dianthus barbatus*
Sunflower	*Helianthus annuus*
Thistle	*Carduus*
Tulip	*Tulipa*
Weeping willow	*Salix babylonica*

LATIN FRUIT AND VEGETABLE NAMES

Apple	*Malus domestica*
Apricot	*Prunus armeniaca*
Avocado	*Persea americana*
Aubergine	*Solanum melongena*
Beetroot	*Beta vulgaris*
Blackberry	*Rubus fruticosus*
Blackcurrant	*Ribes nigrum*
Broccoli (Italia Group)	*Brassica oleracea*
Coconut	*Cocos nucifera*
Cranberry	*Vaccinium oxycoccos*
Cucumber	*Cucumis sativus*
Garlic	*Allium sativum*
Grape	*Vitis vinifera*
Grapefruit	*Citrus paradisi*
Kiwi fruit	*Actinidia deliciosa*
Lemon	*Citrus limon*
Lettuce	*Lactuca sativa*
Lime	*Citrus latifolia*
Mandarin	*Citrus reticulata*
Mango	*Mangifera indica*
Mushroom	*Agaricus bisporus*
Olive	*Olea europaea*
Onion	*Allium cepa*
Orange	*Citrus sinensis*
Pea	*Pisum sativum*
Peach	*Prunus persica*
Pear	*Pyrus communis*
Pepper	*Capsicum annuum*
Pineapple	*Ananas comosus*
Plum	*Prunus domestica*
Pomegranat	*Punica granatum*
Potato	*Solanum tuberosum*
Pumpkin	*Cucurbita pepo*
Raspberry	*Rubus idaeus*
Runner bean	*Phaseolus coccineus*
Satsuma	*Citrus unshiu*
Tomato	*Solanum lycopersicum*
Watermelon	*Citrullus lanatus*

COMMON LATIN PHRASES

a posteriori based on experience

a priori based on knowledge prior to experience

ad absurdum to the point of absurdity

ad hoc for this special purpose

ad hominem a personal attack, or an argument appealing to emotion rather than reason

ad infinitum without limit

ad nauseam to a tedious extent

addenda items to be added

affidavit a sworn written statement usable as evidence in court

alma mater former school or college

alter ego other self

annus horribilis a bad year

annus mirabilis a wonderful year

antebellum before the war

ars gratia artis art for art's sake

bona fide genuine, in good faith

carpe diem seize the day

casus belli the circumstances justifying war

caveat emptor let the buyer beware

circa (abbreviated *c.* and followed by a date) approximately

cogito ergo sum I think, therefore I am (Descartes)

compos mentis sane

cui bono? who benefits?

curriculum vitae a summary of a person's career (*course of life*)

de facto in fact (see *de jure*)

de jure in law, in principle (see *de facto*)

deus ex machina a plot device where a contrived event resolves a problem at the last moment

dramatis personae the list of characters in a play

ecce homo behold the man

ergo therefore

et alii (abbreviated *et al*) and others

ex cathedra (of a pronouncement) formally, with official authority

fiat let it be done – an official decree

habeas corpus you may have the body (the opening words of a prerogative writ requiring a person to be brought before a court or a judge)

ibidem (abbreviated *ibid* in citations) in the same place

in absentia while absent

in extremis the most distant place, or near death

in flagrante delicto in the very act of committing an offence

in loco parentis in the place of a parent

in memoriam in memory

in situ in its original place

in vino veritas in wine there is truth

in vitro outside the living body and in an artificial environment

in vivo within a living organism

infra below or on a later page

inter alia among other things

ipso facto by that very fact

magna cum laude with great honour or distinction

magnum opus great work

mea culpa my fault

memento mori a reminder that you are mortal

mens rea guilty mind

mens sana in corpore sano a sound mind in a sound body

modus operandi manner of working

mutatis mutandis the necessary changes having been made

non sequitur it does not follow

passim in various places (referring to a quoted piece of work) *per annum* for each year

per ardua ad astra through difficulties to the stars

per capita for each person

per centum for each hundred

per diem for each day

per se taken alone – by and in itself

persona non grata a person who is not welcome

post mortem after death (also figuratively)

prima facie on a first view

pro bono done without charge in the public interest

pro forma for the sake of form

pro rata according to the rate

pro tempore (abbreviated to *pro tem*) for the time being

quid pro quo something for something

quo vadis? where are you going?

quod erat demonstrandum (abbreviated QED) which was to be proved

quod vide (abbreviated *q.v.*) which see

reductio ad absurdum reduction to the absurd (disproving the truth of a proposition by showing it leads to a contradiction)

sic thus

sic transit gloria mundi thus passes the glory of the world

sine qua non an indispensable condition

status quo the existing condition

stet let it stand

sub judice before a court or judge

sui generis of its own kind, unique

tempus fugit time flies

terra firma solid ground

terra incognita unknown land

vade mecum go with me – a constant companion or handbook

veni, vedi, vici I came, I saw, I conquered (Caesar)

verbatim word for word

vice versa with the order reversed

vox populi voice of the people

PHOBIAS

NAME	FEAR
Acrophobia	heights
Agoraphobia	open spaces, crowds
Ailurophobia	cats
Algophobia	pain
Aquaphobia	water
Androphobia	men
Anthophobia	flowers
Anthropophobia	people, society
Apiphobia	bees
Arachnophobia	spiders
Ataxophobia	untidiness, disorder
Bogyphobia	bogeymen, goblins
Brontophobia	thunder
Carcinophobia	cancer
Catoptrophobia	mirrors
Chaetophobia	hair
Cheimaphobia	cold
Chorophobia	dancing
Chronophobia	time
Cibophobia	food
Clinophobia	going to bed
Coulrophobia	clowns
Cynophobia	dogs, rabies
Dendrophobia	trees
Dentophobia	dentists
Ergasiophobia	work
Gamophobia	marriage
Gerascophobia	ageing
Gynophobia	women
Hadephobia	hell
Hemaphobia	blood
Herpetophobia	reptiles
Hormephobia	shock
Iatrophobia	doctors

Kenophobia	empty rooms, voids
Lachanaphobia	vegetables
Methyphobia	alcohol
Metrophobia	poetry
Monophobia	solitude
Mysophobia	dirt, germs
Necrophobia	death, corpses
Nosocomephobia	hospitals
Nucleomituphobia	nuclear weapons
Oenophobia	wine
Olfactophobia	smells
Ommatophobia	eyes
Ophidiophobia	snakes
Peladophobia	baldness
Pharmacophobia	medicine
Philemaphobia	kissing
Photophobia	light
Pogonophobia	beards
Pupaphobia	puppets
Pyrophobia	fire
Rhytiphobia	getting wrinkles
Sciophobia	shadows
Scopophobia	being looked at
Selenophobia	the moon
Soceraphobia	parents-in-law
Stasiphobia	standing
Taphephobia	being buried alive
Thaasophobia	sitting
Tocophobia	childbirth
Tomophobia	surgery
Trypanophobia	injections
Venustraphobia	beautiful women
Xenophobia	foreigners, strangers
Xerophobia	dryness
Zelophobia	jealousy
Zeusophobia	God or gods

RHYMING SLANG

Adam and Eve	believe
Apples and pears	stairs
Barnet fair	hair
Boat race	face
Bread and honey	money
Brown bread	dead
China plate	mate
Currant bun	sun
Dog and bone	phone
Frog and toad	road
Half inch	pinch (to steal)
Loaf of bread	head
Mince pies	eyes
Old Joanna	piano
Pen and ink	stink
Plates of meat	feet
Pork pies	lies
Rabbit and pork	talk
Rosy Lee	tea
Ruby Murray	curry
Saucepan lids	kids
Skin and blister	sister
Syrup of fig	wig
Tit for tat	hat
Tom and Dick	sick
Trouble and strife	wife
Whistle and flute	suit

EXPERTS, COLLECTORS AND ENTHUSIASTS

NAME	INTEREST
Ailurophile	cats
Antiquary	antiquities
Arachnologist	spiders and other arachnids
Arctophile	teddy bears
Balletomane	ballet
Bibliopegist	bookbinding
Bibliophile, bibliomane, bibliolatrist	books

Cagophilist	keys	Oenophile	wine
Campanologist	bell-ringing, bells	Ophiophilist	snakes
Canophilist	dogs	Ornithologist	birds
Coleopterist	beetles	Orthoepist	words, correct
Conchologist	shells (molluscs)		pronunciation of
Cruciverbalist	crossword	Philanthropist	humankind, the
	puzzles		welfare of
Cumyxaphilist	matchboxes	Philatelist	stamps
Entomologist	insects	Plangonology	dolls
Gourmet, epicure	food and drink	Pteridophilist	ferns
Herpetologist	reptiles and	Sericulturist	silkworms
	amphibians	Speleologist	caves
Hippophile	horses	Steganographer	writing hidden
Lepidopterist	butterflies, moths		messages
Myrmecologist	ants	Tegestologist	beer mats
Notaphilist	banknotes	Ufologist	UFOs
Numismatist	coins, medals	Vexillologist	flags, banners

ENDANGERED LANGUAGES

There are 2,471 languages under threat, according to UNESCO. These are divided into five categories, which are listed below with selected examples.

Extinct: Dalmatian (Croatia), Dura (Nepal), Nagumi (Cameroon), Wappo (USA)
Critically Endangered: Cornish (UK), Guarasu (Brazil), Hawaiian (USA), Samatao (China)
Severely Endangered: Arawun (Papua New Guinea), Nyikina (Australia), Quichua (Ecuador), Taznatit (Algeria)
Definitely Endangered: Kolami (India), Phuthi (Lesotho), Trukhmen (Russian Federation), Waigali (Afghanistan)
Vulnerable: Kaqchikel (Guatemala), Khalaj (Iran), Rarotongan (Cook Islands), Welsh (UK)

Countries with the most languages in danger (all categories):

India	196
USA	191
Brazil	190
Indonesia	147
China	143

Source: UNESCO *Atlas of Languages in Danger* 2009

LINGUISTIC TERMS

WORD	DEFINITION	EXAMPLE
Acronym	Word formed from the first letters of several words	NATO = North Atlantic Treaty Organisation
Anagram	Word(s) rearranged to produce new word(s)	earth/heart
Antonym	Words with opposite meanings	hot/cold
Archaism	Word or expression that is no longer in use	thou art = you are
Euphemism	Word or phrase used in place of a term considered too direct	pushing up daisies = dead
Homonym	Words with the same pronunciation and spelling but different meanings	mean (average, nasty)
Homophone	Words with the same pronunciation but different spellings and meanings	bear/bare
Litotes	Deliberate understatement	no small victory = very impressive victory
Malapropism	Word or phrase used incorrectly in place of a similar sounding word	Michelangelo painted the Sixteenth Chapel
Metonymy	Substitution of an attribute for the name of the thing itself	Wall Street = USA's financial world
Neologism	Word invented to describe an existing concept	email
Onomatopoeia	Word that imitates the sound it describes	buzz, hiss
Oxymoron	Figure of speech combining two normally contradicting words	wise fool
Palindrome	Word or sentence that reads the same in both directions	Do geese see God?
Pangram	Sentence containing all the letters of the alphabet	Pack my box with five dozen liquor jugs
Portmanteau	New word made from a combination of two or more existing words	Oxbridge = Oxford and Cambridge universities
Spoonerism	Accidental transposition of the first letters or parts of words in speech	belly jeans
Synonym	Different words with the same meaning	chair/seat
Tautology	Redundant repetition of meaning	new innovation
Zeugma	Joining two nouns with a common verb or adjective that takes on a different sense with each	he lost his coat and his temper

-ARCHIES AND -OCRACIES

Anarchy	Social or political disorder
Andrarchy, Androcracy	Rule by men
Aristocracy	Privileged group, nobility
Autarchy	Absolute sovereignty
Autocracy	Absolute rule by one person
Bureaucracy	Rule by administration, officialdom
Democracy	Rule by the people via elected representatives
Despotocracy	Absolute rule by a tyrant or oppressor
Diarchy	Rule by two independent authorities
Ethnocracy	Rule by an ethnic or racial group
Gerontocracy	Rule by the elderly
Gynarchy, Gynocracy	Rule by women
Hierocracy	A body of ruling priests
Matriarchy	Rule by a woman with descent through the female line
Meritocracy	Rule by persons selected according to merit
Monarchy	Rule by monarch
Monocracy	Rule by one person only
Ochlocracy	Mob rule
Oligarchy	Rule by a small group of people
Patriarchy	Rule by a man with descent through the male line
Plutocracy	Rule by the wealthy
Stratocracy	Military rule
Technocracy	Rule by technical experts
Thearchy	Rule by a god or gods
Triarchy	Rule by three people

BOOKS OF THE BIBLE

The following list gives the commonly used abbreviations for the books of the Bible.

OLD TESTAMENT

Genesis	Gen.	Joshua	Josh.
Exodus	Ex.	Judges	Judg.
Leviticus	Lev.	Ruth	Ruth
Numbers	Num.	1 Samuel	1 Sam.
Deuteronomy	Deut.	2 Samuel	2 Sam.
		1 Kings	1 Kings
		2 Kings	2 Kings
		1 Chronicles	1 Chron.
		2 Chronicles	2 Chron.
		Ezra	Ezra

Nehemiah	Neh.
Esther	Est.
Job	Job
Psalms	Ps.
Proverbs	Prov.
Ecclesiastes	Eccl.
Song of Solomon	Song
Isaiah	Isa.
Jeremiah	Jer.
Lamentations	Lam.
Ezekiel	Ezek.
Daniel	Dan.
Hosea	Hos.
Joel	Joel
Amos	Amos
Obadiah	Obad.
Jonah	Jonah
Micah	Mic.
Nahum	Nah.
Habakkuk	Hab.
Zephaniah	Zeph.
Haggai	Hag.
Zechariah	Zech.
Malachi	Mal.

APOCRYPHA

1 Esdras	1 Esd.
2 Esdras	2 Esd.
Tobit	Tobit
Judith	Judith
Rest of Esther	Rest of Est.
Wisdom of Solomon	Wisd. Sol.
Ecclesiasticus	Ecclus.
Baruch with the Epistle of Jeremiah	Bar. and Ep. Jer.
Song of the Three Holy Children	S. of III Ch.

History of Susanna	Sus.
Bel and the Dragon	Bel
Prayer of Manasseh	Pr. Man.
1 Maccabees	1 Macc.
2 Maccabees	2 Macc.
Prayer of Azariah	Pr. Azar.
Psalm 151	Ps. 151

NEW TESTAMENT

Matthew	Matt.
Mark	Mark
Luke	Luke
John	John
Acts	Acts
Romans	Rom.
1 Corinthians	1 Cor.
2 Corinthians	2 Cor.
Galatians	Gal.
Ephesians	Eph.
Philippians	Phil.
Colossians	Col.
1 Thessalonians	1 Thess.
2 Thessalonians	2 Thess.
1 Timothy	1 Tim.
2 Timothy	2 Tim.
Titus	Titus
Philemon	Philem.
Hebrews	Heb.
James	James
1 Peter	1 Peter
2 Peter	2 Peter
1 John	1 John
2 John	2 John
3 John	3 John
Jude	Jude
Revelation	Rev.

THE SEVEN DEADLY SINS

Envy
Gluttony
Greed
Lust
Pride
Sloth
Wrath

THE TEN COMMANDMENTS

1. You shall have no other gods but me.
2. You shall not make or worship any idol.
3. You shall not take the name of the Lord in vain.
4. Remember the Sabbath day and keep it holy.
5. Honour your father and mother.
6. You shall not kill.
7. You shall not commit adultery.
8. You shall not steal.
9. You shall not bear false witness.
10. You shall not covet.

Source: Exodus 20:1–17

POPULAR NAMES

Most popular baby names in the UK in 2008 (change from 2007 is in brackets)

BOYS	GIRLS
1. Jack (–)	1. Olivia (+2)
2. Oliver (+1)	2. Ruby (–)
3. Thomas (–1)	3. Emily (+1)
4. Harry (+1)	4. Grace (–3)
5. Joshua (–1)	5. Jessica (–)
6. Alfie (+4)	6. Chloe (+1)
7. Charlie (–1)	7. Sophie (–1)
8. Daniel (–1)	8. Lily (–)
9. James (–)	9. Amelia (+1)
10. William (–2)	10. Evie (+5)

Most popular baby names in the UK (1904–2004)

YEAR	BOYS	GIRLS
1904	William	Mary
1914	John	Mary
1924	John	Margaret
1934	John	Margaret
1944	John	Margaret
1954	David	Susan
1964	David	Susan
1974	Paul	Sarah
1984	Christopher	Sarah
1994	Thomas	Rebecca
2004	Jack	Emily

THE TWELVE DAYS OF CHRISTMAS

A partridge in a pear tree
Two turtle doves
Three French hens
Four calling birds
Five gold rings
Six geese a-laying
Seven swans a-swimming
Eight maids a-milking
Nine ladies dancing
Ten lords a-leaping
Eleven pipers piping
Twelve drummers drumming

CLASSIFIED AD ABBREVIATIONS

CARS

4wd	four wheel drive
a/c	air conditioning
abs	anti-lock braking system
bhp	brake horsepower
c/l	central locking
e/w	electric windows
fsh	full service history
ono	or nearest offer
pas	power assisted steering
p/x or p/ex	part exchange

DATING

asl	age/sex/location
ddf	drug and disease free
glbt	gay/lesbian/bisexual/transgender
gsoh	good sense of humour
hwp	height and weight proportional
iso	in search of
ldr	long distance relationship
mba	married but available
ohac	own house and car

spark	single parent raising kids
wltm	would like to meet

PROPERTY

b/r	bedroom
ccjs	county court judgements
c/h	central heating
d/g	double glazing
excl	excluding bills
f/f	fully furnished
f/h	freehold
incl	including bills
l/h	leasehold
osp	off street parking
pcm	per calendar month
p/w	per week
u/f	unfurnished

GENERAL

coa	certificate of authenticity
ess	essential
ntw	no time wasters
payg	pay as you go
s/c	self catering
tlc	tender loving care
w/e	weekend
yo	years old

MATHEMATICS

NUMBERS

Binary numbers: the binary system uses only the digits 0 and 1 to represent any number. The more usual decimal system, using all 10 digits from 0 to 9, has a base of 10; the binary system has a base of 2. Binary is the number system most commonly used in computers since the two numerals correspond to the on and off positions of an electronic switch.

The table below shows decimal numbers 1 to 20 with their binary equivalents:

	8 4 2 1			16 8 4 2 1
1	1	11		1 0 1 1
2	1 0	12		1 1 0 0
3	1 1	13		1 1 0 1
4	1 0 0	14		1 1 1 0
5	1 0 1	15		1 1 1 1
6	1 1 0	16		1 0 0 0 0
7	1 1 1	17		1 0 0 0 1
8	1 0 0 0	18		1 0 0 1 0
9	1 0 0 1	19		1 0 0 1 1
10	1 0 1 0	20		1 0 1 0 0

To convert a binary number into a decimal, count the '1's from right to left as 1, 2, 4, 8, 16 and so on. The sum of these values will give the equivalent decimal figure. For example, the binary number 10011 is equivalent to the sum of the value of those columns where a '1' appears (ie, $1 + 2 + 16 = 19$).

Cube root: see Cubic number.

Cubic number: the product of multiplying a whole number by itself, and then the product of that by the whole number again, eg $3 \times 3 \times 3 = 27$. Therefore 3 is the cube root of 27.

Difference: the result when one number is subtracted from another.

Even number: a whole number that divides by 2 exactly, ie to give a whole number without leaving a remainder.

Factor: a whole number that divides into another number without leaving a remainder.

Fibonacci numbers (Leonardo Fibonacci, c.1170–c.1250): beginning 1, 1, a series of numbers in which each number is the sum of the two numbers preceding it, eg 1, 1, 2 (1 + 1), 3 (1 + 2), 5 (2 + 3), 8 (3 + 5), 13, 21, 34, 55 etc. This sequence appears in nature, eg as the number of petals on the rim of a sunflower, the pattern of scales on a pine cone and the spiral shape of a nautilus shell.

Googol and googolplex: A googol is a finite number equal to 10^{100} (ie, 1 followed by 100 zeroes). A googolplex is a large number equal to 10^{googol} (that is, the number 1 followed by a googol zeroes).

Highest common factor (HCF): the largest number that divides into two or more numbers without leaving a remainder is the HCF of the numbers.

Index: a number placed in superscript after another number to show how many times the first number is to be multiplied by itself (eg 4^2). The value of the index is called the power.

Integer: any positive or negative whole number, including zero.

Irrational number: a number that cannot be expressed as a fraction or ratio of two integers.

Lowest common multiple (LCM): the smallest number that divides by two or more numbers without leaving a remainder is the LCM of the numbers.

Modulus (of a number): its magnitude, ignoring sign, eg the modulus of both 3 and –3 is 3. Also referred to as absolute value.

Multiple: a number that is the product of a given number and an integer.

Natural (or whole) number: a number that is a positive integer.

Odd number: an integer that will not divide by 2 without leaving a remainder.

Perfect number: a number that is equal to the sum of its factors, excluding the number itself. Only 30 have been discovered so far, the first of which is 6: factors of 6 (excluding 6 itself) are
1, 2 and 3
1 + 2 + 3 = 6

Prime number: with the exception of 1, any natural number that can only be divided by itself and 1.

Prime numbers between 1 and 100:

2	3	5	7	11
13	17	19	23	29
31	37	41	43	47
53	59	61	67	71
73	79	83	89	97

Product: the result of multiplying numbers together.

Quotient: a whole number resulting from the division of one number by another number (eg 17/5 gives a quotient of 3 with a remainder of 2).

Ratio: the relative magnitudes of two or more quantities.

Rational number: any number that can be expressed as a fraction or ratio of two integers.

Remainder: the amount left over when one number cannot be exactly divided by another.

Square number: the product of multiplying a whole number by itself, eg $3 \times 3 = 9$. Therefore, 3 is the square root of 9.

Whole number: see Natural number

Unity: the number 1

FRACTIONS, DECIMALS AND PERCENTAGES

Fraction: any quantity expressed as a ratio of two numbers, a numerator and a denominator (see below), written one above the other, separated by a line. When the numerator is less than the denominator, the fraction is of magnitude less than unity.

Decimal point: a dot that separates whole numbers from the fractional part in a decimal notation number.

Decimal fraction: a quantity less than unity expressed in decimal notation, eg 0.375.

Denominator: the number below the line in a fraction that denotes the number of equal parts into which the whole is divided.

Improper fraction: a fraction in which the numerator is larger than the denominator, eg $^{13}/_2$.

Mixed number: a number that comprises an integer and a fraction, eg $4^{1}/_2$ (in other words $4 + ^{1}/_2$).

Numerator: the number above the line in a fraction which denotes the number of fractional parts taken.

Proper fraction: one in which the numerator is smaller than the denominator, eg $^{7}/_{12}$.

Recurring (decimals and percentages): a pattern that repeats indefinitely.

Vulgar fraction (also known as simple and common fraction): a quantity expressed as a fraction with integers as numerator and denominator, as opposed to being expressed as a decimal fraction, eg $^{1}/_4$ rather than 0.25.

CORRESPONDING FRACTIONS, DECIMALS AND PERCENTAGES

These are three different ways of showing the same information:

FRACTION	DECIMAL	PER CENT (%)
$^{1}/_{20}$	0.05	5.00
$^{1}/_{10}$	0.10	10.00
$^{1}/_9$	0.11111*	11.11
$^{1}/_8$	0.125	12.50
$^{1}/_7$	0.14286	14.28
$^{1}/_6$	0.16667*	16.67
$^{1}/_5$	0.20	20.00
$^{1}/_4$	0.25	25.00
$^{1}/_3$	0.33333*	33.33
$^{1}/_2$	0.50	50.00
$^{2}/_3$	0.66667*	66.66
$^{3}/_4$	0.75	75.00

* = recurring; by convention a recurring digit equal to or greater than 5 is rounded up

GEOMETRY AND TRIGONOMETRY

Geometry is the branch of mathematics that deals with the properties of lines, points, surfaces and solids.

Acute angle: an angle of less than 90°, eg less than a quarter of a complete rotation.

Cosine of an angle (abbrev. cos): in a right-angled triangle =

the length of the adjacent side
the length of the hypotenuse

Degree (°): the magnitude of an angle of $^{1}/_{360}$ of a complete rotation.

Hypotenuse: the side of a right-angled triangle that is opposite the right angle.

Pythagoras' theorem (Greek mathematician and philosopher, c.580–c.500 BC): the square of the hypotenuse is equal in size to the sum of the squares of the other two sides ($a^2 + b^2 = c^2$).

Right angle: a quarter of a complete rotation in angle (90°).

Sine of an angle (abbrev. sin): in a right-angled triangle =

$$\frac{\text{the length of the opposite side}}{\text{the length of the hypotenuse}}$$

Tangent of an angle (abbrev. tan): in a right-angled triangle =

$$\frac{\text{the length of the opposite side}}{\text{the length of the adjacent side}}$$

Trigonometry: the branch of mathematics that deals with the relations between the sides and angles of triangles.

POLYGONS

A polygon is a closed plane figure with three or more straight sides (usually implies more than four).

NUMBER OF SIDES	NAME OF POLYGON
3	triangle
4	quadrilateral
5	pentagon
6	hexagon
7	heptagon
8	octagon
9	nonagon
10	decagon
12	dodecagon

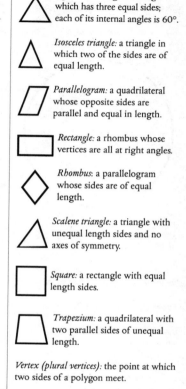

Equilateral triangle: a triangle which has three equal sides; each of its internal angles is 60°.

Isosceles triangle: a triangle in which two of the sides are of equal length.

Parallelogram: a quadrilateral whose opposite sides are parallel and equal in length.

Rectangle: a rhombus whose vertices are all at right angles.

Rhombus: a parallelogram whose sides are of equal length.

Scalene triangle: a triangle with unequal length sides and no axes of symmetry.

Square: a rectangle with equal length sides.

Trapezium: a quadrilateral with two parallel sides of unequal length.

Vertex (plural vertices): the point at which two sides of a polygon meet.

CIRCLES

Circle: a plane figure bounded by one line, every point on which is an equal distance from a fixed point at the centre.

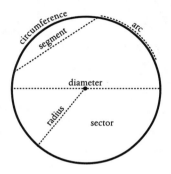

Arc: any part of the circumference of a circle.

Circumference: the line that forms the complete perimeter of a circle.

Diameter: a straight line that passes through the centre of a circle (or other figure) and terminates at the circumference at each end.

pi (indicated by the Greek letter π): the ratio of the circumference of a circle to its diameter (approximately 3.1416).

Radius (plural radii): a straight line from the circumference of a circle to its centre.

Sector: a region of a circle bounded by two radii.

Segment: a region of a circle bounded by a straight line whose ends touch two points of the circumference.

ANGULAR AND CIRCULAR MEASURES

60 seconds (″) = 1 minute (′)

60 minutes = 1 degree (°)

90 degrees = 1 right angle or quadrant

Circumference of circle = diameter (or 2 x radius) x 3.1416, eg πd or $2\pi r$

Area of circle = radius squared x 3.1416, eg πr^2

Surface of sphere = 4 x 3.1416 x radius squared, eg $4\pi r^2$

Volume of sphere = ⅔ x 3.1416 x radius cubed, eg ⅔ πr^3

Radian* = one degree of circumference x 57.3, eg $360/2\pi$

Curved surface of cylinder = circumference of circular base x 3.1416 x length or height, eg $2\pi rh$

Volume of cylinder = area of circular base x length or height, eg $\pi r^2 h$

* Or, one radian (the angle subtended at the centre of a circle by an arc of the circumference equal in length to the radius) = approximately 57.3 degrees

π TO 100 DECIMAL PLACES

3.14159265358979323846264338327
950288419716939937510582097494
459230781640628620899862803482
53421170679

MATHEMATICAL SYMBOLS

$=$	Equal to
$\neq$	Not equal to
$\approx$	Approximately equal to
$\equiv$	Identically equal to
$\div$	Division
$\times$	Multiplication
∞	Infinity
$\propto$	Proportional to
$\parallel$	Parallel to
$\perp$	Perpendicular to
$\geqslant$	Greater than or equal to
$\ngeqslant$	Not greater than or equal to
$>$	Greater than
$\ngtr$	Not greater than
$\ggg$	Much greater than
$\gtrless$	Greater than or less than
$\leqslant$	Less than or equal to
$\nleqslant$	Not less than or equal to
$<$	Less than
$\nless$	Not less than
$\lll$	Much less than
$\lessgtr$	Less than or greater than
$\pm$	Plus or minus
$\int$	Integral sign
$\sqrt{\ }$	Square root
$\sqrt{\ }$	Cube root
$\sqrt{\ }$	n-th root
∂	Partial derivative
Σ	Sum of

ROMAN NUMERALS

1	I	30	XXX
2	II	40	XL
3	III	50	L
4	IV	60	LX
5	V	70	LXX
6	VI	80	LXXX
7	VII	90	XC
8	VIII	100	C
9	IX	200	CC
10	X	300	CCC
11	XI	400	CD
12	XII	500	D
13	XIII	600	DC
14	XIV	700	DCC
15	XV	800	DCCC
16	XVI	900	CM
17	XVII	1000	M
18	XVIII	1500	MD
19	XIX	1900	MCM
20	XX	2000	MM

When a smaller number precedes a larger number (eg CD), the smaller number should be subtracted from the larger number

EXAMPLES

43	XLIII
66	LXVI
98	XCVIII
339	CCCXXXIX
619	DCXIX
988	CMLXXXVIII
996	CMXCVI
1674	MDCLXXIV
1962	MCMLXII
1998	MCMXCVIII
2011	MMXI

A bar placed over a numeral has the effect of multiplying the number by 1,000, eg

6,000	$\overline{\text{VI}}$
16,000	$\overline{\text{XVI}}$
160,000	$\overline{\text{CLX}}$
666,000	$\overline{\text{DCLXVI}}$

PROBABILITY AND STATISTICS

Probability is a branch of mathematics concerned with chance. It usually begins with a collection of data which is then analysed to identify trends and predict likely outcomes.

MEAN
The mean is found by dividing the sum of quantities by the number of quantities. It is often referred to as the average.

MEDIAN
The median is the middle number in a set of numbers arranged in order of size. If there are two middle numbers then the median is the average of the two figures.

MODE
In a set of figures, the number which occurs most often is called the mode.

GAUSSIAN CURVE
Where the values of a variable are distributed symmetrically around the mean, a line graph or bar chart will produce a distinctive-looking 'bell-shaped', or Gaussian curve. This pattern is also known as the normal distribution.

PROBABILITY OF EVENTS

Newborn baby living to 100 years: 1 in 2 (50%)
Rolling six on a single die: 1 in 6 (16.67%)
A 40-year-old living to 100 years: 1 in 10 (10%)
An 'official' white Christmas in London: 1 in 11 (9.09%)
A pregnant woman giving birth to twins: 1 in 32 (3.12%)
Double six on a single roll of two dice: 1 in 36 (2.78%)
Being dealt a royal flush on five cards: 1 in 650,000 (0.00015%)
Being struck by lightning in any one year: 1 in 1.36 million (0.000073%)
Winning the UK Lotto prize jackpot: 1 in 14 million (0.0000071%)
Winning the EuroMillions prize jackpot: 1 in 76 million (0.000000013%)

The above include approximate/mathematically modelled probabilities, given for the UK.

MONEY

WORLD CURRENCIES

Average rate against £1 Sterling on 30 April 2010

COUNTRY/TERRITORY	CURRENCY	VALUE
Albania	Lek (Lk) of 100 qindarka	Lk 158.61
Algeria	Algerian dinar (DA) of 100 centimes	DA 112.37
American Samoa	Currency is that of the USA	US$1.53
Andorra	Euro (€) of 100 cents	€1.15
Angola	Readjusted kwanza (Krzl) of 100 centimos	Kzrl 143.09
Anguilla	East Caribbean dollar (EC$) of 100 cents	EC$4.13
Antigua and Barbuda	East Caribbean dollar (EC$) of 100 cents	EC$4.13
Argentina	Peso of 100 centavos	Pesos 5.95
Aruba	Aruban guilder	Guilder 2.74
Ascension Island	Currency is that of St Helena	—
Australia	Australian dollar ($A) of 100 cents	$A1.64
Austria	Euro (€) of 100 cents	€1.15
Azerbaijan	New manat of 100 gopik	New manat 1.23
The Bahamas	Bahamian dollar (B$) of 100 cents	B$1.53
Bahrain	Bahraini dinar (BD) of 1,000 fils	BD 0.58
Bangladesh	Taka (Tk) of 100 poisha	Tk 106.02
Barbados	Barbados dollar (BD$) of 100 cents	BD$3.06
Belarus	Belarusian rouble of 100 kopeks	BYR 4,533.79
Belgium	Euro (€) of 100 cents	€1.15
Belize	Belize dollar (BZ$) of 100 cents	BZ$2.98
Benin	Franc CFA of 100 centimes	Francs 755.12
Bermuda	Bermuda dollar of 100 cents	$1.53
Bhutan	Ngultrum of 100 chetrum (Indian currency is also legal tender)	Ngultrum 67.90
Bolivia	Boliviano ($b) of 100 centavos	$b10.75
Bosnia and Hercegovina	Convertible marka of 100 fenings	Mark 2.25
Botswana	Pula (P) of 100 thebe	P 10.41
Brazil	Real of 100 centavos	Real 2.65
Brunei	Brunei dollar (B$) of 100 sen	B$2.10
Bulgaria	Lev of 100 stotinki	Leva 2.25
Burkina Faso	Franc CFA of 100 centimes	Francs 755.12
Burundi	Burundi franc of 100 centimes	Francs 1,882.86
Cameroon	Franc CFA of 100 centimes	Francs 755.12
Canada	Canadian dollar (C$) 100 cents	C$1.55

COUNTRY/TERRITORY	CURRENCY	VALUE
Cayman Islands	Cayman Islands dollar (CI$) of 100 cents	CI$1.26
Central African Republic	Franc CFA of 100 centimes	Francs 755.12
Chad	Franc CFA of 100 centimes	Francs 755.12
Chile	Chilean peso of 100 centavos	Pesos 790.58
China	Renminbi yuan of 10 jiao or 100 fen	Yuan 10.45
Colombia	Colombian peso of 100 centavos	Pesos 2,986.83
The Comoros	Comorian franc (KMF) of 100 centimes	Francs 566.34
Congo, Rep. of	Franc CFA of 100 centimes	Francs 755.12
Congo, Dem. Rep. of	Congolese franc (CFr) of 100 cents	CFr 1,370.43
Cook Islands	Currency is that of New Zealand	NZ$2.10
Costa Rica	Costa Rican colón (C) of 100 céntimos	C782.12
Côte d'Ivoire	Franc CFA of 100 centimes	Francs 755.12
Croatia	Kuna of 100 lipa	Kuna 8.35
Cuba	Cuban peso of 100 centavos	Pesos 1.53
Cyprus	Euro (€) of 100 cents	€1.15
Czech Republic	Koruna (Kcs) of 100 haleru	Kcs 29.46
Denmark	Danish krone of 100 ore	Kroner 8.57
Dominica	East Caribbean dollar (EC$) of 100 cents	EC$4.13
Dominican Republic	Dominican Republic peso (RD$) of 100 centavos	RD$56.30
Ecuador	Currency is that of the USA (formerly sucre of 100 centavos)	US$1.53
Egypt	Egyptian pound (£E) of 100 piastres or 1,000 millièmes	£E8.51
El Salvador	Currency is that of the USA	US$1.53
Equatorial Guinea	Franc CFA of 100 centimes	Francs 755.12
Estonia	Kroon of 100 senti (expected to introduce the euro in January 2011)	Kroons 18.01
Ethiopia	Ethiopian birr (EB) of 100 cents	EB 20.68
Faeroe Islands	Currency is that of Denmark	Kroner 8.57
Falkland Islands	Falkland pound of 100 pence	£1.00
Fiji	Fiji dollar (F$) of 100 cents	F$2.94
Finland	Euro (€) of 100 cents	€1.15
France	Euro (€) of 100 cents	€1.15
French Guiana	Euro (€) of 100 cents	€1.15
French Polynesia	Franc CFP of 100 centimes	Francs 137.28
Gabon	Franc CFA of 100 centimes	Francs 755.12
Gambia	Dalasi (D) of 100 butut	D 41.33
Georgia	Lari of 100 tetri	Lari 2.71
Germany	Euro (€) of 100 cents	€1.15
Ghana	Cedi of 100 pesewas	Cedi 2.17

COUNTRY/TERRITORY	CURRENCY	VALUE
Gibraltar	Gibraltar pound of 100 pence	£1.00
Greece	Euro (€) of 100 cents	€1.15
Greenland	Currency is that of Denmark	Kroner 8.57
Grenada	East Caribbean dollar (EC$) of 100 cents	EC$4.13
Guadeloupe	Euro (€) of 100 cents	€1.15
Guam	Currency is that of the USA	US$1.53
Guatemala	Quetzal (Q) of 100 centavos	Q 12.28
Guinea	Guinea franc of 100 centimes	Francs 7,691.53
Guinea-Bissau	Franc CFA of 100 centimes	Francs 755.12
Haiti	Gourde of 100 centimes	Gourdes 60.84
Honduras	Lempira of 100 centavos	Lempiras 28.92
Hong Kong	Hong Kong (HK$) of 100 cents	HK$11.88
Hungary	Forint of 100 filler	Forints 308.21
Iceland	Icelandic krona (Kr) of 100 aurar	Kr 195.75
India	Indian rupee (Rs) of 100 paise	Rs 67.90
Indonesia	Rupiah (Rp) of 100 sen	Rp 13,797.28
Ireland, Republic of	Euro (€) of 100 cents	€1.15
Israel	Shekel of 100 agora	Shekels 5.69
Italy	Euro (€) of 100 cents	€1.15
Jamaica	Jamaican dollar (J$) of 100 cents	J$135.42
Japan	Yen of 100 sen	Yen 143.90
Jordan	Jordanian dinar (JD) of 10 dirhams	JD 1.08
Kazakhstan	Tenge of 100 tiyn	Tenge 224.15
Kenya	Kenyan shilling (Ksh) of 100 cents	Ksh 118.09
Kiribati	Currency is that of Australia	$A1.64
Korea, Republic of	Won of 100 jeon	Won 1,696.50
Kuwait	Kuwaiti dinar (KD) of 1,000 fils	KD 0.44
Kyrgyzstan	Som of 100 tyiyn	Som 69.25
Latvia	Lats of 100 santims	Lats 0.81
Lebanon	Lebanese pound (L£) of of 100 piastres	L£2,297.51
Lesotho	Loti (M) of 100 lisente	M 11.26
Liechtenstein	Currency is that of Switzerland	Francs 1.65
Lithuania	Litas of 100 centas	Litas 3.97
Luxembourg	Euro (€) of 100 cents	€1.15
Macao	Pataca of 100 avos	Pataca 12.24
Macedonia	Denar of 100 deni	Den 70.87
Madagascar	Ariary of 5 iraimbilanja	MGA 3,137.84
Malawi	Kwacha (K) of 100 tambala	MK 230.78
Malaysia	Malaysian ringgit (dollar) (RM) of 100 sen	RM 4.87
Maldives	Rufiyaa of 100 laaris	Rufiyaa 19.59

COUNTRY/TERRITORY	CURRENCY	VALUE
Mali	Franc CFA of 100 centimes	Francs 755.12
Malta	Euro (€) of 100 cents	€1.15
Marshall Islands	Currency is that of the USA	US$1.53
Martinique	Currency is that of France	€1.15
Mauritania	Ouguiya (UM) of 5 khoums	UM 412.51
Mauritius	Mauritius rupee of 100 cents	Rs 47.11
Mayotte	Currency is that of France	€1.15
Mexico	Peso of 100 centavos	Pesos 18.75
Micronesia, Federated States of	Currency is that of the USA	US$1.53
Moldova	Moldovan leu of 100 bani	MDL 19.38
Monaco	Euro (€) of 100 cents	€1.15
Mongolia	Tugrik of 100 mongo	Tugriks 2,099.29
Montenegro	Euro (€) of 100 cents	€1.15
Montserrat	East Caribbean dollar (EC$) of 100 cents	EC$4.13
Morocco	Dirham (DH) of 100 centimes	DH 12.84
Mozambique	New metical (MT) of 100 centavos	MT 51.85
Namibia	Namibian dollar of 100 cents	$11.26
Nauru	Currency is that of Australia	$A1.64
Nepal	Nepalese rupee of 100 paisa	Rs 108.64
The Netherlands	Euro (€) of 100 cents	€1.15
Netherlands Antilles	Netherlands Antilles guilder of 100 cents	Guilders 2.74
New Caledonia	Franc CFP of 100 centimes	Francs 137.28
New Zealand	New Zealand dollar (NZ$) of 100 cents	NZ$2.10
Nicaragua	Córdoba (C$) of 100 centavos	C$32.42
Niger	Franc CFA of 100 centimes	Francs 755.12
Nigeria	Naira (N) of 100 kobo	N 231.05
Niue	Currency is that of New Zealand	NZ$2.10
Norfolk Island	Currency is that of Australia	$A1.64
Northern Mariana Islands	Currency is that of the USA	US$1.53
Norway	Krone of 100 ore	Kroner 9.04
Oman	Rial Omani (OR) of 1,000 baisas	OR 0.59
Pakistan	Pakistan rupee of 100 paisa	Rs 128.57
Palau	Currency is that of the USA	US$1.53
Panama	Balboa of 100 centésimos (US notes are in circulation)	Balboa 1.53
Papua New Guinea	Kina (K) of 100 toea	K 4.21
Paraguay	Guaraní (Gs) of 100 céntimos	Gs 7,224.68
Peru	New Sol of 100 centimos	New Sol 4.36
The Philippines	Philippine peso (P) of 100 centavos	P 68.05

COUNTRY/TERRITORY	CURRENCY	VALUE
Pitcairn Islands	Currency is that of New Zealand	NZ$2.10
Poland	Zloty of 100 groszy	Zlotych 4.51
Portugal	Euro (€) of 100 cents	€1.15
Puerto Rico	Currency is that of the USA	US$1.53
Qatar	Qatar riyal of 100 dirhams	Riyals 5.57
Réunion	Currency is that of France	€1.15
Romania	New leu of 100 bani	Lei 4.75
Russian Federation	Rouble of 100 kopeks	Rbl 44.73
Rwanda	Rwanda franc of 100 centimes	Francs 882.24
St Helena	St Helena pound (£) of 100 pence	£1.00
St Kitts and Nevis	East Caribbean dollar (EC$) of 100 cents	EC$4.13
St Lucia	East Caribbean dollar (EC$) of 100 cents	EC$4.13
St Pierre and Miquelon	Currency is that of France	€1.15
St Vincent and the Grenadines	East Caribbean dollar (EC$) of 100 cents	EC$4.13
Samoa	Tala (S$) of 100 sene	S$3.79
San Marino	Euro (€) of 100 cents	€1.15
Saudi Arabia	Saudi riyal (SR) of 100 halala	SR 5.74
Senegal	Franc CFA of 100 centimes	Francs 755.12
Serbia	New dinar of 100 paras	New dinars 114.29
Seychelles	Seychelles rupee of 100 cents	Rs 18.32
Sierra Leone	Leone (Le) of 100 cents	Le 5,982.87
Singapore	Singapore dollar (S$) of 100 cents (fully interchangeable with Brunei currency)	S$2.10
Slovakia	Euro (€) of 100 cents	€1.15
Slovenia	Euro (€) of 100 cents	€1.15
Solomon Islands	Solomon Islands dollar (SI$) of 100 cents	SI$12.05
South Africa	Rand (R) of 100 cents	R 11.26
Spain	Euro (€) of 100 cents	€1.15
Sri Lanka	Sri Lankan rupee of 100 cents	Rs 174.42
Suriname	Surinamese dollar of 100 cents	Dollar 4.20
Swaziland	Lilangeni (E) of 100 cents (South African currency is also in circulation)	E 11.26
Sweden	Swedish krona of 100 ore	Kronor 11.10
Switzerland	Swiss franc of 100 rappen (or centimes)	Francs 1.65
Taiwan	New Taiwan dollar (NT$) of 100 cents	NT$47.97
Tanzania	Tanzanian shilling of 100 cents	Shillings 2,120.72
Thailand	Baht of 100 satang	Baht 49.52
Timor–Leste	Currency is that of the USA	US$1.53
Togo	Franc CFA of 100 centimes	Francs 755.12

COUNTRY/TERRITORY	CURRENCY	VALUE
Tokelau	Currency is that of New Zealand	NZ$2.10
Tonga	Pa'anga (T$) of 100 seniti	T$2.98
Trinidad and Tobago	Trinidad and Tobago dollar (TT$) of 100 cents	TT$9.72
Tristan da Cunha	Currency is that of the UK	—
Tunisia	Tunisian dinar of 1,000 millimes	Dinars 2.19
Turkey	New Turkish lira (TL) of 100 kurus	TL 2.27
Turks and Caicos Islands	Currency is that of the USA	US$1.53
Tuvalu	Currency is that of Australia	$A1.64
Uganda	Uganda shilling of 100 cents	Shillings 3,248.04
Ukraine	Hryvna of 100 kopiykas	UAH 12.13
United Arab Emirates	UAE dirham (Dh) of 100 fils	Dirham 5.62
United States of America	US dollar (US$) of 100 cents	US$1.53
Uruguay	Uruguayan peso of 100 centésimos	Pesos 29.47
Uzbekistan	Sum of 100 tiyin	Sum 2,397.67
Vanuatu	Vatu	Vatu 152.41
Vatican City State	Euro (€) of 100 cents	€1.15
Venezuela	Bolívar fuerte (Bs. F) of 100 céntimos	Bs. F 6.57
Vietnam	Dong of 10 hao or 100 xu	Dong 29,047.92
Virgin Islands, British	Currency is that of the USA (£ sterling and EC$ also circulate)	US$1.53
Virgin Islands, US	Currency is that of the USA	US$1.53
Wallis and Futuna Islands	Franc CFP of 100 centimes	Francs 137.28
Yemen	Riyal of 100 fils	Riyals 344.85
Zambia	Kwacha (K) of 100 ngwee	K 7,262.94
Zimbabwe	Zimbabwe dollar (Z$) (suspended April 2009; US dollar now base currency)	US$1.53

Source: WM/Reuters Closing Spot Rates

BRITISH CURRENCY

The decimal system was introduced on 15 February 1971. The unit of currency is the pound sterling (£) of 100 pence.

COINS

The coins in circulation are:

DENOMINATION	METAL
Penny	bronze
Penny	copper-plated steel
2 pence	bronze
2 pence	copper-plated steel
5 pence	cupro-nickel
10 pence	cupro-nickel
20 pence	cupro-nickel
50 pence	cupro-nickel
£1	nickel-brass
£2	cupro-nickel, nickel-brass

Bronze is an alloy of copper 97 parts, zinc 2.5 parts and tin 0.5 part. These proportions have been subject to slight variations in the past. Bronze was replaced by copper-plated steel in 1992.

Cupro-nickel is an alloy of copper 75 parts and nickel 25 parts, except for the 20p, composed of copper 84 parts, nickel 16 parts.

BANKNOTES

Bank of England notes are currently issued in denominations of £5, £10, £20 and £50.

The current series of notes portrays on the back the following prominent figures from British history:

£5	Elizabeth Fry
£10	Charles Darwin
£20	Adam Smith
£50	Sir John Houblon

LEGAL TENDER

Gold (dated 1838 onwards, if not below least current weight)	to any amount
*£5 (Crown since 1990)	to any amount
£2	to any amount
£1	to any amount
50p	up to £10
*25p (Crown pre-1990)	up to £10
20p	up to £10
10p	up to £5
5p	up to £5
2p	up to 20p
1p	up to 20p

* Only redeemable at the post office

WITHDRAWN COINS

These coins ceased to be legal tender on the following dates:

Farthing	1960
Halfpenny (½d)	1969
Half-Crown	1970
Threepence	1971
Penny (1d.)	1971
Sixpence (6d.)	1980
Halfpenny (½p)	1984
old 5 pence	1990
old 10 pence	1993
old 50 pence	1998

WITHDRAWN BANKNOTES

£1	Sir Isaac Newton	1978–88
£5	Duke of Wellington	1971–91
	George Stephenson	1990–2003
£10	Florence Nightingale	1975–94
	Charles Dickens	1992–2003
£20	William Shakespeare	1970–93
	Michael Faraday	1991–2001
	Sir Edward Elgar	1999–2010
£50	Sir Christopher Wren	1981–96

The £1 coin was introduced in 1983 to replace the £1 note; no £1 notes have been issued since 1984 and the outstanding £1 notes were written off in March 1998. The 10 shilling note was replaced by the 50p coin in 1969, and ceased to be legal tender in 1970.

SLANG TERMS FOR MONEY

A bob	1 shilling
A quid	£1
A fiver	£5
A tenner	£10
A score	£20
A pony	£25
A monkey	£500
A plum	£100,000
A kite	an accommodation bill
Blunt	silver, or money in general
Browns	copper or bronze
Coppers	copper/bronze small denomination coins
Tin, brass	money generally

THE TRIAL OF THE PYX

The Trial of the Pyx is the examination by a jury to ascertain that coins made by the Royal Mint, which have been set aside in the pyx (or box), are of the proper weight, diameter and composition required by law. The trial is held annually, presided over by the Queen's Remembrancer (the Senior Master of the Supreme Court), with a jury of freemen of the Company of Goldsmiths.

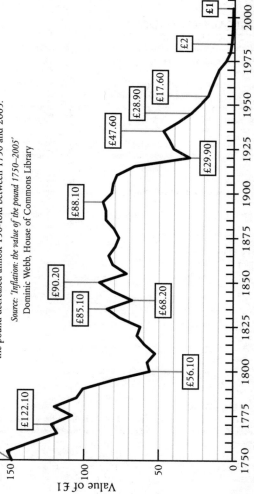

VALUE OF THE POUND 1750–2005

This graph illustrates the purchasing power of the pound relative to £1 sterling in 2005. For instance, to have the same purchasing power as £1 in 1850 you would have needed £90.20 in 2005. The value of the pound decreased almost 150-fold between 1750 and 2005.

Source: 'Inflation: the value of the pound 1750–2005'
Dominic Webb, House of Commons Library

MUSIC

MUSICAL NOTATION

 stave, horizontal lines on which the pitch of a note is indicated

Clef = a sign written at the beginning of the stave to indicate the register in which the music is to be performed. There are three kinds:

𝄞 treble, or G clef, used for the upper stave of keyboard music

𝄢 bass, or F clef, used for the lower stave of keyboard music

𝄡 C clef

INDICATIONS OF PITCH

♭ flat: lowering the note by a semi-tone

♯ sharp: raising the note by a semi-tone

♮ natural: returning a note to its original pitch

♭♭ double flat: lowering the note by a whole tone

𝄪 double sharp: raising the note by a whole tone

NOTE LENGTHS

SYMBOL	NAME	MEANING	REST
𝅝	semibreve	whole note	
𝅗𝅥	minim	half note	
𝅘𝅥	crotchet	quarter note	𝄽
𝅘𝅥𝅮	quaver	eighth note	𝄾
𝅘𝅥𝅯	semi-quaver	sixteenth note	𝄿

CHORD NOTATION

Below is a selection of common chord symbols of the kind found on jazz and popular-music lead sheets. For each example, the root note of the chord shown is C.

SYMBOL(S)	MEANING	SYMBOL(S)	MEANING
C	Major	C7, C^7	Dominant seventh
Cm, Cmin, C–	Minor	C^{M7}, C^{maj7}, C$^{\Delta 7}$, C$^{\Delta}$	Major seventh
C+, Caug	Augmented	Cm^7, Cmin^7, C^{-7}	Minor seventh
C°, Cdim	Diminished	Cm^{M7}, Cm^{maj7}, C$^{-\Delta}$	Minor major seventh

TEMPO (the term used to denote variations in speed)

TERM	MEANING
Accelerando	becoming faster
Rallentando, ritardando, ritenuto	becoming slower
Grave	very slow and solemn
Lento	slow
Largo	broadly
Adagio	in a leisurely manner
Andante	walking pace
Moderato	at a moderate speed
Allegro	fairly fast
Vivace	lively, fast
Presto	very fast
Prestissimo	as fast as possible

INTERPRETATION

TERM	MEANING
A cappella	unaccompanied (choral music)
A punta d'arco	use the point of the bow (of a string instrument)
Alla Marcia	in a marching style
Al tallone	use the heel of the bow (of a string instrument)
Cantabile	in a singing style
Da capo	from the beginning
Dolce	sweetly
Glissando	a rapid sliding scale
Grandioso	grandly
Legato	smoothly
Pizzicato	plucked
Sforzando	accented
Staccato	detached, short

DYNAMICS (the term used to denote the volume of music)

SIGN	TERM	MEANING
pp	*pianissimo*	very soft
p	*piano*	soft
mp	*mezzo-piano*	moderately soft
mf	*mezzo-forte*	moderately loud
f	*forte*	loud
ff	*fortissimo*	very loud
<	*crescendo*	getting louder
>	*diminuendo*	getting softer

PERCUSSION INSTRUMENTS

Definite Pitch
Antique cymbals
Celesta
Cimbalom
Glockenspiel
Marimba
Timpani
Tubular bells
Vibraphone
Xylophone

Indefinite Pitch
Anvil
Bass drums
Bongos
Castanets
Claves
Cymbals
Gong (tam-tam)
Guiro
Maracas
Rattle (ratchet)
Snare drum
Tabor
Temple block
Tenor drum
Tom-toms
Triangle
Whip (slapstick)
Wind machines
Wood block

WIND INSTRUMENTS

Basset horn
Bassoon
Clarinet
Cor anglais
Flute
Oboe
Piccolo
Recorder
Saxophone

STRING INSTRUMENTS

Banjo
Cello
Double Bass
Guitar
Harp
Piano (also percussion)
Sitar
Ukulele
Viola
Violin

BRASS INSTRUMENTS

Bass Trumpet
Bugle
Cornet
Euphonium
Flügel horn
French horn
Horn
Trombone
Trumpet
Tuba

ARRANGEMENT OF THE ORCHESTRA

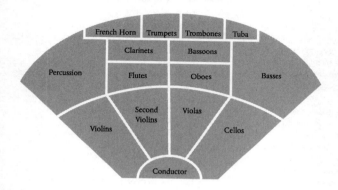

A SELECTION OF NATIONAL ANTHEMS

Bangladesh – 'Amar Shonar Bangla' ['My Golden Bengal']

Bhutan – 'Druk Tsendhen' ['In the Thunder Dragon Kingdom']

Burkina Faso – 'Une Seule Nuit' ['One Single Night']

Dominican Republic – 'Quisqueyanos Valientes' ['Valiant Songs of Quisqueya']

Equatorial Guinea – 'Caminemos Pisando la Senda' ['Let Us Tread the Path']

Ireland – 'Amhran na bhFiann' ['The Soldier's Song']

Lebanon – 'Koullouna Liloutaan Lil Oula Lil Alam' ['All of Us! For our Country, For our Flag and Glory']

Liechtenstein – 'Obem am Jungen Rhein' ['High Above the Young Rhine']

Montenegro – 'Oj, Svijetla Majska Zoro' ['O, Bright Dawn of May']

Nepal – 'Sayaun Thunga Phool Ka' ['Hundreds of Flowers']

Peru – 'Somos Libres, Seamoslo Siempre' ['We Are Free, Let Us Remain So Forever']

Senegal – 'Pincez Tous vos Koras, Frappez les Balafons' ['All Pluck Your Koras, Strike the Balafons']

Slovakia – 'Nad Tatrou sa Blyska' ['Lightning Over the Tatras']

Vanuatu – 'Yumi, Yumi, Yumi' ['We, We, We']

Venezuela – 'Gloria al Bravo Pueblo' ['Glory to the Brave People']

MUSICALS AND COMPOSERS

Annie Get Your Gun (1946)	Irving Berlin
Anything Goes (1934)	Cole Porter
Aspects of Love (1990)	Andrew Lloyd Webber, Don Black, Charles Hart
Avenue Q (2003)	Robert Lopez, Jeff Marx
Billy Elliot (2005)	Elton John
Blood Brothers (1983)	Willy Russell
Carousel (1945)	Richard Rodgers and Oscar Hammerstein
Cats (1982)	Andrew Lloyd Webber
A Chorus Line (1975)	Marvin Hamlisch, Michael Bennett
Chicago (1975)	John Kander
Evita (1978)	Andrew Lloyd Webber, Tim Rice
Fiddler on the Roof (1964)	Sheldon Harnick, Jerry Bock
Godspell (1971)	Stephen Schwartz, John-Michael Tebelak
Guys and Dolls (1950)	Frank Loesser
Hair (1967)	Galt MacDermot, James Rado, Gerome Ragni
Jesus Christ Superstar (1971)	Andrew Lloyd Webber, Tim Rice
Joseph and the Amazing Technicolor Dreamcoat (1968)	Andrew Lloyd Webber, Tim Rice
The King and I (1951)	Richard Rodgers and Oscar Hammerstein
Kiss Me Kate (1948)	Cole Porter
Les Misérables (1945)	Claude-Michel Schönberg, Alain Boublil
The Lion King (1997)	Elton John, Tim Rice
Mamma Mia! (1999)	Benny Andersson, Bjorn Ulvaeus
Me and My Girl (1937)	Noel Gay, Douglas Furber, Arthur Rose
Miss Saigon (1989)	Claude-Michel Schönberg, Alain Boublil
My Fair Lady (1956)	Alan Jay Lerner, Frederick Loewe
Oklahoma! (1943)	Richard Rodgers and Oscar Hammerstein
Oliver! (1960)	Lionel Bart
Paint Your Wagon (1951)	Alan Jay Lerner, Frederick Loewe
The Phantom of the Opera (1986)	Andrew Lloyd Webber, Charles Hart, Richard Stilgoe
The Sound of Music (1959)	Richard Rodgers and Oscar Hammerstein
South Pacific (1949)	Richard Rodgers and Oscar Hammerstein
Starlight Express (1984)	Andrew Lloyd Webber, Richard Stilgoe
Sunset Boulevard (1993)	Andrew Lloyd Webber, Don Black, Christopher Hampton
West Side Story (1957)	Leonard Bernstein, Stephen Sondheim
Wicked (2003)	Stephen Schwartz

OPERAS AND COMPOSERS

Aida (1871)	Giuseppe Verdi
Ariadne auf Naxos (1912)	Richard Strauss
The Barber of Seville (1816)	Gioacchino Rossini
The Bartered Bride (1863)	Bedrich Smetana
Billy Budd (1951)	Benjamin Britten
Bluebeard's Castle (1918)	Béla Bartók
La Bohème (1896)	Giacomo Puccini
Carmen (1875)	Georges Bizet
La Cenerentola (1817)	Gioacchino Rossini
Così fan tutte (1790)	Wolfgang Amadeus Mozart
The Cunning Little Vixen (1924)	Leos Janacek
Dialogues des Carmélites (1957)	Francis Poulenc
Dido and Aeneas (1689)	Henry Purcell
Don Carlos (1867)	Giuseppe Verdi
Don Giovanni (1787)	Wolfgang Amadeus Mozart
Elektra (1909)	Richard Strauss
Eugene Onegin (1879)	Pyotr Tchaikovsky
Faust (1859)	Charles Gounod
Fidelio (1805)	Ludwig van Beethoven
Die Fledermaus (1874)	Johann Strauss
The Flying Dutchman (1843)	Richard Wagner
The Gambler (1929)	Sergei Prokofiev
Götterdämmerung (1876)	Richard Wagner
Hänsel und Gretel (1893)	Engelbert Humperdinck
Jenufa (1904)	Leos Janacek
Julius Caesar (1724)	George Frideric Handel
Katya Kabanova (1921)	Leos Janacek
Lady Macbeth of Mtsensk (1934)	Dmitry Shostakovich
Madame Butterfly (1904)	Giacomo Puccini
The Magic Flute (1791)	Wolfgang Amadeus Mozart
The Marriage of Figaro (1786)	Wolfgang Amadeus Mozart
Mazeppa (1884)	Pyotr Tchaikovsky
Orfeo (1607)	Claudio Monteverdi
The Pearl Fishers (1863)	Georges Bizet
Peter Grimes (1945)	Benjamin Britten
Pelléas et Mélisande (1902)	Claude Debussy
Das Rheingold (1869)	Richard Wagner
Rigoletto (1851)	Giuseppe Verdi
Rusalka (1901)	Antonin Dvorak

Salome (1905)	Richard Strauss
Tales of Hoffmann (1881)	Jacques Offenbach
Tristan and Isolde (1865)	Richard Wagner
Tosca (1900)	Giacomo Puccini
La Traviata (1853)	Giuseppe Verdi
Il Trovatore (1853)	Giuseppe Verdi
Turandot (1926)	Giacomo Puccini
War and Peace (1945)	Sergei Prokofiev
Wozzeck (1925)	Alban Berg

MUSICAL COMPOSITIONS AND SECTIONS

TERM	MEANING
Aria	A self-contained piece for solo voice, often with an accompaniment and occurring within a larger work
Canon	A device in which one melody is repeated, often with creative variation, at regular overlapping intervals
Concerto	A work, usually in three parts, for orchestra and one or more solo instruments
Étude	French 'study': a piece, often difficult, originally designed to help perfect a particular technique or style
Mass	A sacred composition for choir (either accompanied or a cappella) in which the Eucharistic liturgy is set to music
Nocturne	A piece inspired by, or evocative of, the night
Opera	A composition in which vocal and orchestral scores are combined to create a piece of dramatic narrative theatre
Oratorio	A large work for choir, orchestra and soloist, similar to an opera but with a focus on sacred topics
Requiem	A mass for the dead
Rhapsody	A lively, one-movement work, often patriotic
Sonata	An instrumental piece for one or two instruments, often comprising four movements: fast, slow, moderate, fast
Symphony	An orchestral piece, generally in several movements
Toccata	An instrumental piece, often designed to demonstrate the dexterity and technical proficiency of a performer

CHRISTMAS NUMBER ONES

1989 Band Aid II – 'Do They Know It's Christmas'
1990 Cliff Richard – 'Saviour's Day'
1991 Queen – 'Bohemian Rhapsody'/'These are the Days of our Lives'
1992 Whitney Houston – 'I Will Always Love You'
1993 Mr Blobby – 'My Blobby'
1994 East 17 – 'Stay Another Day'
1995 Michael Jackson – 'Earth Song'
1996 Spice Girls – '2 Become 1'
1997 Spice Girls – 'Too Much'
1998 Spice Girls – 'Goodbye'
1999 Westlife – 'I Have a Dream'/'Seasons in the Sun'
2000 Bob the Builder – 'Can We Fix It?'
2001 Robbie Williams & Nicole Kidman – 'Somethin' Stupid'
2002 Girls Aloud – 'Sound of the Underground'
2003 Michael Andrews (feat. Gary Jules) – 'Mad World'
2004 Band Aid 20 – 'Do They Know It's Christmas?'
2005 Shayne Ward – 'That's My Goal'
2006 Leona Lewis – 'A Moment Like This'
2007 Leon Jackson – 'When You Believe'
2008 Alexandra Burke – 'Hallelujah'
2009 Rage Against the Machine – 'Killing in the Name'

EUROVISION

Countries in the 2010 song contest, staged in Oslo:

Albania, Armenia, Azerbaijan, Belarus, Belgium, Bosnia and Hercegovina,
*Bulgaria, *Croatia, Cyprus, Denmark, *Estonia, *Finland, †France, Georgia,
†Germany, Greece, Iceland, Ireland, Israel, *Latvia, *Lithuania, *Macedonia,
*Malta, Moldova, *the Netherlands, Norway, *Poland, Portugal, Romania, Russia,
Serbia, *Slovakia, *Slovenia, †Spain, *Sweden, *Switzerland, Turkey, Ukraine,
†United Kingdom

* countries that did not qualify in the semi-finals

† automatic entry to the final through financial contribution to the contest

WINNERS

1989	Yugoslavia	2000	Denmark
1990	Italy	2001	Estonia
1991	Sweden	2002	Latvia
1992	Ireland	2003	Turkey
1993	Ireland	2004	Ukraine
1994	Ireland	2005	Greece
1995	Norway	2006	Finland
1996	Ireland	2007	Serbia
1997	United Kingdom	2008	Russia
1998	Israel	2009	Norway
1999	Sweden	2010	Germany

THE UNITED KINGDOM'S WINNING EUROVISION ENTRIES

1967	Sandie Shaw	'Puppet On A String'
1969	Lulu	'Boom-bang-a-bang'
1976	Brotherhood of Man	'Save Your Kisses For Me'
1981	Bucks Fizz	'Making Your Mind Up'
1997	Katrina and the Waves	'Love Shine A Light'

NUMBER OF WINS FOR EACH COUNTRY

7	Ireland
5	France, Luxembourg, United Kingdom
4	The Netherlands, Sweden
3	Israel, Norway
2	Denmark, Germany, Italy, Spain, Switzerland
1	Austria, Belgium, Estonia, Finland, Greece, Latvia, Monaco, Russia, Serbia, Turkey, Ukraine, Yugoslavia

Norway holds the record for the most entries in last place, with ten songs finishing at the bottom of the scoreboard since the contest began in 1956.

MERCURY MUSIC PRIZE WINNERS

YEAR	ARTIST	ALBUM	HIGHEST UK CHART POSITION
1992	Primal Scream	Screamadelica	8
1993	Suede	Suede	1
1994	M People	Elegant Slumming	2
1995	Portishead	Dummy	2
1996	Pulp	Different Class	1
1997	Roni Size/Reprazent	New Forms	8
1998	Gomez	Bring It On	11
1999	Talvin Singh	OK	41
2000	Badly Drawn Boy	The Hour of Bewilderbeast	13
2001	PJ Harvey	Stories from the City, Stories from the Sea	23
2002	Ms Dynamite	A Little Deeper	10
2003	Dizzee Rascal	Boy in da Corner	23
2004	Franz Ferdinand	Franz Ferdinand	3
2005	Antony and the Johnsons	I Am a Bird Now	16
2006	Arctic Monkeys	Whatever People Say I Am, That's What I'm Not	1
2007	Klaxons	Myths of the Near Future	2
2008	Elbow	The Seldom Seen Kid	5
2009	Speech Debelle	Speech Therapy	65

PEOPLE

PRESIDENTS OF THE USA

YEAR INAUGURATED

1789	George Washington (1732–99)	*Federalist*
1797	John Adams (1735–1826)	*Federalist*
1801	Thomas Jefferson (1743–1826)	*Democratic-Republican*
1809	James Madison (1751–1836)	*Democratic-Republican*
1817	James Monroe (1758–1831)	*Democratic-Republican*
1825	John Quincy Adams (1767–1848)	*Democratic-Republican*
1829	Andrew Jackson (1767–1845)	*Democrat*
1837	Martin Van Buren (1782–1862)	*Democrat*
1841	William Harrison (1773–1841) (died in office)	*Whig*
1841	John Tyler (1790–1862) (elected as Vice-President)	*Whig*
1845	James Polk (1795–1849)	*Democrat*
1849	Zachary Taylor (1784–1850) (died in office)	*Whig*
1850	Millard Fillmore (1800–74) (elected as Vice-President)	*Whig*
1853	Franklin Pierce (1804–69)	*Democrat*
1857	James Buchanan (1791–1868)	*Democrat*
1861	Abraham Lincoln (1809–65) (assassinated in office)	*Republican*
1865	Andrew Johnson (1808–75) (elected as Vice-President)	*National Union*
1869	Ulysses Grant (1822–85)	*Republican*
1877	Rutherford Hayes (1822–93)	*Republican*
1881	James Garfield (1831–81) (assassinated in office)	*Republican*
1881	Chester Arthur (1830–86) (elected as Vice-President)	*Republican*
1885	Grover Cleveland (1837–1908)	*Democrat*
1889	Benjamin Harrison (1833–1901)	*Republican*
1893	Grover Cleveland (1837–1908)	*Democrat*
1897	William McKinley (1843–1901) (assassinated in office)	*Republican*
1901	Theodore Roosevelt (1858–1919) (elected as Vice-President)	*Republican*
1909	William Taft (1857–1930)	*Republican*

YEAR INAUGURATED

1913	Woodrow Wilson (1856–1924)	*Democrat*
1921	Warren Harding (1865–1923)	
	(died in office)	*Republican*
1923	Calvin Coolidge (1872–1933)	
	(elected as Vice-President)	*Republican*
1929	Herbert Hoover (1874–1964)	*Republican*
1933*	Franklin Roosevelt (1882–1945)	
	(died in office)	*Democrat*
1945	Harry Truman (1884–1972)	
	(elected as Vice-President)	*Democrat*
1953	Dwight Eisenhower (1890–1969)	*Republican*
1961	John Kennedy (1917–63)	
	(assassinated in office)	*Democrat*
1963	Lyndon Johnson (1908–73)	
	(elected as Vice-President)	*Democrat*
1969	Richard Nixon (1913–94)	*Republican*
1974†	Gerald Ford (1913–2006)	*Republican*
1977	James Carter (1924–)	*Democrat*
1981	Ronald Reagan (1911–2004)	*Republican*
1989	George Bush (1924–)	*Republican*
1993	William Clinton (1946–)	*Democrat*
2001	George W. Bush (1946–)	*Republican*
2009	Barack Obama (1961–)	*Democrat*

* Re-elected 5 November 1940, the first case of a third term; re-elected for a fourth term 7 November 1944

† Appointed under the provisions of the 25th Amendment

SECRETARIES-GENERAL OF THE UNITED NATIONS

1946–52	Trygve Lie (Norway)
1953–61	Dag Hammarskjöld (Sweden)
1961–71	U Thant (Burma)
1972–81	Kurt Waldheim (Austria)
1982–91	Javier Pérez de Cuellar (Peru)
1992–96	Boutros Boutros-Ghali (Egypt)
1997–2006	Kofi Annan (Ghana)
2007–	Ban Ki-moon (Republic of Korea)

PRESIDENTS OF THE EUROPEAN PARLIAMENT

1952–54	Paul Henri Spaak (Belgium)	1982–84	Piet Dankert (Netherlands)
1954	Alcide de Gasperi (Italy)	1984–87	Pierre Pflimin (France)
1954–56	Giuseppe Pella (Italy)	1987–89	Lord Plumb (UK)
1956–58	Hans Furler (Germany)	1989–92	Enrique Baron Crespo (Spain)
1958–60	Robert Schuman (France)		
1960–62	Hans Furler (Germany)	1992–94	Egon A. Klepsch (Germany)
1962–64	Gaetano Martino (Italy)	1994–97	Klaus Hansch (Germany)
1964–65	Jean Duvieusart (Belgium)	1997–99	Jose Maria Gil-Robles (Spain)
1965–66	Victor Leemans (Belgium)		
1966–69	Alain Poher (France)	1999–2002	Nicole Fontaine (France)
1969–71	Mario Scelba (Italy)	2002–04	Pat Cox (Ireland)
1971–73	Walter Behrendt (Germany)	2004–07	Josep Borrell Fontelles (Spain)
1973–75	Cornelius Berkhouwer (Netherlands)	2007–09	Hans-Gert Pöttering (Germany)
1975–77	Georges Spénale (France)		
1977–79	Emilio Colombo (Italy)	2009–12	Jerzy Buzek (Poland)
1979–82	Simone Veil (France)		

LEADERS OF THE COMMUNIST PARTY OF THE SOVIET UNION (1922–1991)*

1922–53	Iosif Vissarionovich Stalin†
1953–64	Nikita Sergeyevich Khrushchev
1964–82	Leonid Ilyich Brezhnev
1982–84	Yuriy Vladimirovich Andropov
1984–85	Konstantin Ustinovich Chernenko
1985–91	Mikhail Sergeyevich Gorbachev

* From 1898 to 1918 known as Russian Social Democratic Workers' Party (Bolshevik); from 1918 to 1925 as Russian Communist Party; from 1925 to 1952 as All-Union Communist Party.

†Lenin, regardless of being the party leader to his death in January 1924, was never general secretary of the Central Committee nor chairman of the Politburo.

ARCHBISHOPS OF CANTERBURY

Since the English Reformation
YEAR APPOINTED

1533	Thomas Cranmer	1768	Frederick Cornwallis
1556	Reginald Pole	1783	John Moore
1559	Matthew Parker	1805	Charles Manners-Sutton
1576	Edmund Grindal	1828	William Howley
1583	John Whitgift	1848	John Bird Sumner
1604	Richard Bancroft	1862	Charles Longley
1611	George Abbot	1868	Archibald Campbell Tait
1633	William Laud	1883	Edward White Benson
1660	William Juxon	1896	Frederick Temple
1663	Gilbert Sheldon	1903	Randall Davidson
1678	William Sancroft	1928	Cosmo Lang
1691	John Tillotson	1942	William Temple
1695	Thomas Tenison	1945	Geoffrey Fisher
1716	William Wake	1961	Michael Ramsey
1737	John Potter	1974	Donald Coggan
1747	Thomas Herring	1980	Robert Runcie
1757	Matthew Hutton	1991	George Carey
1758	Thomas Secker	2002	Rowan Williams

POPES

Since the English Reformation
YEAR ELECTED

1523	Clement VII	1605	Leo XI
1534	Paul III	1605	Paul V
1550	Julius III	1621	Gregory XV
1555	Marcellus II	1623	Urban VIII
1555	Paul IV	1644	Innocent X
1559	Pius IV	1655	Alexander VII
1566	St Pius V	1667	Clement IX
1572	Gregory XIII	1670	Clement X
1585	Sixtus V	1676	Blessed Innocent XI
1590	Urban VII	1689	Alexander VIII
1590	Gregory XIV	1691	Innocent XII
1591	Innocent IX	1700	Clement XI
1592	Clement VIII	1721	Innocent XIII
		1724	Benedict XIII

1730	Clement XII	1878	Leo XIII
1740	Benedict XIV	1903	St Pius X
1758	Clement XIII	1914	Benedict XV
1769	Clement XIV	1922	Pius XI
1775	Pius VI	1939	Pius XII
1800	Pius VII	1958	Blessed John XXIII
1823	Leo XII	1963	Paul VI
1829	Pius VIII	1978	John Paul I
1831	Gregory XVI	1978	John Paul II
1846	Blessed Pius IX	2005	Benedict XVI

PATRON SAINTS

OCCUPATION	SAINT
Accountants	Matthew the Apostle
Animals (sick)	Nicholas of Tolentino
Animals (domestic)	Anthony the Abbot
Archaeologists	Damasus
Architects	Thomas the Apostle
Armies	Maurice
Artists	Luke the Apostle
Astronauts	Joseph of Cupertino
Astronomers	Dominic de Guzman
Barbers	Cosmas and Damian
Booksellers	John of God
Brewers	Amand
Bricklayers	Stephen of Hungary
Builders	Thomas the Apostle
Civil Servants	Thomas More
Cooks	Lawrence
Dentists	Apollonia
Doctors	Luke the Apostle
Engineers	Ferdinand III of Castille
Farmers	Isidore the Farmer
Fishermen	Peter the Apostle
Hairdressers	Cosmas and Damian
Lawyers	Raymond of Penyafort
Midwives	Raymund Nonnatus
Mountaineers	Bernard of Menthon
Nurses	Camillus of Lellis
Paratroopers	Michael the Archangel
Policemen	Michael the Archangel
Prison officers	Hippolytus of Rome
Publishers	John the Apostle
Sailors	Erasmus and Nicholas
Scholars	Thomas Aquinas
Scientists	Albertus Magnus
Singers	Cecilia
Swimmers	Adjutor
Taxi drivers	Fiacre
Teachers	John Baptist de la Salle
Travellers	Christopher
Wine merchants	Amand
Writers	Francis de Sales

COUNTRY	SAINT
England	George
Wales	David
Scotland	Andrew
N. Ireland	Patrick

ROMAN EMPERORS

Augustus	27 BC–AD 14
Tiberius	14–37
Gaius Caesar (Caligula)	37–41
Claudius I	41–54
Nero	54–68
Galba	68–69
Otho	69
Vitellius	69
Sabinus	69
Vespasian	69–79
Titus	79–81
Domitian	81–96
Nerva	96–98
Trajan	98–117
Hadrian	117–38
Antoninus Pius	138–61
Marcus Aurelius	161–80
Lucius Verus	161–69
Commodus	177–92
Pertinax	193
Didius Julianus	193
Septimius Severus	193–211
Caracalla	211–17
Geta	211–12
Macrinus	217–18
Elagabalus	218–22
Alexander Severus	222–35
Maximinus Thrax	235–38
Gordian I	238
Gordian II	238
Pupienus	238
Balbinus	238
Gordian III	238–44
Philip	244–49
Decius	249–51
Hostilianus	251
Gallus	251–53
Aemilianus	253
Valerian	253–59
Gallienus	253–68
Claudius II	268–70
Aurelian	270–75
Tacitus	275–76
Florianus	276
Probus	276–82
Carus	282–83
Carinus	283–84
Numerianus	283–84
Diocletian	284–305
Maximian	285–305
Constantius I	305–6
Galerius	305–11
Severus	306–7
Maxentius	307–12
Constantine I	306–37
Constantine II	337–40
Constans	337–50
Constantius II	337–61
Julian	361–63
Jovian	363–64
Valentinian I	364–75
Valens	364–78
Gratian	375–83
Valentinian II	375–92
Maximus	383–88
Eugenius	392–94
Theodosius I	394–95
Arcadius	395–408
Theodosius II	408–50

Marcian	450–57	Valentinian III	425–55
Leo I	457–74	Petronius Maximus	455
Leo II	474	Avitus	455–56
Zeno	474–91	Majorian	457–61
		Libius Severus	461–65
WESTERN EMPERORS		Anthemius	467–72
Honorius	395–423	Olybrius	472
Maximus	408–11	Glycerius	473–74
Constantius III	421	Julius Nepos	474–75
Johannes	423–5	Romulus Augustus	475–76

LONGEST-SERVING HEADS OF STATE *as at July 2010*

	NAME	FROM	YEARS OF SERVICE
1	King Bhumibol Adulyadej of Thailand	June 1946	64
2	Dalai Lama Tenzin Gyatso of Tibet*	Nov 1950	59
3	Queen Elizabeth II of the United Kingdom	Feb 1952	58
4	Sultan Hassanal Bolkiah of Brunei	Oct 1967	42
5	Colonel Muammar al-Gaddafi of Libya	Sept 1969	40
6	Sultan Qaboos bin Said al-Said of Oman	July 1970	40
7	Queen Margrethe II of Denmark	Jan 1972	38
8	King Carl XVI Gustaf of Sweden	Sept 1973	36
9	King Juan Carlos I of Spain	Nov 1975	34
10	President Ali Abdullah Saleh of Yemen	July 1978†	32
11	President Teodoro Obiang Nguema Mbasogo of Equatorial Guinea	Aug 1979	31
12	President Jose Eduardo dos Santos of Angola	Sept 1979	30
13	Queen Beatrix of the Netherlands	April 1980	30
14	President Hosni Mubarak of Egypt	Oct 1981	28
15	President Paul Biya of Cameroon	Nov 1982	27
16	President Yoweri Museveni of Uganda	Jan 1986	24
17	King Mswati III of Swaziland	April 1986	24
18	President Blaise Compaoré of Burkina Faso	Oct 1987	22
19	President Zine al-Abidine Ben Ali of Tunisia	Nov 1987	22
20	President Robert Mugabe of Zimbabwe ‡	Dec 1987	22

* Leader of the Central Tibetan Administration, a government in exile

† The date when Saleh became president of North Yemen, a position he retained following the establishment of Republic of Yemen

‡ Constitutional amendment allowed Mugabe to serve as both president and head of state

PLACES

COUNTRIES OF THE WORLD

COUNTRY	AREA (SQ. KM)	POPULATION	CAPITAL
Afghanistan	652,230	28,396,000	Kabul
Albania	28,748	3,639,453	Tirana
Algeria	2,381,741	34,178,188	Algier
Andorra	468	83,888	Andorra la Vella
Angola	1,246,700	12,799,293	Luanda
Antigua and Barbuda	442.6	85,632	St John's
Argentina	2,780,400	40,913,548	Buenos Aires
Armenia	29,743	2,967,004	Yerevan
Australia	7,741,220	21,262,641	Canberra
Austria	83,871	8,210,281	Vienna
Azerbaijan	86,600	8,238,672	Baku
The Bahamas	13,880	309,156	Nassau
Bahrain	741	727,785	Manama
Bangladesh	143,998	156,050,883	Dhaka
Barbados	430	284,589	Bridgetown
Belarus	207,600	9,648,533	Minsk
Belgium	30,528	10,414,336	Brussels
Belize	22,966	307,899	Belmopan
Benin	112,622	8,791,832	Porto Novo
Bhutan	38,394	691,141	Thimphu
Bolivia	1,098,581	9,775,246	La Paz
Bosnia and Hercegovina	51,197	4,613,414	Sarajevo
Botswana	581,730	1,990,876	Gaborone
Brazil	8,514,877	198,739,269	Brasilia
Brunei	5,765	388,190	Bandar Seri Begawan
Bulgaria	110,879	7,204,687	Sofia
Burkina Faso	274,200	15,746,232	Ouagadougou
Burundi	27,830	9,511,330	Bujumbura
Cambodia	181,035	14,494,293	Phnom Penh
Cameroon	475,440	18,879,301	Yaoundé
Canada	9,984,670	33,487,208	Ottawa
Cape Verde	4,033	429,474	Praia
Central African Republic	622,984	4,511,488	Bangui

COUNTRY	AREA (SQ. KM)	POPULATION	CAPITAL
Chad	1,284,000	10,329,208	N'Djaména
Chile	756,102	16,601,707	Santiago
China	9,596,961	1,338,612,968	Beijing
Colombia	1,138,914	45,644,023	Bogotá
The Comoros	2,235	752,438	Moroni
Democratic Republic of Congo	2,344,858	68,692,542	Kinshasa
Republic of Congo	342,000	4,012,809	Brazzaville
Costa Rica	51,100	4,253,877	San José
Côte d'Ivoire	322,463	20,617,068	Yamoussoukro
Croatia	56,594	4,489,409	Zagreb
Cuba	110,860	11,451,652	Havana
Cyprus	9,251	796,740	Nicosia
Czech Republic	78,867	10,211,904	Prague
Denmark	43,094	5,484,723	Copenhagen
Djibouti	23,200	5,500,510	Djibouti
Dominica	751	72,660	Roseau
Dominican Republic	48,670	9,650,054	Santo Domingo
East Timor	14,874	1,131,612	Dili
Ecuador	283,561	14,573,101	Quito
Egypt	1,001,450	83,082,869	Cairo
El Salvador	21,041	7,185,218	San Salvador
Equatorial Guinea	28,051	633,441	Malabo
Eritrea	117,600	5,647,168	Asmara
Estonia	45,228	1,299,371	Tallinn
Ethiopia	1,104,300	85,237,338	Addis Ababa
Fiji	18,274	944,720	Suva
Finland	338,145	5,250,275	Helsinki
France	643,427	64,057,792	Paris
Gabon	267,667	1,514,993	Libreville
The Gambia	11,295	1,782,893	Banjul
Georgia	69,700	4,615,807	Tbilisi
Germany	357,022	82,329,758	Berlin
Ghana	238,533	23,832,495	Accra
Greece	131,957	10,737,428	Athens
Grenada	344	90,739	St George's
Guatemala	108,889	13,276,517	Guatemala City
Guinea	245,857	10,057,975	Conakry

COUNTRY	AREA (SQ. KM)	POPULATION	CAPITAL
Guinea-Bissau	36,125	1,533,964	Bissau
Guyana	214,969	772,298	Georgetown
Haiti	27,750	9,035,536	Port-au-Prince
Honduras	112,090	7,792,854	Tegucigalpa
Hungary	93,028	9,905,596	Budapest
Iceland	103,000	306,694	Reykjavik
India	3,287,263	1,166,079,217	New Delhi
Indonesia	1,904,569	240,271,522	Jakarta
Iran	1,648,195	66,429,284	Tehran
Iraq	438,317	28,945,657	Baghdad
Ireland	70,273	4,203,200	Dublin
Israel and Palestinian Territories	22,072	7,233,701	Tel Aviv
Italy	301,340	58,126,212	Rome
Jamaica	10,991	2,825,928	Kingston
Japan	377,915	127,078,679	Tokyo
Jordan	89,342	6,342,948	Amman
Kazakhstan	2,724,900	15,399,437	Astana
Kenya	580,367	39,002,772	Nairobi
Kiribati	811	112,850	Tarawa
Democratic People's Republic of Korea	120,538	22,665,345	Pyongyang
Republic of Korea	99,720	48,508,972	Seoul
Kuwait	17,818	2,691,158	Kuwait City
Kyrgyzstan	199,951	5,431,747	Bishkek
Laos	236,800	6,834,942	Vientiane
Latvia	64,589	2,231,503	Riga
Lebanon	10,400	4,017,095	Beirut
Lesotho	30,355	2,130,819	Maseru
Liberia	111,369	3,441,790	Monrovia
Libya	1,759,540	6,310,434	Tripoli
Liechtenstein	160	34,761	Vaduz
Lithuania	65,300	3,555,179	Vilnius
Luxembourg	2,586	491,775	Luxembourg
Macedonia	25,713	2,066,718	Skopje
Madagascar	587,041	20,653,556	Antananarivo
Malawi	118,484	14,268,711	Lilongwe
Malaysia	329,847	25,715,819	Kuala Lumpur

COUNTRY	AREA (SQ. KM)	POPULATION	CAPITAL
Maldives	298	396,334	Male
Mali	1,240,192	12,666,987	Bamako
Malta	316	405,165	Valletta
Marshall Islands	181	64,522	Majuro
Mauritania	1,030,700	3,129,486	Nouakchott
Mauritius	2,040	1,284,264	Port Louis
Mexico	1,964,375	111,211,789	Mexico City
Federated States of Micronesia	702	107,434	Palikir
Moldova	33,851	4,320,748	Chisinau
Monaco	2	32,965	Monaco
Mongolia	1,564,116	3,041,142	Ulaanbaatar
Montenegro	13,812	672,180	Podgorica
Morocco	446,550	34,859,364	Rabat
Mozambique	799,380	21,669,278	Maputo
Myanmar	676,578	48,137,741	Naypyidaw
Namibia	824,292	2,108,665	Windhoek
Nauru	21	14,019	Yaren District
Nepal	147,181	28,563,377	Kathmandu
The Netherlands	41,543	16,715,999	Amsterdam
New Zealand	267,710	4,213,418	Wellington
Nicaragua	130,370	5,891,199	Managua
Niger	1,267,000	15,306,252	Niamey
Nigeria	923,768	149,229,090	Abuja
Norway	323,802	4,660,539	Oslo
Oman	309,500	3,418,085	Muscat
Pakistan	796,095	176,242,949	Islamabad
Palau	459	20,796	Melekeok
Panama	75,420	3,360,474	Panama City
Papua New Guinea	462,840	6,057,263	Port Moresby
Paraguay	406,752	6,995,655	Asunción
Peru	1,285,216	29,546,963	Lima
The Philippines	300,000	97,976,603	Manila
Poland	312,685	38,482,919	Warsaw
Portugal	92,090	10,707,924	Lisbon
Qatar	11,586	833,285	Doha
Romania	238,391	22,215,421	Bucharest
Russia	17,098,242	140,041,247	Moscow

COUNTRY	AREA (SQ. KM)	POPULATION	CAPITAL
Rwanda	26,338	10,473,282	Kigali
St Christopher and Nevis	261	40,131	Basseterre
St Lucia	616	160,267	Castries
St Vincent and The Grenadines	389	104,574	Kingstown
Samoa	2,831	219,998	Apia
San Marino	61	30,324	San Marino
Sao Tome and Principe	964	212,679	Sao Tome
Saudi Arabia	2,149,690	28,686,633	Riyadh
Senegal	196,722	13,711,597	Dakar
Serbia	77,474	7,379,339	Belgrade
Seychelles	455	87,476	Victoria
Sierra Leone	71,740	6,440,053	Freetown
Singapore	697	4,657,542	Singapore
Slovakia	49,035	5,463,046	Bratislava
Slovenia	20,273	2,005,692	Ljubljana
Solomon Islands	28,896	595,613	Honiara
Somalia	637,657	9,832,017	Mogadishu
South Africa	1,219,090	49,052,489	Pretoria
Spain	505,370	40,525,002	Madrid
Sri Lanka	65,610	21,324,791	Colombo
Sudan	2,505,813	41,087,825	Khartoum
Suriname	163,820	481,267	Paramaribo
Swaziland	17,364	1,123,913	Mbabane
Sweden	450,295	9,059,651	Stockholm
Switzerland	41,277	7,604,467	Bern
Syria	185,180	20,178,485	Damascus
Taiwan	35,980	22,974,347	Taipei
Tajikistan	143,100	7,349,145	Dushanbe
Tanzania	947,300	41,048,532	Dodoma
Thailand	513,120	65,905,410	Bangkok
Togo	56,785	6,019,877	Lomé
Tonga	747	120,898	Nuku'alofa on Tongatapu
Trinidad and Tobago	5,128	1,229,953	Port of Spain
Tunisia	163,610	10,486,339	Tunis
Turkey	783,562	76,805,524	Ankara
Turkmenistan	488,100	4,884,887	Ashgabat

COUNTRY	AREA (SQ. KM)	POPULATION	CAPITAL
Tuvalu	26	12,373	Funafuti
Uganda	241,038	32,369,558	Kampala
Ukraine	603,550	45,700,395	Kyiv
United Arab Emirates	83,600	4,798,491	Abu Dhabi
United Kingdom	243,610	61,113,205	London
United States of America	9,826,675	307,212,123	Washington DC
Uruguay	176,215	3,494,382	Montevideo
Uzbekistan	447,400	27,606,007	Tashkent
Vanuatu	12,189	218,519	Port Vila
Vatican City State	0.44	826	Vatican City
Venezuela	912,050	26,814,843	Caracas
Vietnam	331,210	86,967,524	Hanoi
Yemen	527,968	23,822,783	Sana'a
Zambia	752,618	11,862,740	Lusaka
Zimbabwe	390,757	11,392,629	Harare

STATES OF THE USA

STATE (DATE AND ORDER OF ADMISSION)	ABBREVIATION	CAPITAL
Alabama (1819, 22)	AL	Montgomery
Alaska (1959, 49)	AK	Juneau
Arizona (1912, 48)	AZ	Phoenix
Arkansas (1836, 25)	AR	Little Rock
California (1850, 31)	CA	Sacramento
Colorado (1876, 38)	CO	Denver
Connecticut* (1788, 5)	CT	Hartford
Delaware* (1787, 1)	DE	Dover
District of Columbia (1791)	DC	—
Florida (1845, 27)	FL	Tallahassee
Georgia* (1788, 4)	GA	Atlanta
Hawaii (1959, 50)	HI	Honolulu
Idaho (1890, 43)	ID	Boise
Illinois (1818, 21)	IL	Springfield
Indiana (1816, 19)	IN	Indianapolis
Iowa (1846, 29)	IA	Des Moines
Kansas (1861, 34)	KS	Topeka
Kentucky (1792, 15)	KY	Frankfort
Louisiana (1812, 18)	LA	Baton Rouge
Maine (1820, 23)	ME	Augusta
Maryland* (1788, 7)	MD	Annapolis
Massachusetts* (1788, 6)	MA	Boston
Michigan (1837, 26)	MI	Lansing
Minnesota (1858, 32)	MN	St Paul
Mississippi (1817, 20)	MS	Jackson
Missouri (1821, 24)	MO	Jefferson City
Montana (1889, 41)	MT	Helena
Nebraska (1867, 37)	NE	Lincoln
Nevada (1864, 36)	NV	Carson City
New Hampshire* (1788, 9)	NH	Concord
New Jersey* (1787, 3)	NJ	Trenton
New Mexico (1912, 47)	NM	Santa Fé
New York* (1788, 11)	NY	Albany
North Carolina* (1789, 12)	NC	Raleigh
North Dakota (1889, 39)	ND	Bismarck
Ohio (1803, 17)	OH	Columbus

STATE (DATE AND ORDER OF ADMISSION)	ABBREVIATION	CAPITAL
Oklahoma (1907, 46)	OK	Oklahoma City
Oregon (1859, 33)	OR	Salem
Pennsylvania* (1787, 2)	PA	Harrisburg
Rhode Island* (1790, 13)	RI	Providence
South Carolina* (1788, 8)	SC	Columbia
South Dakota (1889, 40)	SD	Pierre
Tennessee (1796, 16)	TN	Nashville
Texas (1845, 28)	TX	Austin
Utah (1896, 45)	UT	Salt Lake City
Vermont (1791, 14)	VT	Montpelier
Virginia* (1788, 10)	VA	Richmond
Washington (1889, 42)	WA	Olympia
West Virginia (1863, 35)	WV	Charleston
Wisconsin (1848, 30)	WI	Madison
Wyoming (1890, 44)	WY	Cheyenne

*The 13 original states

STATES AND TERRITORIES OF AUSTRALIA

	ABBREVIATION	CAPITAL
Australian Capital Territory	ACT	Canberra
New South Wales	NSW	Sydney
Northern Territory	NT	Darwin
Queensland	Qld	Brisbane
South Australia	SA	Adelaide
Tasmania	Tas.	Hobart
Victoria	Vic.	Melbourne
Western Australia	WA	Perth

PROVINCES AND TERRITORIES OF CANADA

	ABBREVIATION	CAPITAL
Alberta	AB	Edmonton
British Columbia	BC	Victoria
Manitoba	MB	Winnipeg
New Brunswick	NB	Fredericton
Newfoundland and Labrador	NF	St John's
Northwest Territories	NT	Yellowknife
Nova Scotia	NS	Halifax

	ABBREVIATION	CAPITAL
Nunavut	NT	Iqaluit
Ontario	ON	Toronto
Prince Edward Island	PE	Charlottetown
Québec	QC	Québec City
Saskatchewan	SK	Regina
Yukon	YT	Whitehorse

UNITED NATIONS MEMBER STATES

as at May 2010 (192 members)

Afghanistan; Albania; Algeria; Andorra; Angola; Antigua and Barbuda; Argentina; Armenia; Australia; Austria; Azerbaijan; Bahamas; Bahrain; Bangladesh; Barbados; Belarus; Belgium; Belize; Benin; Bhutan; Bolivia; Bosnia and Hercegovina; Botswana; Brazil; Brunei; Bulgaria; Burkina Faso; Burundi; Cambodia; Cameroon; Canada; Cape Verde; Central African Republic; Chad; Chile; China; Colombia; Comoros; Congo, Dem. Rep. of; Congo, Rep. of; Costa Rica; Côte d'Ivoire; Croatia; Cuba; Cyprus; Czech Republic; Denmark; Djibouti; Dominica; Dominican Republic; East Timor; Ecuador; Egypt; El Salvador; Equatorial Guinea; Eritrea; Estonia; Ethiopia; Fiji; Finland; France; Gabon; Gambia; Georgia; Germany; Ghana; Greece; Grenada; Guatemala; Guinea; Guinea-Bissau; Guyana; Haiti; Honduras; Hungary; Iceland; India; Indonesia; Iran; Iraq; Ireland; Israel; Italy; Jamaica; Japan; Jordan; Kazakhstan; Kenya; Kiribati; Korea, Dem. Rep. of; Korea, Rep. of; Kuwait; Kyrgyzstan; Laos; Latvia; Lebanon; Lesotho; Liberia; Libya; Liechtenstein; Lithuania; Luxembourg; FYR Macedonia; Madagascar; Malawi; Malaysia; Maldives; Mali; Malta; Marshall Islands; Mauritania; Mauritius; Mexico; Micronesia (Federated States of); Moldova; Monaco; Mongolia; Montenegro; Morocco; Mozambique; Myanmar; Namibia; Nauru; Nepal; Netherlands; New Zealand; Nicaragua; Niger; Nigeria; Norway; Oman; Pakistan; Palau; Panama; Papua New Guinea; Paraguay; Peru; Philippines; Poland; Portugal; Qatar; Romania; Russian Federation; Rwanda; Saint Kitts and Nevis; Saint Lucia; Saint Vincent and the Grenadines; Samoa; San Marino; Sao Tome and Principe; Saudi Arabia; Senegal; Serbia; Seychelles; Sierra Leone; Singapore; Slovakia; Slovenia; Solomon Islands; Somalia; South Africa; Spain; Sri Lanka; Sudan; Suriname; Swaziland; Sweden; Switzerland; Syria; Tajikistan; Tanzania; Thailand; Togo; Tonga; Trinidad and Tobago; Tunisia; Turkey; Turkmenistan; Tuvalu; Uganda; Ukraine; United Arab Emirates; United Kingdom; United States of America; Uruguay; Uzbekistan; Vanuatu; Venezuela; Vietnam; Yemen; Zambia; Zimbabwe.

MEMBERS OF THE COMMONWEALTH

as at May 2010 (54 members)
COUNTRY (YEAR JOINED)
Antigua and Barbuda (1981)
Australia (1931)
The Bahamas (1973)
Bangladesh (1972)
Barbados (1966)
Belize (1981)
Botswana (1966)
Brunei (1984)
Cameroon (1995)
Canada (1931)
Cyprus (1961)
Dominica (1978)
Fiji (1970, currently suspended)
The Gambia (1965)
Ghana (1957)
Grenada (1974)
Guyana (1966)
India (1947)
Jamaica (1962)
Kenya (1963)
Kiribati (1979)
Lesotho (1966)
Malawi (1964)
Malaysia (1957)
The Maldives (1982)
Malta (1964)
Mauritius (1968)
Mozambique (1995)
Namibia (1990)
Nauru (1968)
New Zealand (1931)
Nigeria (1960)
Pakistan (1947)
Papua New Guinea (1975)
Rwanda (2009)
St Kitts and Nevis (1983)
St Lucia (1979)

St Vincent and the Grenadines (1979)
Samoa (1970)
Seychelles (1976)
Sierra Leone (1961)
Singapore (1965)
Solomon Islands (1978)
South Africa (1931)
Sri Lanka (1948)
Swaziland (1968)
Tanzania (1961)
Tonga (1970)
Trinidad and Tobago (1962)
Tuvalu (1978)
Uganda (1962)
United Kingdom
Vanuatu (1980)
Zambia (1964)

FASTEST-GROWING CITIES

CITY	POPULATION (THOUSANDS)	
	1950	2000
Karaj, Iran	10	1,063
Brasilia, Brazil	36	2,746
Monrovia, Liberia	15	776
Abidjan, Cote D'Ivoire	65	3,055
Dubai, UAE	20	938
Faridabad, India	22	1,018
Durg-Bhilainagar, India	20	905
Kaduna, Nigeria	28	1,220
Conakry, Guinea	31	1,222
Las Vegas, USA	35	1,335

Source: Satterthwaite, D. 2007. 'The Transition to a Predominantly Urban World and its Underpinnings.' **W** www.iied.org

LONDON

DISTANCES FROM LONDON BY AIR

The following list details the distances from Heathrow Airport in London to various airports worldwide.

TO	KM	MILES
Abu Dhabi	5,512	3,425
Acapulco	9,177	5,702
Accra	5,097	3,167
Addis Ababa	5,915	3,675
Adelaide	16,283	10,111
Aden	5,907	3,670
Alexandria	3,365	2,091
Algiers	1,666	1,035
Amman	3,681	2,287
Amsterdam	370	230
Anchorage	7,196	4,472
Ankara	2,848	1,770
Atlanta	6,756	4,198
Auckland	18,353	11,404
Bali	12,518	7,779
Bangkok	9,540	5,928
Barcelona	1,146	712
Beijing	8,148	5,063
Beirut	3,478	2,161
Belfast	524	325
Belgrade	1,700	1,056
Belize City	8,340	5,182
Benghazi	2,734	1,699
Berlin	947	588
Bogotá	8,468	5,262
Boston	5,239	3,255
Brasilia	8,775	5,452
Bratislava	1,315	817
Brazzaville	6,368	3,957
Bridgetown	6,748	4,193
Brisbane	16,533	10,273
Brussels	349	217
Bucharest	2,103	1,307
Budapest	1,486	923
Buenos Aires-Ezeiza	11,129	6,915
Cairo	3,531	2,194
Calgary	7,012	4,357
Canberra	16,999	10,563
Cape Town	9,675	6,011
Caracas	7,466	4,639
Cardiff	200	124
Casablanca	2,092	1,300
Chennai	8,229	5,113
Chicago	6,343	3,941
Cologne/Bonn	533	331
Colombo	8,708	5,411
Copenhagen	978	608
Dallas/Fort Worth	7,622	4,736
Damascus	3,577	2,223
Dar es Salaam	7,502	4,662
Darwin	13,861	8,613
Denver	7,492	4,655
Dhaka	8,008	4,976
Doha	5,235	3,253
Douala	5,356	3,328
Dresden	987	613
Dubai	5,494	3,414
Dublin	449	279
Dubrovnik	1,727	1,073
Dundee	579	359
Durban	9,555	5,937
Düsseldorf	500	310
Edmonton	6,805	4,229
Frankfurt	653	406
Gaborone	8,842	5,494
Geneva	754	468
Glasgow	555	345
Gothenburg	1,071	666
Gran Canaria	2,897	1,800
Guatemala City	8,745	5,435
Hamburg	745	463
Hannover	703	437

TO	KM	MILES	TO	KM	MILES
Harare	8,298	5,156	Malmö	1,017	632
Havana	7,479	4,647	Malta	2,100	1,305
Helsinki	1,847	1,147	Manila	10,758	6,685
Hobart	17,430	10,833	Maputo	9,184	5,707
Ho Chi Minh City	10,211	6,345	Marrakech-Menara	2,292	1,424
Hong Kong	9,640	5,990	Marseille	988	614
Honolulu	11,619	7,220	Melbourne	16,897	10,499
Houston	7,759	4,821	Memphis	7,005	4,353
Islamabad	6,062	3,767	Menorca	1,339	832
Isle of Man	403	250	Mexico City	8,899	5,529
Istanbul	2,510	1,560	Miami	7,104	4,414
Jakarta	11,712	7,277	Milan	979	609
Jeddah	4,743	2,947	Minneapolis-St Paul	6,439	4,001
Johannesburg	9,068	5,634			
Kabul	5,726	3,558	Minsk	1,893	1,176
Karachi	6,334	3,935	Mombasa	7,236	4,497
Kathmandu	7,354	4,570	Montego Bay	7,544	4,687
Khartoum	4,943	3,071	Montevideo	11,010	6,841
Kiev	2,184	1,357	Montréal	5,213	3,239
Kigali	6,600	4,101	Moscow	2,543	1,580
Kilimanjaro	7,055	4,384	Mumbai	7,207	4,478
Kingston, Jamaica	7,513	4,668	Munich	940	584
Kinshasa	6,387	3,969	Muscat	5,828	3,621
Kolkata	7,979	4,958	Nairobi	6,837	4,249
Kraków	1,425	886	Naples	1,628	1,011
Kuala Lumpur	10,552	6,557	Nassau	6,973	4,333
Kuwait	4,671	2,903	Natal	7,180	4,462
Lagos	5,000	3,107	N'Djamena	4,588	2,851
Larnaca	3,276	2,036	Newark	5,558	3,454
Lisbon	1,564	972	New Delhi	6,727	4,180
Ljubljana	1,233	767	New York	5,536	3,440
Lomé-Tokoin	5,036	3,129	Nice	1,039	645
Los Angeles	8,753	5,439	Novosibirsk	5,216	3,241
Luanda	6,830	4,243	Orlando	6,954	4,321
Lusaka	7,933	4,929	Osaka	9,555	5,938
Luxor	3,999	2,485	Oslo	1,206	749
Lyon-Saint Exupéry	759	472	Ostend-Bruges	232	144
Madrid	1,244	773	Ottawa	5,344	3,321
Málaga	1,675	1,041	Ouagadougou	4,348	2,702
Malé	8,533	5,302	Palma de Mallorca	1,347	836

TO	KM	MILES	TO	KM	MILES
Panama City	8,448	5,249	Skopje	1,963	1,220
Paris	346	215	Sofia	2,038	1,266
Penang	10,277	6,386	Split-Kastela	1,530	951
Perth, Australia	14,497	9,008	Stockholm	1,461	908
Philadelphia	5,686	3,533	Strasbourg	663	412
Pisa	1,184	736	Stuttgart	754	469
Port of Spain	7,088	4,404	Suva	16,285	10,119
Prague	1,043	649	Sydney	17,008	10,568
Québec	4,979	3,093	Tahiti	15,361	9,545
Quito	9,188	5,709	Taipei	9,775	6,074
Rabat	2,001	1,243	Tbilisi	3,571	2,219
Reykjavik	1,895	1,177	Tehran	4,420	2,747
Rhodes	2,805	1,743	Tel Aviv	3,585	2,227
Riga	1,695	1,054	Thessaloniki	2,164	1,345
Rimini	1,275	793	Tokyo	9,585	5,956
Rio de Janeiro-Galeao	9,245	5,745	Toronto	5,704	3,544
			Tripoli	2,362	1,468
Riyadh	4,936	3,067	Trondheim	1,490	926
Rome	1,441	895	Tunis-Carthage	1,830	1,137
St Lucia	6,785	4,216	Turin	917	570
St Petersburg	2,114	1,314	Ulaanbaatar	6,984	4,340
Salt Lake City	7,806	4,850	Vancouver	7,574	4,707
Salzburg	1,048	651	Venice	1,150	715
San Diego	8,802	5,469	Vienna	1,272	790
San Francisco	8,610	5,351	Vladivostok	8,526	5,298
Sao Paulo	9,483	5,892	Warsaw	1,468	912
Sarajevo	1,636	1,017	Washington	5,898	3,665
Seoul	8,855	5,503	Wellington	18,817	11,692
Seychelles	8,169	5,076	Yangon	8,984	5,582
Shannon	594	369	Zagreb	1,365	848
Shetland Islands	936	582	Zürich-Kloten	787	490
Singapore	10,873	6,756			

THAMES BRIDGES
(from east to west)

Queen Elizabeth II Bridge, opened 1991
Tower Bridge, opened 1894
London Bridge, original opened 1831;
    current bridge opened 1973
Cannon Street Railway Bridge, opened
    1866
Southwark Bridge, original opened
    1819; current bridge opened 1921
Millennium Bridge, opened 2000;
    reopened 2002
Blackfriars, Railway Bridge, opened
    1864, only the columns remain
Blackfriars Bridge, opened 1769
Waterloo Bridge, opened 1817
Golden Jubilee Bridges, opened 2002
Hungerford Railway Bridge, opened 1845
Westminster Bridge, opened 1750
Lambeth Bridge, opened 1862
Vauxhall Bridge, opened 1816
Grosvenor Bridge, opened 1860
Chelsea Bridge, opened 1858
Albert Bridge, opened 1873
Battersea Bridge, opened 1771
Battersea Railway Bridge, opened 1863
Wandsworth Bridge, opened 1873
Putney Railway Bridge, opened 1889
Putney Bridge, original opened 1729;
    current bridge opened 1886
Hammersmith Bridge, built 1827
Barnes Railway Bridge, opened 1849
Chiswick Bridge, opened 1933
Kew Railway Bridge, opened 1869
Kew Bridge, original built 1759; current
    bridge opened 1903
Richmond Lock, opened 1894
Twickenham Bridge, opened 1933
Richmond Railway Bridge, opened 1848
Richmond Bridge, built 1777
Teddington Lock, opened 1889

Kingston Railway Bridge, opened 1863
Kingston Bridge, built 1825–8
Hampton Court Bridge, built 1753

THE LONDON UNDERGROUND

The London Underground map has become a classic of topology and is among the city's most recognisable symbols. Early tube maps (1906–33) tended to be geographically accurate and featured additional information such as street names. Harry Beck, the creator of the modern map, argued that since passengers were below the surface, accurate geographical representation was unnecessary. On his simplified design, every line drawn (including those representing the Thames) runs either horizontally, vertically or at 45 degrees. Beck's map also differentiated between single-line stations (shown as tabs) and interchanges (diamonds, then circles) for the first time.

LINE (YEAR OPENED)	COLOUR
Bakerloo (1906)	brown
Central (1900)	red
Circle (1884)	yellow
District (1868)	green
Docklands Light Railway (1987)	teal
Hammersmith and City (1863)	pink
Jubilee (1879)	silver
London Overground (2007)	orange
Metropolitan (1863)	magenta
Northern (1890)	black
Piccadilly (1906)	dark blue
Victoria (1968)	light blue
Waterloo and City (1898)	turquoise

THE UNITED KINGDOM

AREA

The United Kingdom comprises Great Britain (England, Wales and Scotland) and Northern Ireland.

The Isle of Man and the Channel Islands are Crown dependencies with their own legislative systems, and not part of the United Kingdom.

	KM²	MILES²
United Kingdom	242,495	93,627
England	130,279	50,301
Wales	20,733	8,005
Scotland	77,907	30,080
Northern Ireland*	13,576	5,242
Isle of Man	572	221
Channel Islands	194	75

* Excluding certain tidal waters that are parts of statutory areas in Northern Ireland

POPULATION

The first official census of population in England, Wales and Scotland was taken in 1801 and a census has been taken every ten years since, except in 1941 when there was no census because of war. The last official census in the United Kingdom was taken in April 2001.

The first official census of population in Ireland was taken in 1841. However, all figures given below refer only to the area which is now Northern Ireland. Figures for Northern Ireland in 1921 and 1931 are estimates based on the censuses taken in 1926 and 1937 respectively.

Estimates of the population of England before 1801, calculated from the number of baptisms, burials and marriages, are:

1570	4,160,221
1600	4,811,718
1630	5,600,517
1670	5,773,646
1700	6,045,008
1750	6,517,035

UK CENSUS RESULTS 1811–2001

	TOTAL	MALE	FEMALE
1811	13,368,000	6,368,000	7,000,000
1821	15,472,000	7,498,000	7,974,000
1831	17,835,000	8,647,000	9,188,000
1841	20,183,000	9,819,000	10,364,000
1851	22,259,000	10,855,000	11,404,000
1861	24,525,000	11,894,000	12,631,000
1871	27,431,000	13,309,000	14,122,000
1881	31,015,000	15,060,000	15,955,000
1891	34,264,000	16,593,000	17,671,000
1901	38,237,000	18,492,000	19,745,000
1911	42,082,000	20,357,000	21,725,000
1921	44,027,000	21,033,000	22,994,000
1931	46,038,000	22,060,000	23,978,000
1951	50,225,000	24,118,000	26,107,000
1961	52,709,000	25,481,000	27,228,000
1971	55,515,000	26,952,000	28,562,000
1981	55,848,000	27,104,000	28,742,000
1991	56,467,000	27,344,000	29,123,000
2001	58,789,194	28,581,233	30,207,961

POPULATION BY AGE AND SEX UK CENSUS 2001

AGE RANGE	MALES	FEMALES	AGE RANGE	MALES	FEMALES
	THOUSANDS			THOUSANDS	
0 – 4	1,786	1,700	50 – 54	2,003	2,037
5 – 9	1,915	1,823	55 – 59	1,651	1,687
10 – 14	1,988	1,893	60 – 64	1,410	1,470
15 – 19	1,871	1,793	65 – 69	1,241	1,355
20 – 24	1,765	1,781	70 – 74	1,059	1,280
25 – 29	1,896	1,972	75 – 79	818	1,149
30 – 34	2,200	2,294	80 – 84	483	831
35 – 39	2,278	2,348	85 – 89	227	526
40 – 44	2,057	2,095	90 and over	83	288
45 – 49	1,851	1,885			

RELIGIONS IN THE UK

Christian	42,079,000	71.6%
Muslim	1,591,000	2.7%
Hindu	559,000	1.0%
Sikh	336,000	0.6%
Jewish	267,000	0.5%
Buddhist	152,000	0.3%
Other religion	179,000	0.3%
All religions	45,163,000	76.8%
No religion*/not stated	13,626,000	23.2%
Total	58,789,000	100.0%

Other religions practised in the UK include the Baha'i Faith, Humanism, Jainism, Paganism, Scientology and Zoroastrianism

* This category included agnostics, atheists, heathens and Jedi Knights

THE ANCIENT WORLD

THE SEVEN WONDERS OF THE WORLD

The following sights were identified by classical observers as the pre-eminent architectural and sculptural achievements of the ancient world. Only the pyramids of Egypt are still in existence.

THE COLOSSUS OF RHODES
A bronze statue of Greek sun god, Helios, later identified with Apollo, set up about 280 BC. According to legend it stood 33m (110ft) tall at the harbour entrance of the seaport of Rhodes.

THE HANGING GARDENS OF BABYLON
These adjoined Nebuchadnezzar's palace, 96 km (60 miles) south of Baghdad. The terraced gardens, ranging from 25–90m (75ft to 300ft) above ground level, were watered from storage tanks on the highest terrace.

THE PHAROS OF ALEXANDRIA
A marble watch tower and lighthouse on the island of Pharos in the harbour of Alexandria, built c.270 BC.

THE PYRAMIDS OF EGYPT
The pyramids are found from Gizeh, near Cairo, to a southern limit 96km (60 miles) distant. The oldest is that of Djoser, at Saqqara, built c.2650 BC. The Great Pyramid of Cheops (built c.2580 BC) covers 5.3 hectares (230.4 x 230.4m or 756 x 756ft) at the base and was originally 146.6m (481ft) in height.

THE STATUE OF ZEUS
Located at Olympia in the plain of Elis, 12m (40ft) tall and constructed of marble inlaid with ivory and gold by the sculptor Phidias, about 430 BC.

THE TEMPLE OF ARTEMIS AT EPHESUS
Ionic temple erected about 350 BC in honour of the goddess and burned by the Goths in AD 262.

THE TOMB OF MAUSOLUS
Built at Halicarnassus, in Asia Minor, by the widowed Queen Artemisia about 350 BC. The memorial originated the term mausoleum.

ROMAN NAMES

The following is a list of the Roman names for geographical areas and features and for towns and settlements. The area to which the Roman name for a town or country referred is not necessarily precisely the same area occupied by the modern town or country.

THE BRITISH ISLES

Abergavenny	*Gobannium*
Aldborough	*Isurium Brigantum*
Ambleside	*Galava*
Ancaster	*Causennae*
Anglesey	*Mona*
Armagh	*Armacha*
Avon, R.	*Auvona*
Bath	*Aquae Sulis*
Brancaster	*Branodunum*

Britain	*Britannia*
Caerleon	*Isca*
Caerwent	*Venta Silurum*
Canterbury	*Durovernum Cantiacorum*
Cardigan	*Ceretica*
Carlisle	*Luguvalium*
Carmarthen	*Maridunum*
Caernarvon	*Segontium*
Chelmsford	*Caesaromagus*
Chester	*Deva*
Chichester	*Noviomagus Regnensium*
Cirencester	*Corinium Dobunnorum*
Clyde, R.	*Clota*
Colchester	*Camulodunum*
Corbridge	*Corstopitum*
Dee, R.	*Deva*
Doncaster	*Danum*
Dorchester	*Durnovaria*
Dover	*Dubris*
Dover, Straits of	*Fretum Gallicum*
Dunstable	*Durocobrivae*
Eden, R.	*Ituna*
England	*Anglia*
Exeter	*Isca Dumnoniorum*
Forth, R.	*Bodotria*
Gloucester	*Glevum*
Hebrides	*Ebudae Insulae*
Hexham	*Axelodunum*
Ilkley	*Olicana*
Ireland	*Hibernia*
Jersey	*Caesarea*
Kent	*Cantium*
Lanchester	*Longovicium*
Land's End	*Bolerium Promunturium*
Leicester	*Ratae Corieltauvorum*

Lincoln	*Lindum*
Lizard Point	*Damnonium Promunturium*
London	*Londinium*
Manchester	*Mamucium*
Man, Isle of	*Monapia*
Newcastle upon Tyne	*Pons Aelius*
Orkneys	*Orcades*
Pevensey	*Anderetium*
Portsmouth	*Magnus Portus*
Richborough	*Rutupiae*
Rochester	*Durobrivae*
St Albans	*Verulamium*
Salisbury (Old Sarum)	*Sorviodunum*
Scilly Isles	*Cassiterides*
Scotland	*Caledonia*
Severn, R.	*Sabrina*
Silchester	*Calleva Atrebatum*
Solway Firth	*Ituna aestuarium*
Thames, R.	*Tamesis*
Wales	*Cambria*
Wallsend	*Segedunum*
Wash, The	*Metaris aestuarium*
Wear, R.	*Vedra*
Wight, Isle of	*Vectis*
Winchester	*Venta Belgarum*
Worcester	*Vigornia*
Wroxeter	*Viroconium Cornoviorum*
York	*Eboracum*

CONTINENTS

Africa	*Libya, Africa*
Europe	*Europa*

COUNTRIES AND REGIONS

Belgium	*Belgae*
Brittany	*Armoricae*
China	*Seres*

Denmark	*Dania*	Caspian Sea	*Mare Caspium*
Egypt	*Aegyptus*	Dardanelles	*Hellespontus*
Flanders	*Menapii*	Gibraltar, Straits of	*Fretum*
France	*Gallia*		*Gaditanum*
Germany	*Germania*	Marmora, Sea of	*Propontis*
Gibraltar	*Calpe*	Mediterranean	*Mare Internum*
Greece	*Graecia*	Nile, R.	*Nilus*
Holland	*Batavi*	Persian Gulf	*Sinus Arabicus*
Italy	*Italia*	Red Sea	*Mare Rubrim*
Lebanon	*Libanus*	Rhine, R.	*Rhenus*
Malta	*Melita*	Tyrrhenian Sea	*Mare Inferum*
Morocco	*Mauretania*		
Portugal	*Lusitania*	CITIES	
Spain	*Hispania*	Berlin	*Berolinum*
Switzerland	*Helvetia*	Bern	*Verona*
Tuscany	*Etruria*	Cadiz	*Gades*
		Istanbul	*Byzantium*
SEAS AND RIVERS		Jerusalem	*Hierosolyma*
Atlantic Ocean	*Mare Atlanticum*	Lisbon	*Olisipo*
Black Sea	*Pontus (Euxinus)*	Paris	*Lutetia*

GREEK AND ROMAN GODS

GREEK NAME	ROMAN NAME	SYMBOLISING
The Olympians	*Consentes Dii*	
Aphrodite	Venus	Beauty, love and procreation
Apollo	Apollo	Music, poetry and the Sun
Ares	Mars	War
Artemis	Diana	Hunting and animals
Athene	Minerva	Education and wisdom
Demeter	Ceres	The Earth and agriculture
Dionysus	Bacchus	Revelry, theatre and wine
Hades	Pluto	Death and the Underworld
Hebe	Juventas	Youth
Helios	Sol	The Sun
Hephaestus	Vulcan	Fire and crafts
Hera	Juno	Fidelity and marriage
Hermes	Mercury	Messenger of the gods
Hestia	Vesta	Family and the home
Persephone	Proserpine	Death or fertility
Poseidon	Neptune	The sea
Zeus	Jupiter	Ruler of the gods

The Olympians were the principal gods in Greek mythology (their Roman counterparts were known as the *Consentes Dii*) and lived at the top of Mount Olympus, the tallest peak in Greece. The previous occupants of Mount Olympus were the Titans, a powerful group of deities led by Cronus who ruled the Earth. The Olympians, led by Zeus, overthrew the Titans in the Titan War and imprisoned them in Tartarus in the Underworld.

There were never more than 12 Olympians at any one time, but the gods listed above have all been recognised as Olympians at some point.

ROYALTY

THE BRITISH ROYAL FAMILY

ORDER OF SUCCESSION TO THE THRONE

1. HRH the Prince of Wales
2. HRH Prince William of Wales
3. HRH Prince Henry of Wales
4. HRH the Duke of York
5. HRH Princess Beatrice of York
6. HRH Princess Eugenie of York
7. HRH the Earl of Wessex
8. Viscount Severn
9. Lady Louise Windsor
10. HRH the Princess Royal
11. Peter Phillips
12. Zara Phillips
13. Viscount Linley
14. Hon. Charles Armstrong-Jones
15. Hon. Margarita Armstrong-Jones
16. Lady Sarah Chatto
17. Samuel Chatto
18. Arthur Chatto
19. HRH the Duke of Gloucester
20. Earl of Ulster
21. Lord Culloden
22. Lady Cosima Windsor
23. Lady Davina Lewis
24. Lady Rose Gilman
25. HRH the Duke of Kent
26. Lady Amelia Windsor
27. Lady Helen Taylor
28. Columbus Taylor
29. Cassius Taylor
30. Eloise Taylor
31. Estella Taylor
32. Lord Frederick Windsor
33. Lady Gabriella Windsor
34. HRH Princess Alexandra, the Hon. Lady Ogilvy
35. James Ogilvy
36. Alexander Ogilvy
37. Flora Ogilvy
38. Marina Ogilvy
39. Christian Mowatt

The Earl of St Andrews and HRH Prince Michael of Kent lost their right of succession to the throne through marriage to a Roman Catholic. Lord Nicholas Windsor, Baron Downpatrick and Lady Marina-Charlotte Windsor renounced their rights to the throne on converting to Roman Catholicism in 2001, 2003 and 2008 respectively. Their children remain in succession provided that they are in communion with the Church of England.

KINGS AND QUEENS

ENGLISH KINGS AND QUEENS, 927 TO 1603

HOUSES OF CERDIC AND DENMARK

REIGN

927–39	Æthelstan (?–939)
939–46	Edmund I (921–46)
946–55	Eadred (?–955)
955–59	Eadwig (before 943–?)
959–75	Edgar I (943–75)
975–78	Edward I (the Martyr) (c.962–978)
978–1016	Æthelred (the Unready) (968/9–1016)
1016	Edmund II (Ironside) (before 993–1016)
1016–35	Cnut (Canute) (c.995–1035)
1035–40	Harold I (Harefoot) (1016/17–40)
1040–42	Harthacnut (Harthacanute) (c.1018–42)
1042–66	Edward II (the Confessor) (c.1002/5–66)
1066	Harold II (Godwinesson) (c.1020–66)

THE HOUSE OF NORMANDY

REIGN

1066–87	William I (the Conqueror) (c.1027–87)
1087–1100	William II (Rufus) (c.1056–1100)
1100–35	Henry I (Beauclerk) (1068–1135)
1135–54	Stephen (before 1100–54)

THE HOUSE OF ANJOU (PLANTAGENETS)

REIGN

1154–89	Henry II (Curtmantle) (1133–89)
1189–99	Richard I (Coeur de Lion) (1157–99)
1199–1216	John (Lackland) (1167–1216)
1216–72	Henry III (1207–72)
1272–1307	Edward I (Longshanks) (1239–1307)
1307–27	Edward II (1284–1327)
1327–77	Edward III (1312–77)
1377–99	Richard II (1367–1400)

THE HOUSE OF LANCASTER
REIGN

1399–1413	Henry IV (1366–1413)
1413–22	Henry V (1387–1422)
1422–71	Henry VI (1421–71)

THE HOUSE OF YORK
REIGN

1461–83	Edward IV (1442–83)
1483	Edward V (1470–83)
1483–85	Richard III (1452–85)

THE HOUSE OF TUDOR
REIGN

1485–1509	Henry VII (1457–1509)
1509–47	Henry VIII (1491–1547)
1547–53	Edward VI (1537–53)
1553	Jane (1537–54)
1553–58	Mary I (1516–58)
1558–1603	Elizabeth I (1533–1603)

BRITISH KINGS AND QUEENS SINCE 1603
THE HOUSE OF STUART
REIGN

1603–25	James I (VI of Scotland) (1566–1625)
1625–49	Charles I (1600–49)
INTERREGNUM 1649–60	
1649–53	Government by a council of state
1653–58	Oliver Cromwell, Lord Protector
1658–59	Richard Cromwell, Lord Protector
RESTORATION OF THE MONARCHY	
1660–85	Charles II (1630–85)
1685–88	James II (VII of Scotland) (1633–1701)
INTERREGNUM 11 December 1688 to 12 February 1689	
1689–1702	William III (1650–1702)
1689–94	Mary II (1662–94)
1702–14	Anne (1665–1714)

THE HOUSE OF HANOVER
REIGN

1714–27	George I (Elector of Hanover) (1660–1727)
1727–60	George II (1683–1760)
1760–1820	George III (1738–1820)
	Regency 1811–20
	Prince of Wales regent owing to the insanity of George III
1820–30	George IV (1762–1830)
1830–37	William IV (1765–1837)
1837–1901	Victoria (1819–1901)

THE HOUSE OF SAXE-COBURG AND GOTHA
REIGN

1901–10	Edward VII (1841–1910)

THE HOUSE OF WINDSOR
REIGN

1910–36	George V (1865–1936)
1936	Edward VIII (1894–1972)
1936–52	George VI (1895–1952)
1952–	Elizabeth II (1926–)

KINGS AND QUEENS OF SCOTS, 1016 TO 1603
REIGN

1016–34	Malcolm II (c.954–1034)

THE HOUSE OF ATHOLL
REIGN

1034–40	Duncan I (?–1040)
1040–57	Macbeth (c.1005–57)
1057–58	Lulach (c.1032–58)
1058–93	Malcolm III (Canmore) (c.1031–93)
1093–97	Donald III Ban (c.1033–1100)
	Deposed May 1094, restored November 1094
1094	Duncan II (c.1060–94)
1097–1107	Edgar (c.1074–1107)
1107–24	Alexander I (The Fierce) (c.1077–1124)
1124–53	David I (The Saint) (c.1085–1153)
1153–65	Malcolm IV (The Maiden) (c.1141–65)
1165–1214	William I (The Lion) (c.1142–1214)
1214–49	Alexander II (1198–1249)

| 1249–86 | Alexander III (1241–86) |
| 1286–90 | Margaret (The Maid of Norway) (1283–90) |

FIRST INTERREGNUM 1290–92

Throne disputed by 13 competitors. Crown awarded to John Balliol by adjudication of Edward I of England

THE HOUSE OF BALLIOL
REIGN

| 1292–96 | John (Balliol) (c.1250–1313) |

SECOND INTERREGNUM 1296–1306

Edward I of England declared John Balliol to have forfeited the throne for contumacy in 1296, and took the government of Scotland into his own hands

THE HOUSE OF BRUCE
REIGN

1306–29	Robert I (Bruce) (1274–1329)
1329–71	David II (1324–71)
1332	Edward Balliol (1282–1364), son of John Balliol, crowned King of Scots September, expelled December
1333–36	Edward Balliol restored as King of Scots

THE HOUSE OF STEWART
REIGN

1371–90	Robert II (Stewart) (1316–90)
1390–1406	Robert III (c.1337–1406)
1406–37	James I (1394–1437)
1437–60	James II (1430–60)
1460–88	James III (1452–88)
1488–1513	James IV (1473–1513)
1513–42	James V (1512–42)
1542–67	Mary (1542–87)
1567–1625	James VI (and I of England) (1566–1625) Succeeded 1603 to the English throne, so joining the English and Scottish crowns

WELSH SOVEREIGNS AND PRINCES

Wales was ruled by sovereign princes from the earliest times until the death of Llywelyn in 1282. The first English Prince of Wales was the son of Edward I, who was born in Caernarvon town on 25 April 1284. According to a discredited legend, he was presented to the Welsh chieftains as their prince, in fulfilment of a promise that they should have a prince who 'could not speak a word of English' and should be native born. This son, who

afterwards became Edward II, was created 'Prince of Wales and Earl of Chester' at the Lincoln Parliament on 7 February 1301.

The title Prince of Wales is borne after individual conferment and is not inherited at birth, though some princes have been declared and styled Prince of Wales but never formally so created (marked (s.) in the following lists). The title was conferred on Prince Charles by The Queen on 26 July 1958. He was invested at Caernarvon on 1 July 1969.

INDEPENDENT PRINCES, 844 TO 1282

REIGN

844–78	Rhodri the Great
878–916	Anarawd, son of Rhodri
916–50	Hywel Dda, the Good
950–79	Iago ab Idwal (or Ieuaf)
979–85	Hywel ab Ieuaf, the Bad
985–86	Cadwallon, his brother
986–99	Maredudd ab Owain ap Hywel Dda
999–1008	Cynan ap Hywel ab Ieuaf
1018–23	Llywelyn ap Seisyll
1023–39	Iago ab Idwal ap Meurig
1039–63	Gruffydd ap Llywelyn ap Seisyll
1063–75	Bleddyn ap Cynfyn
1075–81	Trahaern ap Caradog
1081–1137	Gruffydd ap Cynan ab Iago
1137–70	Owain Gwynedd
1170–94	Dafydd ab Owain Gwynedd
1194–1240	Llywelyn Fawr, the Great
1240–46	Dafydd ap Llywelyn
1246–82	Llywelyn ap Gruffydd ap Llywelyn

ENGLISH PRINCES SINCE 1301

1301	Edward (Edward II)
1343	Edward the Black Prince, son of Edward III
1376	Richard (Richard II), son of the Black Prince
1399	Henry of Monmouth (Henry V)
1454	Edward of Westminster, son of Henry VI
1471	Edward of Westminster (Edward V)
1483	Edward, son of Richard III (*d.* 1484)
1489	Arthur Tudor, son of Henry VII
1504	Henry Tudor (Henry VIII)
1610	Henry Stuart, son of James I (*d.* 1612)
1616	Charles Stuart (Charles I)
*c.*1638 (s.)	Charles Stuart (Charles II)
1688 (s.)	James Francis Edward Stuart (The Old Pretender), son of James II
1714	George Augustus (George II)
1729	Frederick Lewis, son of George II (*d.* 1751)
1751	George William Frederick (George III)
1762	George Augustus Frederick (George IV)
1841	Albert Edward (Edward VII)
1901	George (George V)
1910	Edward (Edward VIII)
1958	Charles, son of Elizabeth II

PRINCESSES ROYAL

The style Princess Royal is conferred at the Sovereign's discretion on his or her eldest daughter. It is an honorary title, held for life, and cannot be inherited or passed on. It was first conferred on Princess Mary, daughter of Charles I, in approximately 1642.

*c.*1642	Princess Mary (1631–60), daughter of Charles I
1727	Princess Anne (1709–59), daughter of George II
1766	Princess Charlotte (1766–1828), daughter of George III
1840	Princess Victoria (1840–1901), daughter of Victoria
1905	Princess Louise (1867–1931), daughter of Edward VII
1932	Princess Mary (1897–1965), daughter of George V
1987	Princess Anne (*b.* 1950), daughter of Elizabeth II

THE WIVES OF HENRY VIII

MARRIED	WIFE	ISSUE
1509–33	Catherine of Aragon (divorced)	Henry, Duke of Cornwall (*b. & d.* 1510)
		Mary I (1516–1558)*
1533–6	Anne Boleyn (beheaded)	Elizabeth I (1533–1603)
		Henry, Duke of Cornwall (*b. & d.* 1534)
1536–7	Jane Seymour (died)	Edward VI (1537–1553)
1540	Anne of Cleves (divorced)	–
1540–2	Catherine Howard (beheaded)	–
1543–7	Catherine Parr (outlived Henry VIII)	–

* Catherine of Aragon gave birth to six children in total; two were born alive and only Mary I survived infancy

WORLD MONARCHIES

The following is a list of those countries of the world that are monarchies or principalities, showing the head of state and his/her date of accession to the throne.

Bahrain	King Hamad bin Isa al-Khalifa, acceded as amir 6 March 1999, proclaimed King 14 February 2002
Belgium	King Albert II, acceded 9 August 1993
Bhutan	King Jigme Khesar Namgyel Wangchuk, acceded 14 December 2006, crowned 6 November 2008
Brunei	Sultan Hassanal Bolkiah, acceded 5 October 1967
Cambodia	King Norodom Sihamoni, acceded 14 October 2004
Denmark	Queen Margrethe II, acceded 14 January 1972
Japan	Emperor Akihito, acceded 8 January 1989
Jordan	King Abdullah II, acceded 7 February 1999
Kuwait	Shaikh Sabah al-Ahmad al-Jaber al-Sabah, sworn in 29 January 2006
Lesotho	King Letsie III, acceded 7 February 1996
Liechtenstein	Prince Hans Adam II, acceded 13 November 1989
Luxembourg	Grand Duke Henri, acceded 7 October 2000
Malaysia	Sultan Mizan Zainal Abidin, sworn in 13 December 2006
Monaco	Prince Albert II, acceded 6 April 2005
Morocco	King Mohammed VI, acceded 30 July 1999
The Netherlands	Queen Beatrix, acceded 30 April 1980
Norway	King Harald V, acceded 17 January 1991
Oman	Sultan Qaboos bin Said al-Said, acceded 23 July 1970

Qatar	Shaikh Hamad bin Khalifa al-Thani, assumed power 27 June 1995
Samoa	Susuga Tuiatua Tupua Tamasese Efi, elected 16 June 2007
Saudi Arabia	King Abdullah ibn Abdul Aziz al-Saud, acceded 1 August 2005
Spain	King Juan Carlos I, acceded 22 November 1975
Swaziland	King Mswati III, acceded 25 April 1986
Sweden	King Carl XVI Gustaf, acceded 15 September 1973
Thailand	King Bhumibol Adulyadej, acceded 9 June 1946
Tonga	King George Tupou V, acceded 11 September 2006
United Kingdom	Queen Elizabeth II*, acceded 6 February 1952

* Also head of state in Antigua and Barbuda, Australia, the Bahamas, Barbados, Belize, Canada, Grenada, Jamaica, New Zealand, Papua New Guinea, St Christopher and Nevis, St Lucia, St Vincent and the Grenadines, Solomon Islands and Tuvalu

SCIENCE

THE SOLAR SYSTEM

	MEAN DISTANCE FROM SUN KM 10⁶	PERIOD OF ROTATION ON AXIS DAYS	DIAMETER KM
Sun	—	25–35*	

PLANETS†

Mercury	58	58.646	4,878
Venus	108	243.019r	12,100
Earth	150	0.997	12,756
Mars	228	1.026	6,794
Jupiter	778	0.410e	142,800
Saturn	1,427	0.426e	120,000
Uranus	2,870	0.718r	52,400
Neptune	4,497	0.671	48,400

* depending on latitude, r retrograde, e equatorial

† In August 2006 Pluto was reclassified by the International Astronomical Union as a dwarf planet

SATELLITES OF THE PLANETS

	MEAN DISTANCE FROM PLANET KM	PERIOD OF REVOLUTION ROUND PLANET DAYS
EARTH		
Moon	384,400	27.322
MARS		
Phobos	9,378	0.319
Deimos	23,459	1.262
JUPITER		
Metis	127,960	0.295
Adrastea	128,980	0.298
Amalthea	181,300	0.498
Thebe	221,900	0.675
Io	421,600	1.769
Europa	670,900	3.551
Ganymede	1,070,000	7.155
Callisto	1,883,000	16.689
Leda	11,094,000	239
Himalia	11,480,000	251
Lysithea	11,720,000	259
Elara	11,737,000	260
Ananke	21,200,000	631r
Carme	22,600,000	692r
Pasiphae	23,500,000	735r
Sinope	23,700,000	758r
SATURN		
Pan	133,583	0.575
Atlas	137,670	0.602
Prometheus	139,353	0.613
Pandora	141,700	0.629
Epimetheus	151,422	0.694
Janus	151,472	0.695
Mimas	185,520	0.942
Enceladus	238,020	1.370
Tethys	294,660	1.888

Telesto	294,660	1.888
Calypso	294,660	1.888
Dione	377,400	2.737
Helene	377,400	2.737
Rhea	527,040	4.518
Titan	1,221,830	15.945
Hyperion	1,481,100	21.277
Iapetus	3,561,300	79.330
Phoebe	12,952,000	550.48r

URANUS

Cordelia	49,770	0.335
Ophelia	53,790	0.376
Bianca	59,170	0.435
Cressida	61,780	0.464
Desdemona	62,680	0.474
Juliet	64,350	0.493
Portia	66,090	0.513
Rosalind	69,940	0.558
Belinda	75,260	0.624
Puck	86,010	0.762
Miranda	129,390	1.413
Ariel	191,020	2.520
Umbriel	266,300	4.144
Titania	435,910	8.706
Oberon	583,520	13.463
Caliban	7,169,000	579

NEPTUNE

Naiad	48,230	0.294
Thalassa	50,070	0.311
Despina	52,530	0.335
Galatea	61,950	0.429
Larissa	73,550	0.555
Proteus	117,650	1.122
Triton	354,760	5.877
Nereid	5,513,400	360.136

DWARF PLANETS

Ceres, Eris, Haumea, Makemake, Pluto

r retrograde

SI UNITS

The Système International d'Unités (SI) is an international and coherent system of units devised to meet all known needs for measurement in science and technology; it was adopted in 1960.

The system consists of seven base units and the derived units formed as products or quotients of various powers of the base units.

BASE UNITS

Ampere (A)	= unit of electric current
Candela (cd)	= unit of luminous intensity
Kelvin (K)	= unit of thermodynamic temperature
Kilogram (kg)	= unit of mass
Metre (m)	= unit of length
Mole (mol)	= unit of amount of substance
Second (s)	= unit of time

DERIVED UNITS

Becquerel (Bq)	= unit of activity (of a radionuclide)
Coulomb (C)	= unit of electric charge, quantity of electricity
Degree Celsius (°C)	= unit of Celsius temperature
Farad (F)	= unit of electric capacitance
Gray (Gy)	= unit of absorbed dose, specific energy imparted, kerma, absorbed dose index
Henry (H)	= unit of inductance
Hertz (Hz)	= unit of frequency
Joule (J)	= unit of energy, work, quantity of heat
Katal (kat)	= unit of catalytic activity
Lumen (lm)	= unit of luminous flux
Lux (lx)	= unit of illuminance
Newton (N)	= unit of force
Ohm ($\vert$)	= unit of electric resistance
Pascal (Pa)	= unit of pressure, stress
Radian (rad)	= unit of plane angle
Siemens (S)	= unit of electric conductance
Sievert (Sv)	= unit of dose equivalent, dose equivalent index
Steradian (sr)	= unit of solid angle
Tesla (T)	= unit of magnetic flux density
Volt (V)	= unit of electric potential, potential difference, electromotive force
Watt (W)	= unit of power, radiant flux
Weber (Wb)	= unit of magnetic flux

OTHER DERIVED UNITS

Other derived units are expressed in terms of base units. Some of the more commonly used are:

Ampere per metre (A m^{-1})	= unit of magnetic field strength
Candela per square metre (cd m^{-2})	= unit of luminance
Cubic metre (m^3)	= unit of volume
Joule per kelvin (J K^{-1})	= unit of heat capacity
Joule per kilogram kelvin (J kg^{-1} K^{-1})	= unit of specific heat capacity
Kilogram per cubic metre (kg m^{-3})	= unit of density
Kilogram metre per second (kg m s^{-1})	= unit of momentum
Metre per second (m s^{-1})	= unit of velocity
Metre per second squared (m s^{-2})	= unit of acceleration
Newton per metre (N m^{-1})	= unit of surface tension

Pascal second (Pa s)	= unit of dynamic viscosity
Square metre (m^2)	= unit of area
Volt per metre ($V\ m^{-1}$)	= unit of electric field strength
Watt per square metre ($W\ m^{-2}$)	= unit of heat flux density, irradiance
Watt per metre kelvin ($W\ m^{-1}\ K^{-1}$)	= unit of thermal conductivity

SI PREFIXES

Decimal multiples and submultiples of the SI units are indicated by SI prefixes. These are as follows:

MULTIPLES
yotta (Y) x 10^{24}
zetta (Z) x 10^{21}
exa (E) x 10^{18}
peta (P) x 10^{15}
tera (T) x 10^{12}
giga (G) x 10^{9}
mega (M) x 10^{6}
kilo (k) x 10^{3}
hecto (h) x 10^{2}
deca (da) x 10

SUBMULTIPLES
deci (d) x 10^{-1}
centi (c) x 10^{-2}
milli (m) x 10^{-3}
micro (i) x 10^{-6}
nano (n) x 10^{-9}
pico (p) x 10^{-12}
femto (f) x 10^{-15}
atto (a) x 10^{-18}
zepto (z) x 10^{-21}
yocto (y) x 10^{-24}

SOME SI UNIT DEFINITIONS

1 metre is the distance travelled by light in a vacuum in one 299,792,458th of a second

1 kilogram is a cylinder of platinum-iridium alloy held by the International Bureau of Weights and Measures at Sevres, near Paris (the only remaining artefact-based standard measure in use)

1 second is 9,192,631,770 radiation cycles of the cesium-133 atom

1 ampere is the magnitude of a current that results in a force equal to 2×10^{-7} newtons

1 kelvin is the point immediately above absolute zero, where all atomic activity ceases

1 mole is the amount of a substance that contains as many elementary entities as there are atoms in 12 grams of carbon-12

PHYSICS

DEFINITIONS AND LAWS

Acceleration (symbol: *a*): the rate of change of velocity (a vector quantity). SI unit: metre per second squared (m s^{-2}).

$$\frac{\text{change in velocity}}{\text{time taken for this change}}$$

Archimedes' principle (Greek mathematician, 287–212 BC): a body that is partially or totally immersed in a fluid is buoyed up by a force that is equal to the weight of the fluid displaced by the body.

Density (symbol: ρ): mass divided by volume (a physical quantity). SI unit: kilogram per cubic metre (kg m^{-3}).

Energy (symbol: *E*): the capacity of a body or system to do work (a physical quantity). SI unit: joule (J).

Force (symbol: *F*): that which causes a body to change its state at rest or linear motion (a vector quantity). The magnitude of the force is equal to the product *ma* where

m = mass of the body.
a = acceleration imparted by the force.

Gravitation (Newton's law of): the force of attraction between two given bodies in the universe is directly proportional to the product of their masses and inversely proportional to the square of the distance between them.

Inertia: see Newton's first law of motion.

Mass (symbol: *m*): measures a body's inertia and determines the mutual gravitational attraction between it and another body. Mass is the amount of 'stuff' in the body. Mass does not depend on gravitational attraction. SI unit: kilogram (kg).

Momentum (symbol: *p*): the product of mass and velocity (a physical and vector quantity). SI unit: kilogram metre per second (kg m s^{-1}).

Newton's laws of motion (Sir Isaac Newton, 1642–1727)
1   A body will remain in a state of rest or travel in a straight line at constant speed unless acted upon by an external force (law of inertia).

2   The rate of change of momentum of a moving body is proportional to and in the same direction as the force acting on it.

3   To every action there is always an equal and opposite reaction.

Power (symbol: *P*): the rate of doing work or of heat transfer (a physical quantity). SI unit: watt (w) 1 watt = 1 joule per second.

$$\text{average power} = \frac{\text{work done}}{\text{time taken}} = \frac{\text{energy change}}{\text{time taken}}$$

Pressure (symbol: *p*): the force acting per unit surface area, expressed as

$$\text{pressure} = \frac{\text{force}}{\text{area}}$$

SI unit: pascal (Pa).

Atmospheric pressure is still quoted in millibars. The standard atmospheric pressure at 1013 millibars (Mb) is 1 kilogram cm^{-2}.
NB: tyre pressures are still quoted in lb/sq.in. or, more recently, Bar, eg 2 Bar.

Relativity, theory of: mass and energy are related by the equation $E = mc^2$, where E is energy, m is mass, and c is the speed of light.

Scalar: a physical quantity that has magnitude but not direction, eg mass (see also vector).

Speed (symbol: *v* or *u*): the rate of change of distance travelled with time (a scalar quantity). SI unit: metre per second (m s^{-1}).

$$\text{average speed} = \frac{\text{distance moved}}{\text{time taken}}$$

Time (symbol: *t*): a fundamental physical quantity indicating duration or precise moment. SI unit: second (s).

Vector: a physical quantity that has magnitude and direction, eg acceleration.

Velocity (symbol: *v* or *c*): the rate of change of displacement with time (a vector quantity). SI unit: metre per second (m s^{-1}).

$$\text{average velocity} = \frac{\text{distance moved in a particular direction}}{\text{time taken}}$$

Weight (symbol: W): the gravitational force exerted on a body at a planet's surface, giving it an acceleration equal to the acceleration of free fall *(g)*. It should not be confused with mass *(m)*: $W = mg$, and therefore varies as *g* varies. (SI unit: newton (N), although it is measured in units of mass in everyday usage.)

Work (symbol: W): a physical quantity expressed as force x distance *(Fs)* where the point of application of a force moves through a distance in the direction of the force. SI unit: joule (J).

CONSTANTS
GRAVITY
Acceleration of gravity (standard value of acceleration of free fall) (symbol: g_n): 9.80665 m s^{-2}. The acceleration of gravity varies in different places on the Earth's surface. At Greenwich: 9.81 m s^{-2}.

Gravitational constant (symbol: G): 6.67259 x 10^{-11} N m^2 kg^{-2}

LIGHT
Speed of light in a vacuum (symbol: c): 299,792,458 m s^{-1}

SOUND
Speed of sound (symbol: c): 331.4 m s^{-1} (in dry air at 0°C)

WAVES
A wave is a periodic vibration in space or in a substance. Waves can be grouped in two ways according to:
1) whether or not they result in a transfer of energy from one place to another:
Travelling (or progressive) wave: the vibrations travel, transferring energy from one place to another, eg the waves on the sea
Stationary (or standing) wave: the wave shape remains stationary, rather than moving, and energy is not transferred
2) whether or not the individual points on the wave move in the same direction as the wave itself:
Longitudinal wave: particles move in the same direction as the wave travels, eg in a slinky spring
Transverse wave: particles move in a perpendicular direction to the direction of wave travel, eg in surface ripples on water

PROPERTIES OF WAVES
Amplitude

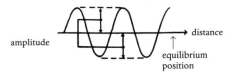

Amplitude is the maximum displacement of a wave from the equilibrium position

Wavelength

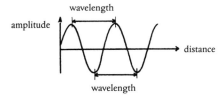

Wavelength is the distance between two successive points along a wave with similar amplitudes

Period

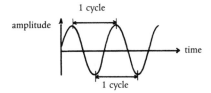

The period of a wave is the time taken for one complete cycle
Frequency = cycles per second. SI unit: hertz (Hz).
1 cycle per second = 1 hertz

Wave Attenuation

 distance

A wave is said to be attenuated when its amplitude becomes progressively reduced as a result of energy loss when it travels through a medium.

SOUND

Decibels (db) are used to measure the power or intensity of sound. Some examples of decibel levels are:

Silence	0db
Pin dropping	20db
Whisper	30db
Ordinary conversation	60db
Vacuum cleaner	70db
In a small car	80db
Damage threshold for noise	*90db*
Orchestra	100db
Street works	110db
Rock music	110db
Pain threshold for noise	*130db*
Earphones on loudest setting	130db
Air raid siren	140db
Bones in the ear may break	*150db*

CHEMISTRY

STATES OF MATTER

The three states of matter are solid, liquid and gas. When heated, a solid melts to form a liquid. Melting point is the temperature above which a solid becomes a liquid. Heating a liquid to its boiling point causes it to boil and form a gas or vapour.

PROPERTY	SOLID	LIQUID	GAS
Volume	Definite	Definite	Variable – expands or contracts to fill container
Shape	Definite	Takes up shape of bottom of container	Takes up shape of whole container
Density	High	Medium	Low
Expansion when heated	Low	Medium	High
Effect of applied pressure	Very slight	Slight decrease in volume	Large decrease in volume
Movement of particles	Very slow	Medium	Fast

ELEMENTS AND COMPOUNDS

ELEMENTS

An element is a pure substance that cannot be split up by chemical reaction. There are 92 known to occur naturally on Earth, and more which have been synthesised under laboratory conditions. Most that occur naturally are solid and metallic at room temperature and pressure, although there are exceptions, eg mercury is a liquid and oxygen is a gas.

COMPOUNDS

Some mixtures of elements react together, usually when heated, to form compounds. These compounds have very different properties from the elements of which they are composed, eg the gases hydrogen and oxygen combine to form water (H_2O).

NAMING COMPOUNDS

Compounds with the prefix **per-** contain extra oxygen
Compounds with the prefix **thio-** contain a sulphur atom in place of an oxygen atom
Compounds that end in **-ide** contain two elements
Compounds that end in **-ate** or **-ite** contain oxygen

FORMULAE OF SOME COMMON COMPOUNDS

Ammonia	NH_3
Carbon dioxide	CO_2
Carbon monoxide	CO
Hydrogen chloride	HCl
Methane	CH_4
Nitrogen dioxide	NO_2
Sulphur dioxide	SO_2
Sulphur trioxide	SO_3
Water	H_2O
Table salt	$NaCl$

CARBON

Carbon can combine with other elements, notably oxygen, nitrogen and hydrogen, to form the large molecules of which living things are made, eg carbohydrates, fats and proteins.

METALS AND ALLOYS

Metals consist of a close-packed, regular arrangement of positive ions surrounded by electrons that hold the ions together (see Atomic Structure). With a few exceptions, they are efficient conductors of heat and electricity, and are both malleable (can be beaten into thin sheets) and ductile (can be extruded into wire). Metals are often combined to form alloys, common examples of which include:

ALLOY	CONSTITUENT ELEMENTS
Brass	Copper and zinc
Bronze	Copper and tin
Duralumin	Aluminium, magnesium, copper and manganese
Solder	Tin and lead
Steel	Iron and carbon, although other metals may be present, eg chromium

ATOMIC STRUCTURE

All elements are made up of atoms. An atom is the smallest unit of an element, and atoms of different elements are made up of different combinations of three basic particles: protons, electrons and neutrons. Protons have a positive charge, electrons have a negative charge and neutrons have no charge.

In an atom, the protons and neutrons are tightly packed in the nucleus, while the electrons move rapidly around the outside. The atomic number of an atom is the number of protons it contains, and the mass number is the total number of protons and neutrons.

Atoms contain the same number of protons as electrons, which means that individual atoms have no overall charge. However, an ion is an electrically charged atom or group of atoms formed by the addition or loss of one or more electrons.

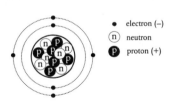

● electron (−)
ⓝ neutron
🅟 proton (+)

Carbon atom

ATOMIC BONDING

When atoms join they are said to bond. Several types of bonding occur in common chemicals.

Ionic (or electrovalent) bonding: involves a complete transfer of electrons from one atom to another.
Covalent bonding: involves the sharing of electrons rather than complete transfer.
Metallic bonding: involves the free movement of the outer shell of electrons between neighbouring atoms. Occurs only in metals.

CHEMICAL GROUPS

Elements can be divided into groups, which include the following.

THE ALKALI METAL GROUP

This is a group of highly reactive metals, the most common of which are Lithium (Li), Sodium (Na) and Potassium (K).

THE HALOGEN GROUP

This is a group of non-metals, all of which are different in appearance but have similar chemical reactions. They include: Fluorine (F), Chlorine (Cl), Bromine (Br) and Iodine (I).

THE NOBLE (OR INERT) GAS GROUP

As their name suggests, these gases are unreactive:

Helium (He)
Neon (Ne)
Argon (Ar)
Krypton (Kr)
Xenon (Xe)
Radon (Rn)

MELTING AND BOILING POINTS OF SELECTED COMPOUNDS AND ELEMENTS

COMPOUND	MELTING POINT (°C)	BOILING POINT (°C)
Ammonia (NH_3)	−77.7	−33.3
Carbon dioxide (CO_2)	−56.6	−78.5
Ethyl alcohol (C_2H_5OH)	−114.1	78.5
Hydrogen chloride (HCl)	−114.0	−85.0
Hydrogen peroxide (H_2O_2)	−0.4	150.2
Methane (CH_4)	−182.5	−162.0
Ozone (O_3)	−192.7	−112.0
Propane (C_3H_8)	−187.6	−42.1
Sulphuric acid (H_2SO_4)	10.4	338.0
Water (H_2O)	0.0	100.0

ELEMENT	MELTING POINT (°C)	BOILING POINT (°C)
Aluminium (Al)	660.3	2,519.0
Arsenic (As)	817.0	603.0
Cadmium (Cd)	321.1	767.0
Calcium (Ca)	842.0	1,484.0
Carbon (C)	3,500.0	4,827.0
Chlorine (Cl)	−101.5	−34.0
Copper (Cu)	1,084.6	2,562.0
Gold (Au)	1,064.2	2,856.0
Hydrogen (H)	−259.3	−252.9
Iron (Fe)	1,538.0	2,861.0
Lead (Pb)	327.5	1,749.0
Lithium (Li)	180.5	1,342.0
Magnesium (Mg)	650.0	1,090.0
Mercury (Hg)	−38.8	356.7
Neon (Ne)	−248.6	−246.1
Nickel (Ni)	1,455.0	2,913.0
Nitrogen (N)	−210.0	−195.8
Oxygen (O)	−218.8	−183.0
Phosphorus (P)	44.2	280.5
Potassium (K)	63.4	759.0
Sodium (Na)	97.8	883.0
Sulphur (S)	119.6	444.6
Tin (Sn)	231.9	2,602.0
Uranium (U)	1,135.0	4,131.0
Zinc (Zn)	419.5	907.0

THE PERIODIC TABLE

	Alkali metals I A								
1	1 Hydrogen **H** 1.01	Alkaline earth metals II A						Transition metals	
2	3 Lithium **Li** 6.94	4 Beryllium **Be** 9.01							
3	11 Sodium **Na** 22.99	12 Magnesium **Mg** 24.31	III B	IV B	V B	VI B	V II		VIII
4	19 Potassium **K** 39.10	20 Calcium **Ca** 40.08	21 Scandium **Sc** 44.96	22 Titanium **Ti** 47.88	23 Vanadium **V** 50.94	24 Chromium **Cr** 52.00	25 Manganese **Mn** 54.94	26 Iron **Fe** 55.85	27 Cobal **Co** 58.9
5	37 Rubidium **Rb** 85.47	38 Strontium **Sr** 87.62	39 Yttrium **Y** 88.91	40 Zirconium **Zr** 91.22	41 Niobium **Nb** 92.91	42 Molybdenum **Mo** 95.96	43 Technetium **Tc** 97.91	44 Ruthenium **Ru** 101.07	45 Rhodiu **Rh** 102.9
6	55 Caesium **Cs** 132.91	56 Barium **Ba** 137.33	Lanthanide series (see below)	72 Hafnium **Hf** 178.49	73 Tantalum **Ta** 180.94	74 Tungsten **W** 183.85	75 Rhenium **Ru** 186.21	76 Osmium **Os** 190.23	77 Iridiu **Ir** 192.2
7	87 Francium **Fr** 223	88 Radium **Ra** 226	Actinide series (see below)	104 Rutherfordium **Rf** 261	105 Dubnium **Db** 262	106 Seaborgium **Sg** 266	107 Bohrium **Bh** 264	108 Hassium **Hs** 277	109 Meitner **Mt** 268

Rare earth elements—Lanthanide series	57 Lanthanum **La** 138.91	58 Cerium **Ce** 140.12	59 Praeseodymium **Pr** 140.91	60 Neodymium **Nd** 144.24	61 Promethium **Pm** 145	62 Samari **Sm** 150.3

Actinide series	89 Actinium **Ac** 227	90 Thorium **Th** 232.04	91 Protactinium **Pa** 231.04	92 Uranium **U** 238.03	93 Neptunium **Np** 237	94 Plutoni **Pu** 244

The Periodic Table arranges the elements into horizontal rows (periods) and vertical columns (groups) according to their ato the left and electronegative to the right. The earliest version of the periodic table was devised in 1869 by Dmitry Mendele

Non-metals

	I B	II B	III A	IV A	V A	VI A	VII A	Noble gases
								2 Helium **He** 4.00
			5 Boron **B** 10.81	6 Carbon **C** 12.01	7 Nitrogen **N** 14.01	8 Oxygen **O** 16.00	9 Fluorine **F** 19.00	10 Neon **Ne** 20.18
			13 Aluminium **Al** 26.98	14 Silicon **Si** 28.09	15 Phosphorus **P** 30.97	16 Sulphur **S** 32.07	17 Chlorine **Cl** 35.45	18 Argon **Ar** 39.95
28 Nickel **Ni** 58.69	29 Copper **Cu** 63.55	30 Zinc **Zn** 65.38	31 Gallium **Ga** 69.72	32 Germanium **Ge** 72.64	33 Arsenic **As** 74.92	34 Selenium **Se** 78.96	35 Bromine **Br** 79.90	36 Krypton **Kr** 83.80
46 alladium **Pd** 106.42	47 Silver **Ag** 107.87	48 Cadmium **Cd** 112.41	49 Indium **In** 114.82	50 Tin **Sn** 118.71	51 Antimony **Sb** 121.76	52 Tellurium **Te** 127.60	53 Iodine **I** 126.90	54 Xenon **Xe** 131.29
78 latinum **Pt** 195.08	79 Gold **Au** 196.97	80 Mercury **Hg** 200.59	81 Thallium **Tl** 204.38	82 Lead **Pb** 207.2	83 Bismuth **Bi** 208.98	84 Polonium **Po** 209	85 Astatine **At** 210	86 Radon **Rn** 222
110 mstadtium **Ds** 271	111 Roentgenium **Rg** 272	112 Copernicium **Cn** 285						

63 ropium **Eu** 51.96	64 Gadolinium **Gd** 157.25	65 Terbium **Tb** 158.93	66 Dysprosium **Dy** 162.50	67 Holmium **Ho** 164.93	68 Erbium **Er** 167.26	69 Thulium **Tm** 168.93	70 Ytterbium **Yb** 173.05	71 Lutetium **Lu** 174.97
95 nericium **Am** 243	96 Curium **Cm** 247	97 Berkelium **Bk** 247	98 Californium **Cf** 251	99 Einsteinium **Es** 252	100 Fermium **Fm** 257	101 Mendelevium **Md** 258	102 Nobelium **No** 259	103 Lawrencium **Lr** 262

ıber. The elements in a group all have similar properties; across each period, atoms are electropositive (form positive ions) to predicted the existence of several elements from gaps in the table.

THE PH SCALE

The pH of a substance is a measure of its alkalinity or acidity. A pH reading below 7 indicates an acidic solution while readings above 7 indicate an alkaline solution.

0	
1	
2	
3	Acid
4	
5	
6	
7	————————Neutral
8	
9	
10	
11	Alkali
12	
13	
14	

Litmus paper shows whether a solution is acidic or alkaline: blue indicates an alkali and red an acid. It is possible to obtain special paper that gives an approximate measure of pH by colour change. For very accurate measurements a pH meter must be used.

APPROX. PH VALUES OF BODY FLUIDS

Blood	7.4–7.5
Breast milk	7.0
Gastric juice	approx. 2
Saliva	6.4–7.4
Semen	7.2
Sweat	4–6.8
Urine	5.7

SCIENTIFIC INSTRUMENTS AND THEIR USES

Altimeter	altitude
Ammeter	electric current
Anemometer	wind speed
Barometer	atmospheric pressure
Calorimeter	heat energy
Chronometer	time
Clinometer	angle of elevation
Craniometer	skull size
Dynamometer	engine power
Endoscope	examining inside the body
Extensometer	ductility
Gravimeter	gravity
Hydrometer	density of liquid
Hygrometer	humidity
Lactometer	density of milk
Manometer	pressure
Micrometer	small distances
Microscope	magnification (of small objects)
Odometer	distance (vehicles)
Pyrometer	high temperatures
Seismometer	earthquakes
Sextant	latitude
Spectroscope	analysing light
Speedometer	speed
Sphygmomanometer	blood pressure
Tachometer	rotational speed
Telescope	magnification (of distant objects)
Thermometer	temperature
Voltmeter	voltage

INVENTIONS AND INVENTORS

Aeroplane	Orville and Wilbur Wright (1903)
Anaesthesia	William Morton (1846)
Aqualung	Jacques Cousteau and Emile Gagnan (1943)
Bagless vacuum cleaner	James Dyson (1991)
Ballpoint pen	Laszlo Biró (1938)
Barbie doll	Ruth Handler (1959)
Battery	Alessandro Volta (1800)
Bifocal lens	Benjamin Franklin (1780)
Bikini	Louis Reard (1946)
Bra	Herminie Cadolle (1889)
Bunsen burner	Robert Wilhelm Bunsen and Peter Desara (1855)
Burglar alarm	Edwin T. Holmes (1858)
Car (petrol driven)	Karl Benz (1886)
Cats' eyes	Percy Shaw (1934)
Cellophane	Dr Jacques Brandenberger (1908)
Centigrade thermometer	Anders Celsius (1742)
Chocolate (solid)	François-Louis Cailler (1819)
Coca-cola	John Pemberton (1886)
Computer	Charles Babbage (1835)
Computer programming language	Ada Lovelace (1843)
Condom	Gabriel Fallopius (1560)
Contact lenses	Adolf E. Fick (1887)
Contraceptive pill	Dr Gregory Pincus, Min Chueh Chang and John Rock (1950)
Crossword puzzle	Arthur Wynne (1913)
Dipped headlights	Emily Canham (1908)
Dishwasher	Josephine Cochran (1886)
Disposable nappy	Marion Donovan (1946)
Dry-cleaning	M. Jolly-Bellin (1849)
Elastic bands	Stephen Perry (1845)
Electric chair	Harold Brown and E. A. Kenneally (1890)
Electric washing machine	Alva J. Fisher (1908)
Escalator	Jesse Reno (1892)
Fax machine	Arthur Korn (1907)
Filter coffee	Melitta Benz (1908)
Fingerprint classification	Francis Galton (1891)
Fountain pen	Lewis Edson Waterman (1884)
Frozen food	Clarence Birdseye (1930)

Genetic fingerprinting	Alec Jeffreys (1985)
Gyroscope	Leon Foucault (1852)
Hovercraft	Christopher Cockerell (1955)
Ice-cream cone	Italo Marcioni (1896)
Inflatable tyre	John Boyd Dunlop (1888)
Jeans	Levi Strauss and Jacob Davis (1873)
Jigsaw puzzle	George Spilsbury (1767)
Locomotive	Richard Trevithick (1804)
Machine gun	James Puckle (1718)
Microchip	Jack St. Clair Kilby and Robert Noyce (1959)
Microwave oven	Percy Lebaron Spencer (1945)
Monopoly	Charles Darrow (1931)
Motorcycle	Gottlieb Daimler (1885)
Non-stick pan	Marc Gregoire (1954)
Paperclip	Johan Vaaler (1899)
Parking meter	Carlton Magee (1935)
Penicillin	Sir Alexander Fleming (1928)
Periodic table	Dmitry Mendeleyev (1869)
Potato crisps	George Crum (1853)
Razor (safety)	King Camp Gillette (1904)
Revolver	Samuel Colt (1835)
Roller skates	Joseph Merlin (1760)
Safety pin	Walter Hunt (1849)
Scrabble	Alfred Butts (1931)
Tampon	Dr Earle Haas (1931)
Thermometer	Galileo Galilei (1593)
Toothbrush	William Addis (1780)
Torpedo guidance system	Hedy Lamarr (1942)
Travel agency	Thomas Cook (1841)
Vaccination	Edward Jenner (1798)
Windscreen wiper	Mary Anderson (1905)
Xerography (basis for the Xerox copier)	Chester Carlson (1938)
X-ray	Wilhelm Konrad Rontgen (1895)
Zip fastener	Whitcomb L. Judson (1893)

LIFE SCIENCES

GENETICS AND EVOLUTION

Most cells have a nucleus containing a fixed number of chromosomes, half derived from each parent. The chromosomes carry genetic (inherited) information along their lengths as genes. In sexual reproduction the parents' genes are mixed and recombined so the offspring usually show characteristics of both.

In 1953, Crick and Watson in Cambridge showed that the genes were short lengths of deoxyribonucleic acid (DNA) and that the genetic information is contained in just four chemical groups taken three at a time. A gene is a sequence of these chemical 'words'. DNA is now used in the identification of individuals.

Charles Darwin (1809–82) described how the enormous variety of living things could have evolved through the 'natural selection' by the environment of those plants and animals best fitted to survive and reproduce themselves in the harshly competitive natural world.

CLASSIFICATION OF PLANTS AND ANIMALS

All species of plants and animals are named according to their genus and their species.

Species: the fundamental unit of biological classification; a group of organisms capable of breeding to produce fertile offspring. They are very similar, but do show variety.
Genus: a category of biological classification; a group of organisms with a large number of similarities but whose different sub-groups or species are usually unable to interbreed successfully.

All species are named according to the binomial system published by Carl Linnaeus in 1735. Under this system the genus name is written first, with a capital letter, eg *Homo* (man). The species name, which starts with a small letter, is written second, eg *sapiens* (modern).

GROUPS AND SUB-GROUPS

Just as species are sub-groups of genera, so Linnaeus grouped genera into larger and larger groups. They are listed as follows, from the largest (kingdom) to smallest (species):

Kingdom
Phylum (for animals) or Division (for plants)
Class
Order
Family
Genus
Species

	Kingdom ANIMALIA	Phylum CHORDATA	Class MAMMALIA	Order PRIMATES	Family HOMINIDAE	Genus HOMO	Species SAPIENS
Hydra							
Earthworm							
Crab							
Insect							
Fish							
Frog							
Lizard							
Bird							
Rat							
Wolf							
Elephant							
Giraffe							
Tree Shrew							
Lemur							
Monkey							
Ape							
Early Human							
Modern Human							

PARTS OF A FLOWER

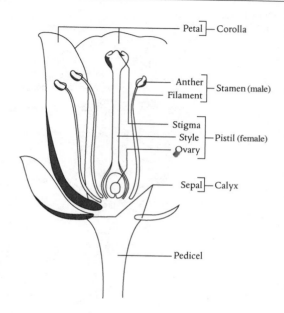

COLOURS OF THE RAINBOW

Red, orange, yellow, green, blue, indigo and violet

THE HUMAN BODY

THE SKELETON – FRONT VIEW

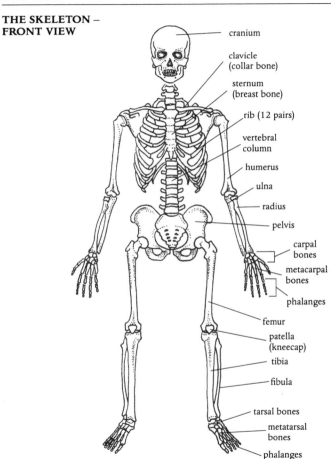

cranium

clavicle
(collar bone)

sternum
(breast bone)

rib (12 pairs)

vertebral
column

humerus

ulna

radius

pelvis

carpal
bones

metacarpal
bones

phalanges

femur

patella
(kneecap)

tibia

fibula

tarsal bones

metatarsal
bones

phalanges

THE SKELETON –
SIDE VIEW

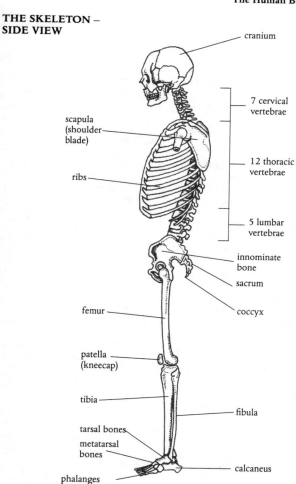

cranium

7 cervical
vertebrae

scapula
(shoulder-
blade)

12 thoracic
vertebrae

ribs

5 lumbar
vertebrae

innominate
bone

sacrum

coccyx

femur

patella
(kneecap)

tibia

fibula

tarsal bones

metatarsal
bones

calcaneus

phalanges

MAIN MUSCLE GROUPS

MUSCLE GROUP	BODY PART	PRIMARY FUNCTIONS
abductors (gluteus medius and minimus)	outer thigh	draw hip outwards
adductors	inner thigh	draw hip inwards
anterior tibialis	shin	draws ball of the foot upwards
biceps brachii	upper arm, front	bends elbow swings shoulder joint forward
biceps femoris (hamstrings)	back of thigh	straightens hip bends knee and rotates it outwards
deltoideus	shoulder/upper arm	involved in all movements of upper arm
erector spinae	lower back	straightens spine
gastrocnemius	calf	bends knee straightens ankle (points toes)
gluteus maximus	buttocks	straightens hip rotates thigh outwards
iliopsoas (psoas major and minor, iliacus)	hip	bends hip rotates leg outwards
latissimus dorsi (broad back muscle)	back	draws arm backwards
obliques (internal and external)	waist	rotate torso bend torso to side
pectoralis major (greater chest muscle)	chest	draws arm inwards pulls arm in front of chest from any position
quadriceps femoris (rectus femoris, vastus medialis, intermedialis, lateralis)	thigh	straightens knee bends hip
rectus abdominus	stomach	bends spine forwards
sartorius (tailor's muscle)	thigh	bends and rotates hip outwards bends and rotates knee inwards
soleus (flounder muscle)	lower calf	standing on toes
trapezius	neck and upper back	draws shoulder blades back turns head bends neck backwards
triceps brachii	upper arm, back	straightens elbow

PERIODS OF GESTATION OR INCUBATION

This table shows approximate periods of gestation or incubation for some common animals and birds; in some cases the periods may vary.

SPECIES	SHORTEST PERIOD (DAYS)	USUAL PERIOD (DAYS)	LONGEST PERIOD (DAYS)
Camel	315	—	440
Canary	12	14	14
Cat	58	62	65
Chicken	20	21	22
Chimpanzee	216	237	261
Cow	273	280	294
Coyote	60	63	65
Dog	55	63	70
Duck	28	28	32
Elephant (African)	—	640	—
Fox	49	52	55
Goat	147	151	155
Giraffe	395	410	425
Goose	28	30	32
Guinea Pig	63	—	70
Hedgehog	35	38	40
Horse	305	336	340
Human	240	273	313
Mouse	18	—	21
Orangutan	245	260	275
Pig	109	112	125
Pigeon	17	18	19
Rabbit	30	32	35
Reindeer	215	230	245
Rat	21	—	24
Sheep	140	148	160
Tiger	105	107	109
Turkey	25	28	28
Zebra	—	392	—

BRAIN AND BODY WEIGHTS OF ANIMALS

ANIMAL	BRAIN WEIGHT (G)	BODY WEIGHT (KG)
Cat	26	3
Chimpanzee	440	52
Cow	423	465
Dog (beagle)	72	14
Horse	655	521
Human	1,320	62
Pig	180	192
Rat	2	0.3
Sheep	175	56
Sperm whale	7,800	13,500

ENDANGERED SPECIES

The International Union for Conservation of Nature (IUCN) categorises endangered species according to their rate of decline, population size, area of geographic distribution and degree of population and distribution fragmentation.

EX (Extinct): dodo, Steller's sea cow
EW (Extinct in the Wild): Abingdon Island tortoise (Lonesome George)
CR (Critically Endangered): angel shark, jellyfish tree
EN (Endangered): chimpanzee, snow leopard
VU (Vulnerable): polar bear, common hippopotamus
NT (Near Threatened): gentoo penguin, tiger shark
LC (Least Concern): house sparrow, brown pelican

The IUCN's Red List is the most comprehensive information published on endangered species. Over 45,000 species of plants, animals, birds, reptiles etc are included each year, almost 17,000 of them are threatened with extinction. Species introduced to the 2009 Red List update as endangered or threatened include:

Eastern voalavo, 12 species of Malaysian mollusc, margarya monodi (snail), Panay monitor lizard, Rabb's fringe-limbed treefrog and the sail-fin water lizard.

Countries with the most endangered species appearing on the 2009 Red List are:

Ecuador	2,211
United States	1,203
Malaysia	1,166
Indonesia	1,126
Mexico	900

THE KINGDOM OF LIVING THINGS

Facts and figures about some record-breaking animals and plants

MAMMALS
Fastest mammal: cheetah (eastern and southern Africa) – up to 110 km/h (68mph)
Tallest mammal: giraffe (western and southern Africa) – up to 5.5m (18ft) in height
Largest mammal: blue whale (Pacific, Indian and Southern oceans) – up to 35m (115ft) in length
Largest land mammal: African bush elephant (central Africa) – up to 3.2m (10.5ft) in height, 7m (22.9ft) in length and 10,000kg (1,574.7 stone) in weight
Loudest mammal: blue whale – up to 188db

BIRDS
Fastest bird: peregrine falcon (worldwide) – up to 350km/h (217mph)
Fastest land bird: ostrich (north Africa) – up to 65km/h (40mph)
Biggest wingspan: wandering albatross (Southern ocean) – up to 3.7m (12.1ft)
Longest migration: Arctic tern (Arctic to Antarctic) – average 80,500km (50,000 miles)

FISH AND REPTILES
Biggest fish: whale shark (Pacific, Atlantic and Indian oceans) – up to 13m (43ft) in length
Biggest amphibian: Chinese giant salamander (China) – up to 1.8m (5.9ft) in length
Biggest reptile estuarine or saltwater crocodile (south-east Asia, northern Australia) – up to 6m (19.7ft) in length
Biggest spider: Goliath bird-eating spider (South America) – leg span of 30cm (11.8in)
Longest snake: reticulated python (south-east Asia) – up to 10m (32.8ft) in length

PLANTS
Tallest living tree: Hyperion (Redwood National Park, Northern California) – 115.5m (378.9ft) tall
Biggest tree: Lindsey Creek tree (Pacific Coast, USA) – trunk volume of 2,550 cubic m (90,000 cubic ft), mass of 3,630,000kg (580,800 stone)
Biggest seed: double coconut or coco de mer (Seychelles) – up to 20kg
Biggest leaves: raffia palm (Madagascar, South America, tropical Africa) – up to 21m (68.9ft) long and 3m (9.8ft) wide

SPORT

THE COMMONWEALTH GAMES

The Games were originally called the British Empire Games. From 1954 to 1966 the Games were known as the British Empire and Commonwealth Games, and from 1970 to 1974 as the British Commonwealth Games. Since 1978 the Games have been called the Commonwealth Games.

BRITISH EMPIRE GAMES
1930   Hamilton, Canada
1934   London, England
1938   Sydney, Australia
1950   Auckland, New Zealand

BRITISH EMPIRE AND COMMONWEALTH GAMES
1954   Vancouver, Canada
1958   Cardiff, Wales

1962   Perth, Australia
1966   Kingston, Jamaica

BRITISH COMMONWEALTH GAMES
1970   Edinburgh, Scotland
1974   Christchurch, New Zealand

COMMONWEALTH GAMES
1978   Edmonton, Canada
1982   Brisbane, Australia
1986   Edinburgh, Scotland
1990   Auckland, New Zealand
1994   Victoria, Canada
1998   Kuala Lumpur, Malaysia
2002   Manchester, England
2006   Melbourne, Australia
2010   Delhi, India
2014   Glasgow, Scotland

THE OLYMPIC GAMES

VANCOUVER WINTER OLYMPICS 2010 MEDAL TABLE

COUNTRY	GOLD	SILVER	BRONZE	TOTAL
Canada	14	7	5	26
Germany	10	13	7	30
United States	9	15	13	37
Norway	9	8	6	23
Korea	6	6	2	14
Switzerland	6	0	3	9
China	5	2	4	11
Sweden	5	2	4	11
Austria	4	6	6	16
Netherlands	4	1	3	8
Russian Federation	3	5	7	15
France	2	3	6	11
Australia	2	1	0	3
Czech Republic	2	0	4	6

COUNTRY	GOLD	SILVER	BRONZE	TOTAL
Poland	1	3	2	6
Italy	1	1	3	5
Belarus	1	1	1	3
Slovakia	1	1	1	3
Great Britain	1	0	0	1
Japan	0	3	2	5
Croatia	0	2	1	3
Slovenia	0	2	1	3
Latvia	0	2	0	2
Finland	0	1	4	5
Estonia	0	1	0	1
Kazakhstan	0	1	0	1

MODERN OLYMPIC GAMES

1896	Athens, Greece
1900	Paris, France
1904	St Louis, USA
1908	London, England
1912	Stockholm, Sweden
1920	Antwerp, Belgium
1924	Paris, France
1928	Amsterdam, Netherlands
1932	Los Angeles, USA
1936	Berlin, Germany
1948	London, England
1952	Helsinki, Finland
1956	Melbourne, Australia (equestrian events held in Stockholm, Sweden)
1960	Rome, Italy
1964	Tokyo, Japan
1968	Mexico City, Mexico
1972	Munich, West Germany
1976	Montreal, Canada
1980	Moscow, USSR
1984	Los Angeles, USA
1988	Seoul, South Korea
1992	Barcelona, Spain
1996	Atlanta, USA
2000	Sydney, Australia
2004	Athens, Greece
2008	Beijing, China
2012	London, UK
2016	Rio de Janeiro, Brazil

The following summer Games were scheduled but did not take place owing to World Wars:

1916	Berlin, Germany
1940	Tokyo, Japan; then Helsinki, Finland
1944	London, England

WINTER OLYMPIC GAMES

1924	Chamonix, France
1928	St Moritz, Switzerland
1932	Lake Placid, USA
1936	Garmisch-Partenkirchen, Germany
1948	St Moritz, Switzerland
1952	Oslo, Norway
1956	Cortina d'Ampezzo, Italy
1960	Squaw Valley, USA
1964	Innsbruck, Austria
1968	Grenoble, France
1972	Sapporo, Japan
1976	Innsbruck, Austria
1980	Lake Placid, USA
1984	Sarajevo, Yugoslavia
1988	Calgary, Canada
1992	Albertville, France

1994	Lillehammer, Norway
1998	Nagano, Japan
2002	Salt Lake City, USA
2006	Turin, Italy
2010	Vancouver, Canada
2014	Sochi, Russian Federation

The following winter games were scheduled but did not take place owing to World Wars:

| 1940 | Sapporo, Japan |
| 1944 | Cortina d'Ampezzo, Italy |

A-Z OF OLYMPIC SPORTS

SUMMER

Aquatics
Archery
Athletics
Badminton
Basketball
Boxing
Canoe/kayak
Cycling
Equestrian
Fencing
Football
Gymnastics
Handball
Hockey
Judo
Modern pentathlon
Rowing
Sailing
Shooting
Table tennis
Taekwondo
Tennis
Triathlon
Volleyball
Weightlifting
Wrestling

WINTER

Biathlon
Bobsleigh
Curling
Ice hockey
Luge
Skating
Skiing

PARALYMPIC SPORTS (SUMMER AND WINTER)

Alpine skiing
Archery
Athletics
Basketball
Boccia
Curling
Cycling
Nordic skiing
Powerlifting
Rowing
Rugby
Sailing
Equestrian
Fencing
Football
Goalball
Ice sledge hockey
Judo
Shooting
Swimming
Table tennis
Tennis
Volleyball

DISCONTINUED SPORTS	YEAR(S) PLAYED
Baseball	1992/96/00/04/08
Cricket	1900
Croquet	1900
Golf	1900/04
Jeu de paume	1908
Lacrosse	1904/08
Pelote Basque	1900
Polo	1900/08/20/24/36
Powerboating	1908
Rackets	1908
Rink hockey	1920
Roque	1904
Rugby union	1900/08/20/24
Softball	1996/00/04/08
Tug-of-war (part of athletics)	1900–20

ATHLETICS

WORLD RECORDS

MEN

Track

100m Usain Bolt (Jamaica) 2009	9.58sec
200m Usain Bolt (Jamaica) 2009	19.19sec
400m Michael Johnson (USA) 1999	43.18sec
800m Wilson Kipketer (Denmark) 1997	1min 41.11sec
1,500m Hicham El Guerrouj (Morocco) 1998	3min 26.00sec
Marathon Haile Gebrselassie (Ethiopia) 2008	2hr 03min 59sec
110m hurdles Dayron Robles (Cuba) 2008	12.87sec
400m hurdles Kevin Young (USA) 1992	46.78sec

Field

High jump Javier Sotomayor (Cuba) 1993	2.45m
Pole vault Sergei Bubka (Ukraine) 1994	6.14m
Long jump Mike Powell (USA) 1991	8.95m
Triple jump Jonathan Edwards (GB) 1995	18.29m
Shot Randy Barnes (USA) 1980	23.12m
Discus Jurgen Schult (GDR) 1986	74.08m
Hammer Yuriy Sedykh (USSR) 1986	86.74m
Javelin Jan Zelezny (Czech Rep.) 1996	98.48m
Decathlon Roman Sebrle (Czech Rep.) 2001	9,026pts

WOMEN

Track

100m Florence Griffith-Joyner (USA) 1988		10.49sec
200m Florence Griffith-Joyner (USA) 1988		21.34sec
400m Marita Koch (GDR) 1985		47.60sec
800m Jarmila Kratochvilova (Czechoslovakia) 1983		1min 53.28sec
1,500m Qu Yunxia (China) 1993		3min 50.46sec
Marathon Paula Radcliffe (GB) 2003		2hr 15min 25sec
100m hurdles Yordanka Donkova (Bulgaria) 1988		12.21sec
400m hurdles Yulia Pechonkina (Russia) 2003		52.34sec

Field

High jump Stefka Kostadinova (Bulgaria) 1987	2.09m
Pole vault Yelena Isinbayeva (Russia) 2009	5.06m
Long jump Galina Chistiakova (USSR) 1988	7.52m
Triple jump Inessa Kravets (Ukraine) 1995	15.50m
Shot Natalya Lisovskaya (USSR) 1987	22.63m
Discus Gabriele Reinsch (GDR) 1988	76.80m
Hammer Anita Wlodarczyk (Poland) 2010	78.30m
Javelin Barbora Spotakova (Czech Rep.) 2008	72.28m
Heptathlon Jackie-Joyner Kersee (USA) 1988	7,291pts

LONDON MARATHON

First held 1981

YEAR	MEN	WOMEN
1981	Dick Beardsley (USA) Inge Simonson (Norway)	Joyce Smith (GB)
1982	Hugh Jones (GB)	Joyce Smith (GB)
1983	Mike Gratton (GB)	Grete Waitz (Norway)
1984	Charlie Spedding (GB)	Ingrid Kristiansen (Norway)
1985	Steve Jones (GB)	Ingrid Kristiansen (Norway)
1986	Toshihiko Seko (Japan)	Grete Waitz (Norway)
1987	Hiromi Taniguchi (Japan)	Ingrid Kristiansen (Norway)
1988	Henrik Jorgensen (Denmark)	Ingrid Kristiansen (Norway)
1989	Douglas Wakiihuri (Kenya)	Veronique Marot (GB)
1990	Allister Hutton (GB)	Wanda Panfil (Poland)
1991	Yakov Tolstikov (EUN)	Rosa Mota (Portugal)
1992	Antonio Pinto (Portugal)	Katrin Dörre (Germany)
1993	Eamonn Martin (GB)	Katrin Dörre (Germany)
1994	Dionicio Cerón (Mexico)	Katrin Dörre (Germany)
1995	Dionicio Cerón (Mexico)	Malgorzata Sobanska (Poland)
1996	Dionicio Cerón (Mexico)	Liz McColgan (GB)
1997	António Pinto (Portugal)	Joyce Chepchumba (Kenya)

YEAR	MEN	WOMEN
1998	Abel Antón (Spain)	Catherina McKiernan (Ireland)
1999	Abdelkader El Mouaziz (Morocco)	Joyce Chepchumba (Kenya)
2000	António Pinto (Portugal)	Tegla Loroupe (Kenya)
2001	Abdelkader El Mouaziz (Morocco)	Deratu Tulu (Ethiopia)
2002	Khalid Khannouchi (USA)	Paula Radcliffe (GB)
2003	Gezahegne Abera (Ethiopia)	Paula Radcliffe (GB)
2004	Evans Rutto (Kenya)	Margaret Okayo (Kenya)
2005	Martin Lel (Kenya)	Paula Radcliffe (GB)
2006	Felix Limo (Kenya)	Deena Kastor (USA)
2007	Martin Lel (Kenya)	Zhou Chunxiu (China)
2008	Martin Lel (Kenya)	Irina Mikitenko (Germany)
2009	Samuel Wanjiru (Kenya)	Irina Mikitenko (Germany)
2010	Tsegaye Kebede (Ethiopia)	Lilya Shobukhova (Russia)

CRICKET

WORLD CUP WINNERS

First held 1975

YEAR	WINNER
1975	West Indies
1979	West Indies
1983	India
1987	Australia
1992	Pakistan
1996	Sri Lanka
1999	Australia
2003	Australia
2007	Australia

COUNTY CHAMPIONS

First held 1864

YEAR	WINNER
1980	Middlesex
1981	Nottinghamshire
1982	Middlesex
1983	Essex
1984	Essex
1985	Middlesex
1986	Essex
1987	Nottinghamshire
1988	Worcestershire
1989	Worcestershire
1990	Middlesex
1991	Essex
1992	Essex
1993	Middlesex
1994	Warwickshire
1995	Warwickshire
1996	Leicestershire
1997	Glamorgan
1998	Leicestershire
1999	Surrey
2000	Surrey
2001	Yorkshire
2002	Surrey
2003	Sussex
2004	Warwickshire
2005	Nottinghamshire
2006	Sussex
2007	Sussex
2008	Durham
2009	Durham

TEST CRICKET

Leading Batsmen as at April 2010

Sachin Tendulkar (India)	13,447 runs at an average of 55.56
Brian Lara (West Indies)	11,953 at 52.88
Ricky Ponting	11,928 at 55.22
Rahul Dravid	11,395 at 53.75
Allan Border	11,174 at 50.56

Leading Bowlers as at April 2010

Muttiah Muralitharan (Sri Lanka)	792 wickets at an average of 22.71
Shane Warne (Australia)	708 at 25.41
Anil Kumble (India)	619 at 29.65
Glenn McGrath (Australia)	563 at 21.64
Courtney Walsh (West Indies)	519 at 24.44

FOOTBALL

WORLD CUP WINNERS

First held 1930

YEAR	VENUE	WINNER
1930	Uruguay	Uruguay
1934	Italy	Italy
1938	France	Italy
1950	Brazil	Uruguay
1954	Switzerland	West Germany
1958	Sweden	Brazil
1962	Chile	Brazil
1966	England	England
1970	Mexico	Brazil
1974	West Germany	West Germany
1978	Argentina	Argentina
1982	Spain	Italy
1986	Mexico	Argentina
1990	Italy	West Germany
1994	USA	Brazil
1998	France	France
2002	Korea/Japan	Brazil
2006	Germany	Italy
2010	South Africa	Spain

WORLD CUP: GOLDEN SHOE WINNERS

The Golden Shoe (also known as the Golden Boot) is awarded to the top goal-scorer of the tournament.

YEAR	PLAYER	NUMBER OF GOALS
1982	Paolo Rossi (Italy)	6
1986	Gary Lineker (England)	6
1990	Salvatore Schillaci (Italy)	6
1994	Hristo Stoichkov (Bulgaria)	6
	Oleg Salenko (Russia)	
1998	Davor Suker (Croatia)	6
2002	Ronaldo (Brazil)	8
2006	Miroslav Klose (Germany)	5
2010	Thomas Müller (Germany)	5

LEAGUE CHAMPIONS

First held 1889

YEAR	WINNER
1980	Liverpool

YEAR	WINNER
1981	Aston Villa
1982	Liverpool
1983	Liverpool
1984	Liverpool
1985	Everton
1986	Liverpool
1987	Everton
1988	Liverpool
1989	Arsenal
1990	Liverpool
1991	Arsenal
1992	Leeds United
1993	Manchester United
1994	Manchester United
1995	Blackburn Rovers
1996	Manchester United
1997	Manchester United
1998	Arsenal
1999	Manchester United
2000	Manchester United
2001	Manchester United
2002	Arsenal
2003	Manchester United
2004	Arsenal
2005	Chelsea
2006	Chelsea
2007	Manchester United
2008	Manchester United
2009	Manchester United
2010	Chelsea

FA CUP WINNERS

First held 1872

YEAR	WINNER
1980	West Ham United
1981	Tottenham Hotspur
1982	Tottenham Hotspur
1983	Manchester United
1984	Everton
1985	Manchester United
1986	Liverpool

YEAR	WINNER
1987	Coventry
1988	Wimbledon
1989	Liverpool
1990	Manchester United
1991	Tottenham Hotspur
1992	Liverpool
1993	Arsenal
1994	Manchester United
1995	Everton
1996	Manchester United
1997	Chelsea
1998	Arsenal
1999	Manchester United
2000	Chelsea
2001	Liverpool
2002	Arsenal
2003	Arsenal
2004	Manchester United
2005	Arsenal
2006	Liverpool
2007	Chelsea
2008	Portsmouth
2009	Chelsea
2010	Chelsea

WEALTHIEST FOOTBALL CLUBS

The world's wealthiest football clubs by revenue.

Real Madrid	€401.4m (£354.8m)
Barcelona	€365.9m (£323.4m)
Manchester United	€327m (£289m)
Bayern Munich	€289.5m (£255.9m)
Arsenal	€263m (£232.5m)
Chelsea	€242.3m (£214.2m)
Liverpool	€217m (£191.8m)
Juventus	€203.2m (£179.4m)
Inter Milan	€196.5m (£173.7m)
AC Milan	€196.5.m (£173.7m)

Source: Deloitte 2008/9

GOLF

MAJORS*

Jack Nicklaus (USA)	18
Tiger Woods (USA)	14
Walter Hagen (USA)	11
Ben Hogan (USA)	9
Gary Player (South Africa)	9

* Majors = Masters, US Open, British Open, PGA

OPEN CHAMPIONS

First held 1860
Played over 72 holes since 1892

YEAR	WINNER
1980	Tom Watson (USA)
1981	Bill Rogers (USA)
1982	Tom Watson (USA)
1983	Tom Watson (USA)
1984	Severiano Ballesteros (Spain)
1985	Sandy Lyle (GB)
1986	Greg Norman (Australia)
1987	Nick Faldo (GB)
1988	Severiano Ballesteros (Spain)
1989	Mark Calcavecchia (USA)
1990	Nick Faldo (GB)
1991	Ian Baker-Finch (Australia)
1992	Nick Faldo (GB)
1993	Greg Norman (Australia)
1994	Nick Price (Zimbabwe)
1995	John Daly (USA)
1996	Tom Lehman (USA)
1997	Justin Leonard (USA)
1998	Mark O'Meara (USA)
1999	Paul Lawrie (GB)
2000	Tiger Woods (USA)
2001	David Duval (USA)
2002	Ernie Els (South Africa)
2003	Ben Curtis (USA)
2004	Todd Hamilton (USA)
2005	Tiger Woods (USA)
2006	Tiger Woods (USA)

YEAR	WINNER
2007	Padraig Harrington (Ireland)
2008	Padraig Harrington (Ireland)
2009	Stewart Cink (USA)

RYDER CUP WINNERS

First held 1927. Played over 2 days
1927–61; over 3 days 1963 to date

YEAR	WINNER
1981	USA
1983	USA
1985	Europe
1987	Europe
1989	Match drawn
1991	USA
1993	USA
1995	Europe
1997	Europe
1999	USA
2002	Europe
2004	Europe
2006	Europe
2008	USA

US OPEN CHAMPIONS

First held 1895

YEAR	WINNER
1980	Jack Nicklaus (USA)
1981	David Graham (Australia)
1982	Tom Watson (USA)
1983	Larry Nelson (USA)
1984	Fuzzy Zoeller (USA)
1985	Andy North (USA)
1986	Raymond Floyd (USA)
1987	Scott Simpson (USA)
1988	Curtis Strange (USA)
1989	Curtis Strange (USA)
1990	Hale Irwin (USA)
1991	Payne Stewart (USA)
1992	Tom Kite (USA)
1993	Lee Janzen (USA)
1994	Ernie Els (South Africa)

YEAR	WINNER
1995	Corey Pavin (USA)
1996	Steve Jones (USA)
1997	Ernie Els (South Africa)
1998	Lee Janzen (USA)
1999	Payne Stewart (USA)
2000	Tiger Woods (USA)
2001	Retief Goosen (South Africa)
2002	Tiger Woods (USA)
2003	Jim Furyk (USA)
2004	Retief Goosen (South Africa)
2005	Michael Campbell (New Zealand)
2006	Geoff Ogilvy (Australia)
2007	Angel Cabrera (Argentina)
2008	Tiger Woods (USA)
2009	Lucas Glover (USA)
2010	Graeme McDowell (GB)

US MASTERS CHAMPIONS

First held 1934

YEAR	WINNER
1980	Severiano Ballesteros (Spain)
1981	Tom Watson (USA)
1982	Craig Stadler (USA)
1983	Severiano Ballesteros (Spain)
1984	Ben Crenshaw (USA)
1985	Bernhard Langer (W. Germany)
1986	Jack Nicklaus (USA)
1987	Larry Mize (USA)
1988	Sandy Lyle (GB)
1989	Nick Faldo (GB)
1990	Nick Faldo (GB)
1991	Ian Woosnam (GB)
1992	Fred Couples (USA)
1993	Bernhard Langer (Germany)
1994	José María Olazábal (Spain)
1995	Ben Crenshaw (USA)
1996	Nick Faldo (GB)
1997	Tiger Woods (USA)
1998	Mark O'Meara (USA)
1999	José María Olazábal (Spain)
2000	Vijay Singh (Fiji)

YEAR	WINNER
2001	Tiger Woods (USA)
2002	Tiger Woods (USA)
2003	Mike Weir (Canada)
2004	Phil Mickelson (USA)
2005	Tiger Woods (USA)
2006	Phil Mickelson (USA)
2007	Zach Johnson (USA)
2008	Trevor Immelman (South Africa)
2009	Angel Cabrera (Argentina)
2010	Phil Mickelson (USA)

HORSE RACING

DERBY WINNERS

First run in 1780

YEAR	WINNING HORSE
1980	Henbit
1981	Shergar
1982	Golden Fleece
1983	Teenoso
1984	Secreto
1985	Slip Anchor
1986	Shahrastani
1987	Reference Point
1988	Kahyasi
1989	Nashwan
1990	Quest For Fame
1991	Generous
1992	Dr Devious
1993	Commander In Chief
1994	Erhaab
1995	Lammtarra
1996	Shaamit
1997	Benny The Dip
1998	High Rise
1999	Oath
2000	Sinndar
2001	Galileo
2002	High Chaparral
2003	Kris Kin
2004	North Light

YEAR	WINNER
2005	Motivator
2006	Sir Percy
2007	Authorized
2008	New Approach
2009	Sea The Stars
2010	Workforce

GRAND NATIONAL WINNERS

First run in 1839

YEAR	WINNING HORSE
1980	Ben Nevis
1981	Aldaniti
1982	Grittar
1983	Corbiere
1984	Hallo Dandy
1985	Last Suspect
1986	West Tip
1987	Maori Venture
1988	Rhyme 'N' Reason
1989	Little Polveir
1990	Mr Frisk
1991	Seagram
1992	Party Politics
1993	*Race declared void*
1994	Minnehoma
1995	Royal Athlete
1996	Rough Quest
1997	Lord Gyllene
1998	Earth Summit
1999	Bobbyjo
2000	Papillon
2001	Red Marauder
2002	Bindaree
2003	Monty's Pass
2004	Amberleigh House
2005	Hedgehunter
2006	Numbersixvalverde
2007	Silver Birch
2008	Comply or Die
2009	Mon Mome
2010	Don't Push It

MOTOR RACING

FORMULA ONE WORLD CHAMPIONS

First held 1950

YEAR	WINNER
1980	Alan Jones (Australia)
1981	Nelson Piquet (Brazil)
1982	Keke Rosberg (Finland)
1983	Nelson Piquet (Brazil)
1984	Niki Lauda (Austria)
1985	Alain Prost (France)
1986	Alain Prost (France)
1987	Nelson Piquet (Brazil)
1988	Ayrton Senna (Brazil)
1989	Alain Prost (France)
1990	Ayrton Senna (Brazil)
1991	Ayrton Senna (Brazil)
1992	Nigel Mansell (GB)
1993	Alain Prost (France)
1994	Michael Schumacher (Germany)
1995	Michael Schumacher (Germany)
1996	Damon Hill (GB)
1997	Jacques Villeneuve (Canada)
1998	Mika Hakkinen (Finland)
1999	Mika Hakkinen (Finland)
2000	Michael Schumacher (Germany)
2001	Michael Schumacher (Germany)
2002	Michael Schumacher (Germany)
2003	Michael Schumacher (Germany)
2004	Michael Schumacher (Germany)
2005	Fernando Alonso (Spain)
2006	Fernando Alonso (Spain)
2007	Kimi Raikkonen (Finland)
2008	Lewis Hamilton (GB)
2009	Jenson Button (GB)

ROWING

THE UNIVERSITY BOAT RACE

First held 1829

1829–2010: Cambridge 80 wins, Oxford 75; one dead heat (1877)

YEAR	WINNER
1980	Oxford
1981	Oxford
1982	Oxford
1983	Oxford
1984	Oxford
1985	Oxford
1986	Cambridge
1987	Oxford
1988	Oxford
1989	Oxford
1990	Oxford
1991	Oxford
1992	Oxford
1993	Cambridge
1994	Cambridge
1995	Cambridge
1996	Cambridge
1997	Cambridge
1998	Cambridge
1999	Cambridge
2000	Oxford
2001	Cambridge
2002	Oxford
2003	Oxford
2004	Cambridge
2005	Oxford
2006	Oxford
2007	Cambridge
2008	Oxford
2009	Oxford
2010	Cambridge

RUGBY LEAGUE

WORLD CUP WINNERS

First held 1954

YEAR	WINNER
1954	Great Britain
1957	Australia
1960	Great Britain
1968	Australia
1970	Australia
1972	Great Britain
1975	Australia
1977	Australia
1988	Australia
1992	Australia
1995	Australia
2000	Australia
2008	New Zealand

CHALLENGE CUP WINNERS

First held 1897

YEAR	WINNER
1980	Hull Kingston Rovers
1981	Widnes
1982	Hull
1983	Featherstone Rovers
1984	Widnes
1985	Wigan
1986	Castleford
1987	Halifax
1988	Wigan
1989	Wigan
1990	Wigan
1991	Wigan
1992	Wigan
1993	Wigan
1994	Wigan
1995	Wigan
1996	St Helens
1997	St Helens
1998	Sheffield
1999	Leeds

2000	Bradford
2001	St Helens
2002	Wigan Warriors
2003	Bradford Bulls
2004	St Helens
2005	Hull
2006	St Helens
2007	St Helens
2008	St Helens
2009	Warrington Wolves

RUGBY UNION

WORLD CUP WINNERS
First held 1987

YEAR	WINNER
1987	New Zealand
1991	Australia
1995	South Africa
1999	Australia
2003	England
2007	South Africa

FOUR/FIVE/SIX NATIONS CHAMPIONS
First held 1883

YEAR	WINNER
1980	England
1981	France
1982	Ireland
1983	France/Ireland
1984	Scotland
1985	Ireland
1986	France/Scotland
1987	France
1988	Wales/France
1989	France
1990	Scotland
1991	England
1992	England
1993	France
1994	Wales
1995	England
1996	England
1997	France
1998	France
1999	Scotland
2000	England
2001	England
2002	France
2003	England
2004	France
2005	Wales
2006	France
2007	France
2008	Wales
2009	Ireland
2010	France

SNOOKER

WORLD PROFESSIONAL CHAMPIONS
First held 1927

YEAR	WINNER
1980	Cliff Thorburn (Canada)
1981	Steve Davis (England)
1982	Alex Higgins (N. Ireland)
1983	Steve Davis (England)
1984	Steve Davis (England)
1985	Dennis Taylor (N. Ireland)
1986	Joe Johnson (England)
1987	Steve Davis (England)
1988	Steve Davis (England)
1989	Steve Davis (England)
1990	Stephen Hendry (Scotland)
1991	John Parrott (England)
1992	Stephen Hendry (Scotland)
1993	Stephen Hendry (Scotland)

1994	Stephen Hendry (Scotland)
1995	Stephen Hendry (Scotland)
1996	Stephen Hendry (Scotland)
1997	Ken Doherty (Ireland)
1998	John Higgins (Scotland)
1999	Stephen Hendry (Scotland)
2000	Mark Williams (Wales)
2001	Ronnie O'Sullivan (England)
2002	Peter Ebdon (England)

2003	Mark Williams (Wales)
2004	Ronnie O'Sullivan (England)
2005	Shaun Murphy (England)
2006	Graeme Dott (Scotland)
2007	John Higgins (Scotland)
2008	Ronnie O'Sullivan (England)
2009	John Higgins (Scotland)
2010	Neil Robertson (Australia)

FASTEST 147 BREAKS

1. Ronnie O'Sullivan (vs Mick Price)	21 April 1997	5min 20sec
2. Ronnie O'Sullivan (vs Marco Fu)	22 April 2003	6min 30sec
3. Ronnie O'Sullivan (vs Drew Henry)	17 October 2001	6min 36sec

TENNIS

WORLD RANKINGS

As at 8 June 2010

Highest number of weeks spent as world number one:

MEN (since 1973)

	WEEKS
Pete Sampras (USA)	286
Roger Federer (Switzerland)	285
Ivan Lendl (Czech Republic)	270
Jimmy Connors (USA)	268
John McEnroe (USA)	170

WOMEN (since 1975)

	WEEKS
Steffi Graf (Germany)	377
Martina Navratilova (USA)	332
Chris Evert (USA)	260
Martina Hingis (Switzerland)	209
Monica Seles (USA)	178

WIMBLEDON MEN'S SINGLES CHAMPIONS

First held 1877

YEAR	WINNER
1980	Bjorn Borg (Sweden)
1981	John McEnroe (USA)
1982	Jimmy Connors (USA)
1983	John McEnroe (USA)
1984	John McEnroe (USA)
1985	Boris Becker (W. Germany)
1986	Boris Becker (W. Germany)
1987	Pat Cash (Australia)
1988	Stefan Edberg (Sweden)
1989	Boris Becker (W. Germany)
1990	Stefan Edberg (Sweden)
1991	Michael Stich (Germany)
1992	Andre Agassi (USA)
1993	Pete Sampras (USA)
1994	Pete Sampras (USA)
1995	Pete Sampras (USA)
1996	Richard Krajicek (Netherlands)

1997	Pete Sampras (USA)
1998	Pete Sampras (USA)
1999	Pete Sampras (USA)
2000	Pete Sampras (USA)
2001	Goran Ivanisevic (Croatia)
2002	Lleyton Hewitt (Australia)
2003	Roger Federer (Switzerland)
2004	Roger Federer (Switzerland)
2005	Roger Federer (Switzerland)
2006	Roger Federer (Switzerland)
2007	Roger Federer (Switzerland)
2008	Rafael Nadal (Spain)
2009	Roger Federer (Switzerland)
2010	Rafael Nadal (Spain)

WIMBLEDON WOMEN'S SINGLES CHAMPIONS

First held 1884

YEAR	WINNER
1980	Evonne Cawley (Australia)
1981	Chris Evert Lloyd (USA)
1982	Martina Navratilova (USA)
1983	Martina Navratilova (USA)
1984	Martina Navratilova (USA)
1985	Martina Navratilova (USA)
1986	Martina Navratilova (USA)
1987	Martina Navratilova (USA)
1988	Steffi Graf (W. Germany)
1989	Steffi Graf (W. Germany)
1990	Martina Navratilova (USA)
1991	Steffi Graf (Germany)
1992	Steffi Graf (Germany)
1993	Steffi Graf (Germany)
1994	Conchita Martinez (Spain)
1995	Steffi Graf (Germany)
1996	Steffi Graf (Germany)
1997	Martina Hingis (Switzerland)
1998	Jana Novotna (Czech Republic)
1999	Lindsay Davenport (USA)
2000	Venus Williams (USA)
2001	Venus Williams (USA)
2002	Serena Williams (USA)
2003	Serena Williams (USA)
2004	Maria Sharapova (Russia)
2005	Venus Williams (USA)
2006	Amelie Mauresmo (France)
2007	Venus Williams (USA)
2008	Venus Williams (USA)
2009	Serena Williams (USA)
2010	Serena Williams (USA)

TIME

TIME ZONES

Standard time differences from the
Greenwich meridian
+ hours ahead of GMT
− hours behind GMT
* may vary from standard time at some
  part of the year (Summer Time or
  Daylight Saving Time)
† some areas may keep another time
  zone
‡ unofficial time zone
h hours
m minutes

	h	*m*
Afghanistan	+ 4	30
*Albania	+ 1	
Algeria	+ 1	
*Andorra	+ 1	
Angola	+ 1	
Antigua and Barbuda	− 4	
*†Argentina	− 3	
*Armenia	+ 4	
*Australia		
*ACT, NSW (except Broken Hill area and Lord Howe Island), Tas, Vic, Whitsunday Islands	+ 10	
Northern Territory	+ 9	30
Queensland	+ 10	
*South Australia	+ 9	30
*†Western Australia	+ 8	
Christmas Island (Indian Ocean)	+ 7	
Cocos (Keeling) Islands	+ 6	30
Norfolk Island	+ 11	30
*Austria	+ 1	
*Azerbaijan	+ 4	
*Bahamas	− 5	

	h	*m*
Bahrain	+ 3	
Bangladesh	+ 6	
Barbados	− 4	
*Belarus	+ 2	
*Belgium	+ 1	
Belize	− 6	
Benin	+ 1	
Bhutan	+ 6	
Bolivia	− 4	
*Bosnia and Hercegovina	+ 1	
Botswana	+ 2	
*Brazil		
*central states	− 4	
*N. and N. E. coastal states	− 2	
*S. and E. coastal states, including Brasilia	− 3	
*Fernando de Noronha Island	− 2	
Brunei	+ 8	
*Bulgaria	+ 2	
Burkina Faso	0	
Burundi	+ 2	
Cambodia	+ 7	
Cameroon	+ 1	
*Canada		
*Alberta	− 7	
*†British Columbia	− 8	
*Manitoba	− 6	
*New Brunswick	− 4	
*†Newfoundland and Labrador	− 3	30
*†Northwest Territories	− 7	
*Nova Scotia	− 4	
*Nunavut		
central	− 6	
eastern	− 5	
mountain	− 7	
*Ontario		
east of 90° W.	− 5	
west of 90° W.	− 6	
*Prince Edward Island	− 4	

	h	m		h	m
*Québec			*Estonia	+ 2	
east of 63° W.	− 4		Ethiopia	+ 3	
*west of 63° W.	− 5		Fiji	+ 12	
*†Saskatchewan	− 6		*Finland	+ 2	
*Yukon	− 8		*France	+ 1	
Cape Verde	− 1		French Guiana	− 3	
Central African Republic	+ 1		†French Polynesia	− 10	
Chad	+ 1		Guadeloupe	− 4	
*Chile	− 4		Martinique	− 4	
Easter Island	− 6		Mayotte	+ 2	
China (inc. Hong Kong and			New Caledonia	+ 11	
Macao)	+ 8		Réunion	+ 4	
Colombia	− 5		St Barthélemy	− 4	
The Comoros	+ 3		*St Pierre and Miquelon	− 3	
Congo, Dem. Rep. of			Wallis and Futuna	+ 12	
eastern	+ 2		Gabon	+ 1	
western	+ 1		The Gambia	0	
Congo, Republic of	+ 1		Georgia	+ 4	
Costa Rica	− 6		*Germany	+ 1	
Côte d'Ivoire	0		Ghana	0	
*Croatia	+ 1		*Greece	+ 2	
*Cuba	− 5		Grenada	− 4	
*Cyprus	+ 2		Guatemala	− 6	
*Czech Republic	+ 1		Guinea	0	
*Denmark	+ 1		Guinea-Bissau	0	
*Faeroe Islands	0		Guyana	− 4	
*Greenland	− 3		Haiti	− 5	
Danmarks Havn,			Honduras	− 6	
Mesters Vig	0		*Hungary	+ 1	
*Scoresby Sund	− 1		Iceland	0	
*Thule area	− 4		India	+ 5	30
Djibouti	+ 3		Indonesia		
Dominica	− 4		Java, Kalimantan (west and		
Dominican Republic	− 4		central), Madura, Sumatra	+ 7	
East Timor	+ 9		Bali, Flores, Kalimantan		
Ecuador	− 5		(south and east), Lombok,		
Galápagos Islands	− 6		Sulawesi, Sumbawa,		
*Egypt	+ 2		West Timor	+ 8	
El Salvador	− 6		Irian Jaya, Maluku	+ 9	
Equatorial Guinea	+ 1		*Iran	+ 3	30
Eritrea	+ 3		Iraq	+ 3	

	h	m
*Ireland, Republic of	0	
*Israel	+ 2	
*Italy	+ 1	
Jamaica	− 5	
Japan	+ 9	
*Jordan	+ 2	
Kazakhstan		
western	+ 5	
eastern	+ 6	
Kenya	+ 3	
Kiribati	+ 12	
Line Islands	+ 14	
Phoenix Islands	+ 13	
Korea, Dem. People's Rep. of	+ 9	
Korea, Republic of	+ 9	
Kuwait	+ 3	
Kyrgyzstan	+ 6	
Laos	+ 7	
*Latvia	+ 2	
*Lebanon	+ 2	
Lesotho	+ 2	
Liberia	0	
Libya	+ 2	
*Liechtenstein	+ 1	
*Lithuania	+ 2	
*Luxembourg	+ 1	
*Macedonia	+ 1	
Madagascar	+ 3	
Malawi	+ 2	
Malaysia	+ 8	
Maldives	+ 5	
Mali	0	
*Malta	+ 1	
Marshall Islands	+ 12	
Mauritania	0	
*Mauritius	+ 4	
*Mexico	− 6	
*Nayarit, Sinaloa, S. Baja California	− 7	
*N. Baja California	− 8	
Sonora	− 7	

	h	m
Micronesia, Fed. States of		
Chuuk, Yap	+ 10	
Kosrae, Pingelap, Pohnpei	+ 11	
*Moldova	+ 2	
*Monaco	+ 1	
†Mongolia	+ 8	
*Montenegro	+ 1	
Morocco	0	
Mozambique	+ 2	
Myanmar	+ 6	30
*Namibia	+ 1	
Nauru	+ 12	
Nepal	+ 5	45
*The Netherlands	+ 1	
Aruba	− 4	
Netherlands Antilles	− 4	
*New Zealand	+ 12	
Chatham Islands	+ 12	45
Cook Islands	− 10	
Niue	− 11	
Tokelau Island	− 10	
Nicaragua	− 6	
Niger	+ 1	
Nigeria	+ 1	
*Norway	+ 1	
*Svalbard, Jan Mayen	+ 1	
Oman	+ 4	
*Pakistan	+ 5	
Palau	+ 9	
Panama	− 5	
Papua New Guinea	+ 10	
*Paraguay	− 4	
Peru	− 5	
The Philippines	+ 8	
*Poland	+ 1	
*Portugal	0	
*Azores	− 1	
*Madeira	0	
Qatar	+ 3	
*Romania	+ 2	

	h	m
*Russia		
Kaliningrad	+ 2	
Moscow	+ 3	
Yekaterinburg	+ 5	
Omsk	+ 6	
Krasnoyarsk	+ 7	
Irkutsk	+ 8	
Yakutsk	+ 9	
Vladivostok	+ 10	
Magadan	+ 11	
Rwanda	+ 2	
St Christopher and Nevis	− 4	
St Lucia	− 4	
St Vincent and the Grenadines	− 4	
*Samoa	− 11	
*San Marino	+ 1	
São Tomé and Príncipe	0	
Saudi Arabia	+ 3	
Senegal	0	
*Serbia	+ 1	
Seychelles	+ 4	
Sierra Leone	0	
Singapore	+ 8	
*Slovakia	+ 1	
*Slovenia	+ 1	
Solomon Islands	+ 11	
Somalia	+ 3	
South Africa	+ 2	
*Spain	+ 1	
*Canary Islands	0	
Sri Lanka	+ 5	30
Sudan	+ 3	
Suriname	− 3	
Swaziland	+ 2	
*Sweden	+ 1	
*Switzerland	+ 1	
*Syria	+ 2	
Taiwan	+ 8	
Tajikistan	+ 5	
Tanzania	+ 3	
Thailand	+ 7	

	h	m
Togo	0	
Tonga	+ 13	
Trinidad and Tobago	− 4	
*Tunisia	+ 1	
*Turkey	+ 2	
Turkmenistan	+ 5	
Tuvalu	+ 12	
Uganda	+ 3	
*Ukraine	+ 2	
United Arab Emirates	+ 4	
*United Kingdom	0	
Anguilla	− 4	
*Bermuda	− 4	
††British Antarctic Territory	− 3	
British Indian Ocean Territory	+ 6	
British Virgin Islands	− 4	
Cayman Islands	− 5	
*Channel Islands	0	
*Falkland Islands	− 4	
*Gibraltar	+ 1	
Montserrat	− 4	
Pitcairn Islands	− 8	
St Helena and Dependencies	0	
South Georgia and South Sandwich Islands	− 2	
*Turks and Caicos Islands	− 5	
*United States of America		
*Alaska	− 9	
Aleutian Islands, east of 169° 30′ W.	− 9	
Aleutian Islands, west of 169° 30′ W.	− 10	
*central time	− 6	
*eastern time	− 5	
Guam	+ 10	
Hawaii	− 10	
*mountain time	− 7	
Northern Mariana Islands	+ 10	

	h	m		h	m
*Pacific time	− 8		Vanuatu	+ 11	
Puerto Rico	− 4		*Vatican City State	+ 1	
Samoa, American	− 11		Venezuela	− 4	30
Virgin Islands	− 4		Vietnam	+ 7	
*Uruguay	− 3		Yemen	+ 3	
Uzbekistan	+ 5		Zambia	+ 2	
			Zimbabwe	+ 2	

TIME MEASUREMENT

Measurements of time are based on the time taken:

> by the Earth to rotate on its axis (day)
> by the Moon to revolve around the Earth (month)
> by the Earth to revolve around the Sun from equinox to equinox (year)

The orbits on which these timescales are based are not uniform, so average or mean periods have been adopted for everyday use.

PERIOD	ACTUAL LENGTH	MEAN LENGTH
Day	23 hours, 56 minutes, 4 seconds	24 hours, each of 60 minutes
Month (from New Moon to New Moon)	29 days, 12 hours, 44 minutes	varies from 28 to 31 days
Year (tropical)	365 days, 5 hours, 48 minutes, 45 seconds	365 days (366 in leap years), each of 24 hours

LEAP YEARS

The tropical year (the period of the Earth's orbit around the Sun) is 365 days 6 hours minus about 11 minutes 15 seconds. Because of the difference between the length of the tropical year and the mean year used for calendar purposes, the natural timescale and the calendar get out of step by 11 minutes 15 seconds each year. The growing difference between the two is corrected by having a leap year every four years.

However, a leap year brings the calendar back by 45 minutes too much. To correct this, the last year of a century is in most cases not a leap year, but the omission corrects the calendar by six hours too much; compensation for this is made by every fourth end-century year being a leap year.

A year is a leap year if the date of the year is divisible by four without remainder, unless it is the last year of the century. The last year of the century is a leap year if the date of the year is divisible by 400 without remainder, eg the years 1800 and 1900 were not leap years but the year 2000 was a leap year.

THE SEASONS

Because the Earth's axis is tilted at 66.5° to the plane in which it orbits the Sun, each hemisphere alternately leans towards or away from the Sun, causing the seasons. The seasons are defined as:

SEASON	ASTRONOMICAL DEFINITION	POPULAR DEFINITION
Spring	vernal equinox to summer solstice	March, April, May
Summer	summer solstice to autumnal equinox	June, July, August
Autumn	autumnal equinox to winter solstice	September, October, November
Winter	winter solstice to vernal equinox	December, January, February

THE SOLSTICE

A solstice is the point in the tropical year at which the Sun is at its greatest distance north or south of the Equator. In the northern hemisphere, the furthest point north is the summer solstice (longest day) and the furthest point south is the winter solstice (shortest day).

THE EQUINOX

The equinox is the point at which the Sun crosses the Equator and day and night are of equal length all over the world. This occurs around 20 or 21 March (vernal equinox) and 22 or 23 September (autumnal equinox).

CALENDARS

The year-numbering system and the calendar now used more or less worldwide are those of western Europe, ie Christian chronology and the Gregorian calendar.

CHRISTIAN CHRONOLOGY

The Christian era is numbered from the birth of Christ. Years after the birth of Christ are denoted by AD (*Anno Domini* – In the Year of Our Lord). Years before the birth of Christ are denoted by the letters BC (Before Christ) or, more rarely, AC (*Ante Christum*). The actual date of the birth of Christ is uncertain.

The system was introduced into Italy in the sixth century. Though first used in France in the seventh century, it did not become universally used there until the eighth century. The system was reputedly introduced into England by St Augustine in the sixth century, but it was not generally used until the Council of Chelsea (AD 816) ordered its use.

THE GREGORIAN CALENDAR

The Gregorian calendar is based on the Julian calendar adopted in the Roman Republic in 45 BC at the instigation of Julius Caesar (*see* Roman Calendar). The Julian calendar had a year of 365 days, with a leap year of 366 days every four years, including the last year of each century.

Because the end-century years in the Julian calendar were leap years, by the end of the 16th century there was a difference of ten days between the tropical year and the calendar year; the vernal equinox fell on 11 March. In 1582 Pope Gregory ordained that 5 October should be called 15 October and that of the end-century years only the fourth should be a leap year.

NAMES OF THE DAYS

The names of the days are derived from Old English translations or adaptations of the Roman names of the Sun, Moon and five planets:

DAY	OLD ENGLISH DERIVATION	ROMAN NAME
Sunday	Sun	Sol
Monday	Moon	Luna
Tuesday	Tiw/Tyr (god of war)	Mars
Wednesday	Woden/Odin	Mercury
Thursday	Thor	Jupiter
Friday	Frigga/Freyja (goddess of love)	Venus
Saturday	Saeternes	Saturn

NAMES OF THE MONTHS

The names of the months are derived from the pre-Julian Roman calendar, which originally had a year of ten months, beginning with March. Two months, January and February, were subsequently added to make a year of 12 months.

MONTH	DERIVATION
January	*Janus*, god of the portal, facing two ways, past and future
February	*Februa*, the Roman festival of purification
March	*Mars*, god of battle
April	*Aperire*, to open; the Earth opens to receive seed
May	*Maia*, goddess of growth and increase
June	*Junius*, goddess of marriage
July	the emperor *Julius* Caesar (originally Quintilis, the fifth month)
August	the emperor *Augustus* (originally Sextilis, the sixth month)
September	*Septem*, the seventh month (of the original Roman calendar)
October	*Octo*, the eighth month
November	*Novem*, the ninth month
December	*Decem*, the tenth month

RELIGIOUS CALENDARS

CHRISTIAN

The Roman Catholic and Protestant Churches use the Gregorian calendar. The Church year begins with the first Sunday in the season of Advent and its principal seasons are:

Advent	preparation for Christmas
Christmas	celebration of the birth of Jesus Christ
Epiphany	celebration of the manifestation of Jesus Christ
Lent	preparation for Easter
Easter	celebration of the death and resurrection of Jesus Christ

The principal feasts and holy days in the Church of England are:

Christmas Day	25 December
The Epiphany	6 January
Presentation of Christ in the Temple	2 February
Ash Wednesday	first day of Lent, 40 days before Easter Day
Annunciation to the Blessed Virgin Mary	25 March
Maundy Thursday	Thursday before Easter Day
Good Friday	Friday before Easter Day
Easter Day*	date varies according to the Moon
Ascension Day	40 days after Easter Day
Pentecost (Whit Sunday)	nine days after Ascension Day
Trinity Sunday	Sunday after Pentecost
All Saints' Day	1 November

*Easter Day can fall at the earliest on 22 March and at the latest on 25 April

THE EASTERN ORTHODOX CHURCHES

Some of the Eastern Orthodox Churches use the Julian calendar and some a modified version of the Julian calendar. The Orthodox Church year begins on 1 September. There are four fast periods and, in addition to Pascha (Easter) 12 great feasts, as well as commemorations of the saints of the Old and New Testaments throughout the year.

HINDU

The Hindu calendar is a luni-solar calendar of 12 months, each containing 29 days 12 hours. Each month is divided into a light fortnight (Shukla or Shuddha) and a dark fortnight (Krishna or Vadya) based on the waxing and waning of the Moon. A leap month occurs about every 32 lunar months, whenever the difference between the Hindu year of 360 lunar days (354 days 8 hours solar time) and the 365 days 6 hours of the solar year reaches the length of one Hindu lunar month (29 days 12 hours).

The names of the days of the week are derived from the Sanskrit names of the Sun, the Moon and the planets Mars, Mercury, Jupiter, Venus and Saturn. The months have Sanskrit names derived from 12 asterisms (constellations).

The days are: Raviwar, Somawar, Mangalwar, Budhawar, Guruwar, Shukrawar and Shaniwar. The months are: Chaitra, Vaishakh, Jyeshtha, Ashadh, Shravan, Bhadrapad, Ashvin, Kartik, Margashirsh, Paush, Magh and Phalgun.

The major festivals are:

Chaitra	Spring New Year
Dasara*	victory of Rama over the demon army
Diwali*	New Year (festival of lights)
Durga Puja*	dedicated to the goddess Durga
Ganesh Chaturthi*	worship of Ganesh
Holi*	spring festival
Janmashtami*	birth festival of the god Krishna
Makara Sankranti	winter solstice festival
Navaratri*	nine-night festival dedicated to the goddess Parvati
Raksha Bandhan*	renewal of kinship bond between brothers and sisters
Ramanavami*	birth festival of the god Rama
Sarasvati Puja*	dedicated to the goddess Sarasvati

* The main festivals celebrated by Hindus in the UK

JEWISH

The epoch, or starting point, of Jewish chronology corresponds to 7 October 3761 BC. The calendar is luni-solar; the hour is divided into 1,080 minims and the period between one New Moon and the next is reckoned as 29 days 12 hours 793 minims.

The Jewish day begins between sunset and nightfall. The time used is that of the meridian of Jerusalem, which is 2 hours 21 minutes in advance of GMT. Rules for the beginning of sabbaths and festivals were laid down for the latitude of London in the 18th century; hours for nightfall are now fixed annually by the Chief Rabbi. The length of a Jewish year varies between 353 and 385 days. The months are: Tishri (30 days), Marcheshvan (29/30), Kislev (30/29), Tebet (29), Shebat (30), Adar (29), Nisan (30), Iyar (29), Sivan (30), Tammuz (29), Ab (30) and Elul (29). In a leap year, there is an additional month called Adar Sheni and the month of Adar becomes Adar Rishon.

The main festivals are:

Rosh Hashanah	New Year
Yom Kippur	Day of Atonement
Succoth	Feast of Tabernacles
Chanucah	Dedication of the Temple
Purim	Festival of Lots
Pesach	Passover
Shavuot	Feast of Weeks

MUSLIM

The Muslim era is dated from the Hijrah, or flight of the Prophet Muhammad from Mecca to Medina; the date corresponds to 16 July AD 622. The calendar is based on a lunar year of about 354 days, consisting of 12 months containing alternate months of 30 and 29 days. A leap day is added at the end of the 12th month at stated intervals in each cycle of 30 years. The purpose of the leap day is to reconcile the date of the first day of the month with the date of the actual New Moon. In each cycle of 30 years, 19 years are common (354 days) and 11 years are leap (kabisah) years (355 days).

Some Muslims still take the date of the evening of the first physical sighting of the crescent of the New Moon as that of the first of the month. If cloud obscures the Moon the present month may be extended to 30 days, after which the new month will begin automatically regardless of whether the Moon has been seen.

The months are: Muharram (30 days), Safar (29), Rabi' I (30), Rabi' II (29), Jumada I (30), Jumada II (29), Rajab (30), Sha'ban (29), Ramadan (30), Shawwal (29), Dhu'l-Qa'da (30) and Dhu'l-Hijjah (29).

The main festivals are:

Eid-ul-Fitr	marks the end of Ramadan
Eid-ul-Adha	celebrates the submission of the Prophet Ibrahim (Abraham) to God
Ashura	the day Prophet Noah left the Ark and Prophet Moses was saved from Pharaoh (Sunni)
	death of the Prophet's grandson Husain (Shi'ite)
Mawlid al-Nabi	birthday of the Prophet Muhammad
Laylat al-Isra' wa'l-Mi'raj	Night of Journey and Ascension
Laylat al-Qadr	Night of Power

SIKH

The Sikh calendar is a lunar calendar of 365 days divided into 12 months. The length of the months varies between 29 and 32 days.

The main celebrations are:

Baisakhi Mela	New Year
Diwali Mela	festival of light
Hola Mohalla Mela	spring festival (in the Punjab)
the Gurpurbs	anniversaries associated with the ten Gurus

OTHER CALENDARS

CHINESE

Although the Gregorian calendar is used in China for business and official purposes, the ancient luni-solar calendar still plays an important part in everyday life. The luni-solar calendar has a cycle of 60 years. The new year begins at the first New Moon after the Sun enters the sign of Aquarius, ie between 21 January and 19 February in the Gregorian calendar.

Each year in the Chinese calendar is associated with one of 12 animals: the rat, the ox, the tiger, the rabbit, the dragon, the snake, the horse, the goat or sheep, the monkey, the chicken or rooster, the dog and the pig.

ANIMAL					YEAR				
Rat	1912	1924	1936	1948	1960	1972	1984	1996	2008
Ox	1913	1925	1937	1949	1961	1973	1985	1997	2009
Tiger	1914	1926	1938	1950	1962	1974	1986	1998	2010
Rabbit	1915	1927	1939	1951	1963	1975	1987	1999	2011
Dragon	1916	1928	1940	1952	1964	1976	1988	2000	2012
Snake	1917	1929	1941	1953	1965	1977	1989	2001	2013
Horse	1918	1930	1942	1954	1966	1978	1990	2002	2014
Goat	1919	1931	1943	1955	1967	1979	1991	2003	2015
Monkey	1920	1932	1944	1956	1968	1980	1992	2004	2016
Rooster	1921	1933	1945	1957	1969	1981	1993	2005	2017
Dog	1922	1934	1946	1958	1970	1982	1994	2006	2018
Pig	1923	1935	1947	1959	1971	1983	1995	2007	2019

CHINESE DYNASTIES AND PERIODS

During the imperial period, the numeration of years was based on a complicated system of reign-titles and other important events. The main periods and dynasties in Chinese history are:

DATE	PERIOD/DYNASTY
	Pre-Imperial China
c.21st–16th century BC	Xia
c.16th–11th century BC	Shang
c.11th century–770 BC	Western Zhou
770–221 BC	Eastern Zhou (Spring and Autumn and Warring States periods)
	Early Empire
221–207 BC	Qin
206 BC–AD 24	Western Han
25–220	Eastern Han
220–65	Three Kingdoms (Wei, Shu and Wu)
265–316	Western Jin
	Middle Empire
317–420	Eastern Jin
420–589	Southern and Northern Dynasties
581–618	Sui
618–907	Tang
907–60	Five Dynasties
960–1127	Northern Song
1127–1279	Southern Song
	Late Empire
1279–1368	Yuan
1368–1644	Ming
1644–1911	Qing
	Post-Imperial China
1912–49	Republic
1949–present	People's Republic

JAPANESE

The Japanese calendar is essentially the same as the Gregorian calendar, the years, months and days being of the same length and beginning on the same days.

The numeration of years is different, based on a system of reign-titles, each of which begins at the accession of a new emperor or other important event. The three latest epochs are defined by the reigns of emperors, whose actual names are not necessarily used:

REIGN-TITLE	DURATION
Taisho	1 August 1912 to 25 December 1926
Showa	26 December 1926 to 7 January 1989
Heisei	8 January 1989 to present

Each year of the epoch begins on 1 January and ends on 31 December.

The months are known as First Month, Second Month, etc, First Month being equivalent to January. The days of the week are:

Nichiyobi	Sun-day
Getsuyobi	Moon-day
Kayobi	Fire-day
Suiyobi	Water-day
Mokuyobi	Wood-day
Kinyobi	Metal-day
Doyobi	Earth-day

ROMAN

In 46 BC Julius Caesar found that the calendar had fallen into some confusion. He sought the help of the Egyptian astronomer Sosigenes, which led to the construction and adoption in 45 BC of the Julian calendar.

In the Roman (Julian) calendar, the days of the month were counted backwards from three fixed points, or days: the Kalends, the Nones and the Ides. The Kalends was the first day of each month; the Nones fell on the fifth or seventh day; and the Ides on the 13th or 15th day, depending on the month. For example, the Ides of March was on the 15th day of the month and the days preceding the 15th were known as the seventh day before the Ides, the sixth day before the Ides, the fifth day before the Ides, etc.

The Julian calendar included an extra day in every fourth year. A year containing 366 days was called bissextillis annus because it had a doubled sixth day (bissextus dies) before the Kalends of March, ie on 24 February.

FRENCH REVOLUTIONARY

The French Revolutionary or Republican calendar was introduced in 1793. It took as its starting point 22 September 1792, the foundation of the first Republic. It was abolished in 1806 on Napoleon's orders.

The year was divided into 12 months, each of 30 days, with five or six extra days at the end. The beginning of the year was the autumnal equinox and the names of the months were intended to reflect the changes of the seasons and the activities of the agricultural year.

Vendémiaire (month of grape harvest)	23 September–22 October
Brumaire (month of mist)	23 October–21 November
Frimaire (month of frost)	22 November–21 December
Nivôse (month of snow)	22 December–20 January
Pluviôse (month of rain)	21 January–19 February
Ventôse (month of wind)	20 February–21 March
Germinal (month of buds)	22 March–20 April
Floréal (month of flowers)	21 April–20 May
Prairial (month of meadows)	21 May–19 June
Messidor (month of harvest)	20 June–19 July
Thermidor (month of heat)	20 July–18 August
Fructidor (month of fruit)	19 August–22 September

WATCHES AT SEA

First watch	8pm – midnight	Afternoon watch	midday – 4pm
Middle watch	midnight – 4am	First dog watch	4pm – 6pm
Morning watch	4am – 8am	Last dog watch	6pm – 8pm
Forenoon watch	8am – midday		

WEDDING ANNIVERSARIES

1st	Paper	10th	Tin
2nd	Cotton	11th	Steel
3rd	Leather	12th	Silk and Fine Linen
4th	Linen	13th	Lace
5th	Wood	14th	Ivory
6th	Iron	15th	Crystal
7th	Wool or Copper	20th	China
8th	Bronze	25th	Silver
9th	Pottery	30th	Pearl

35th	Coral	55th	Emerald
40th	Ruby	60th	Diamond
45th	Sapphire	65th	Blue Sapphire
50th	Gold	70th	Platinum

SIGNS OF THE ZODIAC

In astronomy, the zodiac is an imaginary belt in the heavens containing the apparent paths of the Sun, Moon and major planets. It is bounded by two parallels generally taken as lying 8° on either side of the ecliptic or path of the Sun in its annual course. The zodiac is divided into 12 equal areas, each of 30°.

In astrology, each of the 12 signs of the zodiac takes its name from a constellation with which it once coincided; due to precession, the signs no longer coincide with the constellations whose names they bear, but astrology uses the original signs. The dates can vary slightly from year to year according to the day and hour of the Sun's transition from one sign to another; the dates given below are approximate. The signs are considered to begin at the vernal equinox with Aries.

SIGN	SYMBOL	DATES
Aries	Ram	21 March–19 April
Taurus	Bull	20 April–20 May
Gemini	Twins	21 May–21 June
Cancer	Crab	22 June–22 July
Leo	Lion	23 July–22 August
Virgo	Virgin	23 August–22 September
Libra	Balance	23 September–23 October
Scorpio	Scorpion	24 October–21 November
Sagittarius	Archer	22 November–21 December
Capricorn	Goat	22 December–19 January
Aquarius	Water Carrier	20 January–18 February
Pisces	Fish	19 February–20 March

A 13th sign is used by some astrologers: Ophiuchus, the Serpent Bearer, between Scorpio and Sagittarius.

WEIGHTS AND MEASURES

METRIC UNITS

The metric primary standards are the metre as the unit of measurement of length, and the kilogram as the unit of measurement of mass. Other units of measurement are defined by reference to the primary standards.

MEASUREMENT OF LENGTH

Kilometre (km)	= 1,000 metres

Metre (m) is the length of the path travelled by light in a vacuum during a time interval of $\frac{1}{299792458}$ of a second

Decimetre (dm)	= $\frac{1}{10}$ metre
Centimetre (cm)	= $\frac{1}{100}$ metre
Millimetre (mm)	= $\frac{1}{1000}$ metre

MEASUREMENT OF AREA

Hectare (ha)	= 100 ares
Decare	= 10 ares
Are (a)	= 100 square metres
Square metre	= a superficial area equal to that of a square each side of which measures one metre
Square decimetre	= $\frac{1}{100}$ square metre
Square centimetre	= $\frac{1}{100}$ square decimetre
Square millimetre	= $\frac{1}{100}$ square centimetre

MEASUREMENT OF VOLUME

Cubic metre (m^3)	= a volume equal to that of a cube each edge of which measures one metre
Cubic decimetre	= $\frac{1}{1000}$ cubic metre
Cubic centimetre (cc)	= $\frac{1}{1000}$ cubic decimetre
Hectolitre	= 100 litres
Litre	= a cubic decimetre
Decilitre	= $\frac{1}{10}$ litre
Centilitre	= $\frac{1}{100}$ litre
Millilitre	= $\frac{1}{1000}$ litre

MEASUREMENT OF CAPACITY

Hectolitre (hl)	= 100 litres
Litre (l or L)	= a cubic decimetre
Decilitre (dl)	= $\frac{1}{10}$ litre
Centilitre (cl)	= $\frac{1}{100}$ litre
Millilitre (ml)	= $\frac{1}{1000}$ litre

MEASUREMENT OF MASS OR WEIGHT

Tonne (t)	= 1,000 kilograms

Kilogram (kg) is equal to the mass of the international prototype of the kilogram

Hectogram (hg)	= $\frac{1}{10}$ kilogram
Gram (g)	= $\frac{1}{1000}$ kilogram
Carat, metric*	= $\frac{1}{5}$ gram
Milligram (mg)	= $\frac{1}{1000}$ gram

* Used only for transactions in precious stones or pearls

IMPERIAL UNITS

The imperial primary standards are the yard as the unit of measurement of length and the pound as the unit of measurement of mass. Other units of measurement are defined by reference to the primary standards. Most of these units are no longer authorised for use in trade in the UK.

MEASUREMENT OF LENGTH

Mile	= 1,760 yards
Furlong	= 220 yards
Chain	= 22 yards
Yard (yd)	= 0.9144 metre
Foot (ft)	= ⅓ yard
Inch (in)	= 1/36 yard

MEASUREMENT OF AREA

Square mile	= 640 acres
Acre	= 4,840 square yards
Rood	= 1,210 square yards
Square yard (sq. yd)	= a superficial area equal to that of a square each side of which measures one yard
Square foot (sq. ft)	= ⅑ square yard
Square inch (sq. in)	= 1/144 square foot

MEASUREMENT OF VOLUME

Cubic yard	= a volume equal to that of a cube each edge of which measures one yard
Cubic foot	= 1/27 cubic yard
Cubic inch	= 1/1278 cubic foot

MEASUREMENT OF CAPACITY

Bushel	= 8 gallons
Peck	= 2 gallons
Gallon (gal)	= 4.54609 cubic decimetres
Quart (qt)	= ¼ gallon
Pint (pt)*	= ½ quart
Gill	= ¼ pint
Fluid ounce (fl oz)*	= 1/20 pint
Fluid drachm	= ⅛ fluid ounce
Minim (min)	= 1/60 fluid drachm

MEASUREMENT OF MASS OR WEIGHT

Ton	= 2,240 pounds
Hundredweight (cwt)	= 112 pounds
Cental	= 100 pounds
Quarter	= 28 pounds
Stone	= 14 pounds
Pound (lb)	= 0.45359237 kilogram
Ounce (oz)	= 1/16 pound
Ounce troy (oz tr)*†	= 12/175 pound
Dram (dr)	= 1/16 ounce
Grain (gr)	= 1/7000 pound
Pennyweight (dwt)	= 24 grains
Ounce apothecaries	= 480 grains

† Used only for transactions in gold, silver or other precious metals, and articles made therefrom

MILLIONS AND BILLIONS

The long- and short-scale systems result in different numerical values for sums greater than a million. Many European countries use the long-scale system while the short-scale system is used by the USA and most English-speaking countries. The UK government officially adopted the short-scale system in 1974, but the use of the terms billion and trillion in the UK can still be ambiguous.

LONG SCALE

Million	thousand x thousand	10^6
Billion	million x million	10^{12}
Trillion	million x billion	10^{18}
Quadrillion	million x trillion	10^{24}

SHORT SCALE

Million	thousand x thousand	10^6
Billion	thousand x million	10^9
Trillion	million x million	10^{12}
Quadrillion	million x billion US	10^{15}

PAPER SIZES

A SERIES (magazines, books)

	MM
A0	841 x 1,189
A1	594 x 841
A2	420 x 594
A3	297 x 420
A4	210 x 297
A5	148 x 210
A6	105 x 148
A7	74 x 105
A8	52 x 74
A9	37 x 52
A10	26 x 37

BOOK SIZES

TRADITIONAL

	MM
Royal Quarto	250 × 320
Demy Quarto	220 × 290
Crown Quarto	190 × 250
Royal Octavo	150 × 250
Demy Octavo	143 × 222
Large Crown Octavo	129 × 198

MODERN

	MM
Crown Royal	210 × 280
Royal	191 × 235
Demy	152 × 229
C format paperback	143 × 222
B format or trade paperback	129 × 198
A format	111 × 175

NAUTICAL MEASURES

DISTANCE

Distance at sea is measured in nautical miles. The British standard nautical mile was 6,080 feet, but this measure has been obsolete since 1970, when the international nautical mile of 1852 metres was adopted by the Ministry of Defence.

The cable (600 feet or 100 fathoms) was a measure approximately one-tenth of a nautical mile. Such distances are now expressed in decimal parts of a sea mile or in metres.

Soundings at sea were recorded in fathoms (6 feet); depths are now expressed in metres on Admiralty charts.

SPEED

Speed is measured in nautical miles per hour, called knots. A ship moving at the rate of 30 nautical miles per hour is said to be doing 30 knots.

KNOTS	M.P.H.
1	1.1515
2	2.3030
3	3.4545
4	4.6060
5	5.7575
6	6.9090
7	8.0606
8	9.2121
9	10.3636
10	11.5151
15	17.2727
20	23.0303
25	28.7878
30	34.5454
35	40.3030
40	46.0606

DISTANCE OF THE HORIZON

The distance to the horizon can be calculated, in metric units, using the equation $D = 3.83733\sqrt{H}$ where D is the distance in kilometres and H is the height of the observer in metres, and in imperial units using the equation $D = 1.31573\sqrt{H}$ where D is the distance in miles and H is the height of the observer in feet. The resulting distances are those following a straight line from the observer to the horizon; it is not the distance along the curvature of the Earth. The difference between these two figures, however, is minimal for heights below 100km (62 miles).

HEIGHT IN METRES (FEET)	RANGE IN KM (MILES)
*1.7 (5.6)	5.0 (3.1)
5 (16)	8.6 (5.3)
10 (32.8)	12.1 (7.5)
50 (164)	27.1 (16.8)
100 (328)	38.4 (23.8)
†509 (1,670)	86.6 (53.8)
1,000 (3,281)	121.34 (75.4)
5,000 (16,404)	271.3 (168.5)
‡8,850 (29,035)	361.0 (224.2)
§9,144 (30,000)	366.9 (228.0)

* Average human height in the UK
† Height of the tallest inhabited building (Taipei 101)
‡ Height of Mt Everest
§ Height of cruising aeroplane

WATER AND LIQUOR MEASURES

1 litre weighs 1 kg
1 cubic metre weighs 1 tonne
1 gallon weighs 10 lb

WATER FOR SHIPS

Kilderkin	= 18 gallons
Barrel	= 36 gallons
Puncheon	= 72 gallons
Butt	= 110 gallons
Tun	= 210 gallons

BOTTLES OF WINE
Traditional equivalents in standard champagne bottles:

Magnum	= 2 bottles
Jeroboam	= 4 bottles
Rehoboam	= 6 bottles
Methuselah	= 8 bottles
Salmanazar	= 12 bottles
Balthazar	= 16 bottles
Nebuchadnezzar	= 20 bottles

A quarter of a bottle is known as a nip
An eighth of a bottle is known as a baby

TEMPERATURE SCALES

The Fahrenheit scale is related to the Celsius scale by the equations:

temperature °F = (temperature °C x 1.8) + 32

temperature °C = (temperature °F – 32) ÷ 1.8

°C	°F
100	212
95	203
90	194
85	185
80	176
75	167
70	158
65	149
60	140
55	131
50	122
45	113
40	104
35	95
30	86
25	77
20	68
15	59
10	50
5	41
zero	32
–5	23
–10	14
–15	5

The freezing point of water is 0°C and 32°F

The boiling point of water is 99.974°C and 211.953°F

Body temperature varies between 36.5°C and 37.2°C (97.70–98.9°F)

CONVERSION TABLES

Bold figures equal units of either of the columns beside them; thus: 1 cm = 0.394 inches and 1 inch = 2.540 cm

LENGTH

CENTIMETRES		INCHES
2.540	**1**	0.394
5.080	**2**	0.787
7.620	**3**	1.181
10.160	**4**	1.575
12.700	**5**	1.969
15.240	**6**	2.362
17.780	**7**	2.756
20.320	**8**	3.150
22.860	**9**	3.543
25.400	**10**	3.937
50.800	**20**	7.874
76.200	**30**	11.811
101.600	**40**	15.748
127.000	**50**	19.685
152.400	**60**	23.622
177.800	**70**	27.559
203.200	**80**	31.496
228.600	**90**	35.433
254.000	**100**	39.370

METRES		YARDS
0.914	**1**	1.094
1.829	**2**	2.187
2.743	**3**	3.281
3.658	**4**	4.374
4.572	**5**	5.468
5.486	**6**	6.562
6.401	**7**	7.655
7.315	**8**	8.749
8.230	**9**	9.843
9.144	**10**	10.936
18.288	**20**	21.872
27.432	**30**	32.808
36.576	**40**	43.745
45.720	**50**	54.681

METRES		YARDS
54.864	**60**	65.617
64.008	**70**	76.553
73.152	**80**	87.489
82.296	**90**	98.425
91.440	**100**	109.361

KILOMETRES		MILES
1.609	**1**	0.621
3.219	**2**	1.243
4.828	**3**	1.864
6.437	**4**	2.485
8.047	**5**	3.107
9.656	**6**	3.728
11.265	**7**	4.350
12.875	**8**	4.971
14.484	**9**	5.592
16.093	**10**	6.214
32.187	**20**	12.427
48.280	**30**	18.641
64.374	**40**	24.855
80.467	**50**	31.069
96.561	**60**	37.282
112.654	**70**	43.496
128.748	**80**	49.710
144.841	**90**	55.923
160.934	**100**	62.137

AREA

SQUARE CM		SQUARE IN
6.452	**1**	0.155
12.903	**2**	0.310
19.355	**3**	0.465
25.806	**4**	0.620
32.258	**5**	0.775
38.710	**6**	0.930
45.161	**7**	1.085
51.613	**8**	1.240
58.064	**9**	1.395
64.516	**10**	1.550
129.032	**20**	3.100
193.548	**30**	4.650

SQUARE CM		SQUARE IN
258.064	**40**	6.200
322.580	**50**	7.750
387.096	**60**	9.300
451.612	**70**	10.850
516.128	**80**	12.400
580.644	**90**	13.950
645.160	**100**	15.500

SQUARE M		SQUARE YD
0.836	**1**	1.196
1.672	**2**	2.392
2.508	**3**	3.588
3.345	**4**	4.784
4.181	**5**	5.980
5.017	**6**	7.176
5.853	**7**	8.372
6.689	**8**	9.568
7.525	**9**	10.764
8.361	**10**	11.960
16.723	**20**	23.920
25.084	**30**	35.880
33.445	**40**	47.840
41.806	**50**	59.799
50.168	**60**	71.759
58.529	**70**	83.719
66.890	**80**	95.679
75.251	**90**	107.639
83.613	**100**	119.599

HECTARES		ACRES
0.405	**1**	2.471
0.809	**2**	4.942
1.214	**3**	7.413
1.619	**4**	9.844
2.023	**5**	12.355
2.428	**6**	14.826
2.833	**7**	17.297
3.327	**8**	19.769
3.642	**9**	22.240
4.047	**10**	24.711
8.094	**20**	49.421

HECTARES		ACRES
12.140	30	74.132
16.187	40	98.842
20.234	50	123.555
24.281	60	148.263
28.328	70	172.974
32.375	80	197.684
36.422	90	222.395
40.469	100	247.105

VOLUME

CUBIC CM		CUBIC IN
16.387	1	0.061
32.774	2	0.122
49.161	3	0.183
65.548	4	0.244
81.936	5	0.305
98.323	6	0.366
114.710	7	0.427
131.097	8	0.488
147.484	9	0.549
163.871	10	0.610
327.742	20	1.220
491.613	30	1.831
655.484	40	2.441
819.355	50	3.051
983.226	60	3.661
1147.097	70	4.272
1310.968	80	4.882
1474.839	90	5.492
1638.710	100	6.102

CUBIC M		CUBIC YD
0.765	1	1.308
1.529	2	2.616
2.294	3	3.924
3.058	4	5.232
3.823	5	6.540
4.587	6	7.848
5.352	7	9.156
6.116	8	10.464
6.881	9	11.772

CUBIC M		CUBIC YD
7.646	10	13.080
15.291	20	26.159
22.937	30	39.239
30.582	40	52.318
38.228	50	65.398
45.873	60	78.477
53.519	70	91.557
61.164	80	104.636
68.810	90	117.716
76.455	100	130.795

LITRES		GALLONS
4.546	1	0.220
9.092	2	0.440
13.638	3	0.660
18.184	4	0.880
22.730	5	1.100
27.276	6	1.320
31.822	7	1.540
36.368	8	1.760
40.914	9	1.980
45.460	10	2.200
90.919	20	4.400
136.379	30	6.599
181.839	40	8.799
227.298	50	10.999
272.758	60	13.199
318.217	70	15.398
363.677	80	17.598
409.137	90	19.798
454.596	100	21.998

WEIGHT (MASS)

KILOGRAMS		POUNDS
0.454	1	2.205
0.907	2	4.409
1.361	3	6.614
1.814	4	8.819
2.268	5	11.023
2.722	6	13.228
3.175	7	15.432

KILOGRAMS		POUNDS
3.629	8	17.637
4.082	9	19.842
4.536	10	22.046
9.072	20	44.092
13.608	30	66.139
18.144	40	88.185
22.680	50	110.231
27.216	60	132.277
31.752	70	154.324
36.287	80	176.370
40.823	90	198.416
45.359	100	220.464

METRIC TONNES		TONS (UK)
1.016	1	0.984
2.032	2	1.968
3.048	3	2.953
4.064	4	3.937
5.080	5	4.921
6.096	6	5.905
7.112	7	6.889
8.128	8	7.874
9.144	9	8.858
10.161	10	9.842
20.321	20	19.684
30.481	30	29.526
40.642	40	39.368
50.802	50	49.210
60.963	60	59.052
71.123	70	68.894
81.284	80	78.737
91.444	90	88.579
101.605	100	98.421

METRIC TONNES		TONS (US)
0.907	1	1.102
1.814	2	2.205
2.722	3	3.305
3.629	4	4.409
4.536	5	5.521
5.443	6	6.614
6.350	7	7.716
7.257	8	8.818
8.165	9	9.921
9.072	10	11.023
18.144	20	22.046
27.216	30	33.069
36.287	40	44.092
45.359	50	55.116
54.431	60	66.139
63.503	70	77.162
72.575	80	88.185
81.647	90	99.208
90.719	100	110.231

CLOTHING SIZE CONVERSIONS

MEN'S				WOMEN'S			
ITEM	UK	USA	EUROPE	ITEM	UK	USA	EUROPE
Suits	36	36	46	*Clothing*	8	6	36
	38	38	48		10	8	38
	40	40	50		12	10	40
	42	42	52		14	12	42
	44	44	54		16	14	44
	46	46	56		18	16	46
Shirts	14	14	36		20	18	48
	14½	14½	37		22	20	50
	15	15	38		24	22	52
	15½	15½	39–40	*Shoes*	4	5½	37
	16	16	41		4½	6	37
	16½	16½	42		5	6½	38
	17	17	43		5½	7	38
	17½	17½	44–45		6	7½	39
Shoes	6½	7	39		6½	8	39
	7	7½	40		7	8½	40
	7½	8	41		7½	9	40
	8	8½	42		8	9½	41
	8½	9	43				
	9	9½	43				
	9½	10	44				
	10	10½	44				
	10½	11	45				

OVEN TEMPERATURES

GAS MARK	ELECTRIC °C	°F	GAS MARK	ELECTRIC °C	°F
—	110	225	5	190	375
—	130	250	6	200	400
1	140	275	7	220	425
2	150	300	8	230	450
3	170	325	9	240	475
4	180	350			